ISBN 0-7974-1608-0

First published in Zimbabwe in 1996 by
Thorntree Press (Pvt) Ltd, PO Box 9243 Hillside, Bulawayo, Zimbabwe

RUPERT

FOTHERGILL

BRIDGING A CONSERVATION ERA

by

KEITH MEADOWS

WITH AN INTRODUCTION
BY
DR JOHN CONDY

ILLUSTRATED WITH ORIGINAL LINE DRAWINGS
BY
IAN HENDERSON

'There are two Africas and I do not know which I love the best - the green, lush bright country when the sap is running and the earth is wet; or the dry brown-gold wastes of the drought, when the sky closes down, hazy and smoke dimmed and the sun is copper coloured and distorted.'

Doris Lessing (Title: Going Home)

This book is for Mana.

May there be campfires and lion music

in wild places for her children.

Also, this is for the stalwarts, the small band of brothers,

past and present, who tried, who still try,

to stop the wild life disappearing.

ACKNOWLEDGEMENTS

It took a lot of help for this book to see the light of day.
By the time I returned from Mozambique, where Rupert and I first discussed a book seriously — in April 1975 — he had died. Putting his story together, of chronicling the events of an era that had slipped into history almost unnoticed, meant a lot of legwork. Although I had access to his diaries and other personal papers, and had talked with him on many aspects of his life, I still had to rely on the memories and reminiscences of people who knew him in one context or another to join the dots. So the list of thanks is long, and, I'm sad to say, the ranks have thinned. If I have inadvertently left anyone out — my sincere apologies. It has been a long time.

His wife, Christine, was always gracious and made her time freely available, even though I detected a note of incredulity at times that the modern world would find Rupert's story interesting. His daughter, Hilary, was equally supportive.
Dr Graham Child, the then Director of the Department of National Parks & Wildlife Management, was always helpful, ready to check parts of the manuscript, and answer obscure questions.
I am indebted to Dr John Condy, for his time and reminiscences and, latterly, for agreeing to write the Introduction.
For the most part, Rupert's colleagues and friends in the Department of National Parks & Wildlife Management were very helpful. In particular – Archie Fraser, Frank Junor, Tommy Orford, Boyd Reese, Mike van Rooyen, Peter Moore, Ian Nyschens, Ron Thomson, Ron van Heerden, Greg Gregory, Game Scouts California, Teguru and Manweri.
Also Barry Ball, Ted Davison, Tinkey Haslam, Paul Coetsee, Basil Williamson, John White and Graham Hall.
Ranchers, journalists, prospecting companions, district officers, family, research specialists, even poachers — Rupert's story would not be complete without more gaps filled by a host of people with whom he came in contact during his game ranging days, and again my thanks to –

George Style, Richard Rayner, Mervyn Hamilton, Peter Turnbull-Kemp, Lord Dalhousie, Bob Woollacott, Ian Findlay, Bertie Bowerman, Tubby Calder, Jeff Cartwright, Rupert's brothers, Eric and William Fothergill, for long informative letters; Roma and John Williamson, Dr Toni Harthoorn for his interest and permission to quote from *'The Flying Syringe'*. Gill Knight, wife of the late Stephen Knight, for unearthing the Sengwa photos. Jack Russell White, for services rendered beyond the call of duty and friendship. Tony Conway, for his first hospitality in Matusadona, and other times thereafter. Shaw Dods-Brooks, for flying me to places with improbable co-ordinates and standing out elephant charges with aplomb.
TIME magazine for permission to use Rupert's epitaph in their June 9, 1975 issue.

In recent times, as the book became more reality than woodsmoke –
Nigel Hattle, for pointing me in the right direction. Sally Norvall, for her long hours transferring the manuscript onto disc – often amidst chaos, and her constructive judgement and enthusiasm. Vivian Mitchell, Sally Wynn and Prof Norman Atkinson for their editing of the manuscript and balanced critisism. Janet Duff for her excellent artwork, on the promotional flyer that helped initially sell the book. Ant Williams for his support. Louis Bolze for his advice. Prof Joe Daniel Jnr, Madeleine Cina, Jeannette Dappen, Julia Ducray, Don and Bonnie Sutherland, fine campfire companions and converts to the cause.
I thank, especially, my friend Ian Henderson, for contributing his fine artwork in this book.
And, of course, *Angelicus domesticus* – friend, wife, and midnight guru.

Note: the use of old names, often the Anglicised corruption of the correct name, for places and rivers, does not reflect disrespect of the new terminology. Those were the names in use then, within the time frame of this story. The same yardstick applies to the use of imperial measurements in these metric times, as well as any phraseology in use at that time.

AUTHOR'S NOTE

This book has had an incredibly long gestation period.
It was conceived in a grove of palm trees fringing a pristine stretch of the Mozambique coast, in April 1975… over 20 years ago. A lot of water has flowed down the Zambezi since then. The manuscript has been around, gathered dust in Rhodesia, South Africa, Botswana and Zimbabwe. And the wildlife and wilderness of Africa, indeed the world, has taken a pounding in that time. Philosophies and parameters have been re-evaluated. Guidelines and boundaries have been re-drawn, rubbed out, drawn again. Goal-posts have been moved.
In 1950 there were 221 million humans living in Africa. By the end of the century there will be 853 million people, give or take a few million. This does not bode well for what is left of the wildlife. In the words of Peter Beard, in his timeless apocalyptic END OF THE GAME…

"The wilderness of only a half a century ago, then so completely itself, has been reduced, tree by tree, animal by animal, shadow by shadow, rock by rock, to its last rutted corners. The few remaining spaces have been infiltrated, divided up, domesticated, deprived of natural systems, denuded of natural processes, systemised, artificialised, sterilised, commercialised…"

It is mid morning as I write this, in a therapeutically peaceful bay where the Chura River enters Lake Kariba by way of the Ume estuary. My mind is becalmed, as always, by the timelessness of this region. In the distance the escarpment is blue-hazed and ethereal, beckoning like Shangri-la. Closer, within a stone's throw, a trio of old buffalo bulls are hull down in the sedge and hyacinth at the edge of the water, their moneylenders' gaze sweeping occasionally across our boat. A pair of pied kingfishers, ever insouciant, hunt-dive amongst the oxygen weed. A goliath heron stands glued to its reflection in the water, so still that it looks like some extraordinarily good art piece. Hippo talk, distant and mellifluous, echoes across the bay, briefly drowning out the hoarse rutting challenges of impala rams further along the shoreline.

How different this part of the Zambezi Valley is now, to half a lifetime ago, when the Tonga people lived along the river in harmony with nature, in the land where their ancestors were buried. To when the new lake spread across the valley, and Rupert and his men, his band of brothers, slogged under the hard African sun to save the wild animals who did not know that this flood would be different.

Yet, now, it seems as if the lake has been here forever.

Will the wildlife be here forever? Staying as a kind of living monument to a small band of men who got on with a job of work, so long ago?

Who knows? I do not.

Whenever I ruminate about wildlife and the future, about conservation past and present, and I feel the depression creeping in, I think of the words on the grave of that conservation icon, Bernhard Grzimek, up on the rim of his beloved Ngorongoro Crater.

"It is better to light a candle than to curse the darkness"

Keith Meadows Kariba April 1996

INTRODUCTION

This book is a true historical record of a remarkable man whose efforts left this world a better place. It is a book written about an era during which many values, and life in general, were different to those we know and take as the norm today. It is therefore necessary to paint a picture of what life was like, and what was going on in the world at that time. The world was not as conservation conscious as it is now. Most people did not know the difference between preservation and conservation. Many do not know the difference to this day. The words ecosystem, ecology and environment were seldom heard. Catch phrases like ecotourism, or the green movement were as yet unthought of.

In the Zambezi Valley, and many other places, wildlife was in abundance. The river itself ran pure and clean. The population of humans was increasing, but had not yet reached the staggering numbers that inhabit our planet today. Pollution was minimal. The houseboat explosion on Kariba Lake with its accompanying detrius of muck and spillage was far ahead in the future. There was no commercialisation of our wildlife resources. There were no professional safari hunters or guides. And there was no huge unwieldy bureaucracy regulating wildlife matters.

Insecticides were being used more and more in agriculture. DDT was a new "success story", the great saviour from insect pests. Rachel Carson had not yet brought the world's attention to the devastating effects these insecticides had already caused. '*Silent Spring*' had not yet been published.

In the main it was a happy era, this time before the massive onslaught of rhino and elephant poaching. Before those people in high places, forever hungry for more money, and less thoughts of a balanced garden of Eden and all the creatures that lived there, persuaded the innocent rural hunters in isolated areas to kill those animals for a few dollars, when previously they had been content with the meat their hunting prowess had provided for their families. They were the days before the endless series of wildlife conferences, congresses, seminars, workshops, discussions, talks - they were the days when people worked more, and talked less.

Many of the anecdotes in this book about Rupert Fothergill reflect on the days when, because of an expanding human population, pockets of elephants became isolated from each other. Elephant society was being split up. Confused groups of elephants inadvertently got into trouble, and so conflict between elephant and man grew.
There was not the knowledge or experience at that time to translocate whole herds, as Zimbabwean pioneers are doing today.

Rupert Fothergill was an outstanding example of a breed of men who just got on with doing an honest constructive job, accepting as out of their control the manoeuvring and manipulating of power hungry politicians that have plagued mankind for centuries. He was unfettered by academic superiors from the seat of higher learning. He had many unpleasant tasks to carry out, such as the shooting of wounded and trouble making elephants, lions and buffalos. Someone had to do these tasks. There are many emotionally motivated people, particularly in the northern hemisphere who, excessively brainwashed by an ill-informed media, have never been in touch with the real issues of practical conservation. They do not appreciate the fact that there are frequently dangerous wild animals, wounded by poachers or hurt in the natural wild course of events that kill innocent people each year. There is no place for emotional sentiment in dealing with these problems.

Many of the problems Rupert had to solve were caused by the policies of big companies "developing" the country. There was a strange lack of general understanding of wildlife, and its rightful place in a community.
He spent a lot of his life working virtually alone in isolated parts of the country, with poor or non existent communications with his base or the outside world. He was often the first government official in many of the remote parts of the Lowveld, for example, to expose and frame the reality of conflict on wildlife matters between individuals, companies, and other government departments.

Rupert is best known and remembered for his handling of the largest animal rescue operation since Biblical days - the rescue of game from the receding islands of the growing lake, Kariba. Operation Noah.
When he and a small group of men saved the lives of more than 6000 wild animals that inhibited a part of the Zambezi Valley.... literally with their bare hands.

Should Operation Noah have taken place today, the country would have been inundated with Aid. There would have been offers to help by hundreds of experts, academic and otherwise, from the international wildlife organisations, from the lunatic fringe "bunny lovers", and, of course, the United Nations Organisation. But no. Led by Rupert Fothergill, with a handful of dedicated men, an average of thirty or so people carried out this remarkable operation in spite of, not because of, the weather, equipment, Aid and advice.
It should be remembered that when rescue started, there was no such weapon known as a dart gun. This weapon, which appeared first in 1959, was to revolutionise wild animal management. The immobilising drug, M99, would only appear after Operation Noah had ceased. And no-one in the world knew anything of the swimming capabilities of the many species that inhibited the Zambezi Valley; there was just no relevant experience to draw from. Noah had never kept a log book of his activities! Rupert led his men by example, never expecting anyone to do anything he could not do himself. His total genuine lack of fear was legendary. He never dismissed any staff, but there were many hardy young men who went to work for him who gave up, simply unable to take the pace that Rupert set.

It was a great privilege for me to have known and worked with Rupert Fothergill, and it is a fitting tribute to his efforts that an island on Kariba Lake was named after him.
Apart from general interest, history is always worth studying, because we can learn from this study. We can learn from those who have toiled effectively for ideals divorced from personal, political or financial gain, in this world that seems to have forgotten its God.

John Condy 10.3.96

UGANDA
KENYA
CONGO
GABON
REPUBLIC OF THE CONGO
(ZAIRE)
TANGANYIKA
(TANZANIA)
NORTHERN
RHODESIA
(ZAMBIA)
ANGOLA
FEDERATION OF RHODESIA
AND NYASALAND
NYASALAND
(MALAWI)
SOUTHERN
RHODESIA
(ZIMBABWE)
MOZAMBIQUE
SOUTH WEST AFRICA
(NAMIBIA)
PORTUGUESE
EAST AFRICA
BECHUANALAND
(BOTSWANA)
SOUTH AFRICA

CONTENTS

PART ONE

EARLY DAYS

CHAPTER I

BACKTRACKING

TO GAME OFFICER. GAME DEPT. CAUSEWAY SALISBURY. MEDICAL SATISFACTORY WILL ARRIVE SBY TUESDAY OR WEDNESDAY 15TH FOR DUTY R.B. FOTHERGILL.

.... This story starts, really, with a telegram. It is June 1955, early winter in Southern Rhodesia. The cold, crisp nights give way reluctantly to the dry, flat heat of the winter sun. The veld is fast losing its colour, the greenness is going, giving way to the parched drab brown uniformity of the season. The trees are becoming skeleton-like and the smoke from this year's first bushfires hazes the horizon even more. It is the time when the wild animals start to forage further from the rivers and waterholes for their food.

The telegram came to the rapidly developing Southern Rhodesian capital of Salisbury from the small, picturesque eastern border town of Umtali. It was addressed to Archie Fraser, the game officer in charge of the relatively new Game Section of the Department of Mines, Lands and Surveys, formed three years earlier. It was from one Rupert Bellamy Fothergill, then in the throes of winding up his partnership in an engineering business and packing his wife and two young children off to Salisbury. He was 43 years old and had been promised the fine sum of £750 a year in his new position with the Game Department. His application had been one of many that had ended up on Archie Fraser's desk in the sparse, cluttered office that was, for the moment, temporarily tagged on to the Entomology Department, out on the edge of town, on the red dust Domboshawa road.

Archie Fraser's parish was the entire country - a self-governing British colony that was one- and-a-half times the size of the United Kingdom, and almost the same area as the state of California. From the sluggish brown waters of the Limpopo River in the south, to the green- cloaked buttresses of the Eastern Highlands; and from the wide, hippo and crocodile infested expanses of the mighty Zambezi River to the vast, fertile, featureless expanses of the Lowveld - this was his responsibility. So far his staff consisted of three people: a lady clerk, himself, and one roving game ranger. Fothergill would be the third man to join the small nucleus of what, over the long years ahead, would evolve into one of the most progressive wildlife conservation bodies in the world: the Department of National Parks and Wildlife Management.

The man already in the field was Ian Nyschens. There were few parts of central and southern Africa upon which the tough, steel-eyed Nyschens had not left his stamp. He was a renowned elephant hunter and his haunts had been the French and Belgian Congos, Tanganyika, Portuguese East Africa, Chad, the Sudan, Nyasaland and the Rhodesias. He had shared campfires with many of the ivory hunters of the day, including Marcus Daly, J. A. Hunter and Pondoro Taylor. Indeed, his own ivory hunting in Southern Rhodesia had attracted the attention of the authorities on more than one occasion. Far too wily to be caught red-handed, he stayed always a step ahead of the crowd. Eventually, in a paradoxical reversal of loyalties, he accepted Archie Fraser's offer to join the newly formed Game Section. With African settlements spreading rapidly across the country, and their ubiquitous patches of maize continually suffering from the depredations of elephants and other game, it had become a full time job to control the wild animals' toll of the crops. Nyschens was told that he could keep whatever ivory he obtained from any elephant control duties, and so it happened that one of the region's main ivory hunters became the Game Department's first game ranger.

The Chief Game Officer, A D (Archie) Fraser, had been in government service almost all his adult life. He was 42, Rhodesian born, and administration had been his *forte* almost from the time he left school. He served first with the Treasury Department and then with the Ministry of Justice. The years from 1940 to 1947 had seen him as a member of the Southern Rhodesian Air Force, with the rank of flight lieutenant, holding a dual commission in the S.R.A.F. and R.A.F.

It was the dark-haired, solidly-built Fraser who had first punted the formation of a game department in Southern Rhodesia, and he it was who set the steps in motion in 1952. In June 1955 he occupied a small office in the warren of run-down government buildings in the Salisbury administrative centre of Causeway, stuccoed on to the Department of Mines. Here, amidst stuffed specimens of African birds, map covered walls, and an immense clutter of paperwork, Archie Fraser would meet the third male member of his team.

★ ★ ★ ★ ★ ★ ★ ★

In the twilight world of the Pungwe forest in Portuguese East Africa, Rupert Fothergill had shot his first lion. He was 16 years old and the lion had turned man-eater. Searching for his father, who prospected for the even then powerful Lonrho mining monolith, young Rupert, never a keen scholar, had bunked out of boarding school in Salisbury, and jumped a train to Umtali. Amidst the kraals surrounding the small eastern border trading centre, he searched for news of Fothergill senior. It took time, but eventually he found a local honey-gatherer who had reasonably recent news of his father. A half crown changed hands and they crossed the border on foot. A week passed. Two. Several weeks! Village after village. The trail led ever deeper into the little-known Portuguese-ruled territory. Ever eastwards they walked, seeking news of Fothergill senior. On the fringe of the brooding ethereal Pungwe forest that stood like a vast, shadowed sentinel over the river of the same name, he found his father. And there, for the next six months, he stayed. He left only after Christmas, and the beginning of a new school year.

This was the preface for his second quest. To find the man-eater! The lion had been terrorising the local population for weeks. Bush telegraph sent word that the lion was concentrating its attention on a village some 40 miles away. Leaving his father to continue with his prospecting, Rupert set off for the latest target area. He got to the sprawling concentration of huts late on the second day. That night the lion roared and grunted all through the dark hours, falling silent with the first glimmer of light in the east. Unable to select a human victim, the creature forced its way into a cattle enclosure, killed a young calf, and retired to the forest with its meal. At first light Rupert took up the spoor. Within an hour he made contact with the marauder, a scrubby-maned male in his prime. As the lion bunched itself, tail flailing, for a charge, Rupert shot it.

All too soon he was back at Prince Edward School. Academically, Rupert was not amongst the heavyweights. Rugby and boxing were the only aspects of the schooling he enjoyed, and he was impatient to get out. Both he and his younger brother, Eric, were looked on as above-average boxers, the speed of the smaller boy countering the tall, tough ranginess of his elder brother. In a boxing joust that would be unparalleled for many a year, the two brothers, slugged it out in a stubborn no-quarter match lasting nearly three hours. The result ... a draw.

By now his parents were divorced, his mother remaining in the small mining town of Gatooma, where they had settled on their trek from the Union of South Africa. His father continued to prospect, prisoner to the wanderlust that was always bubbling just beneath the surface. Rupert was the eldest of four children, having two brothers, Eric and William, and a sister, Roma. Rupert had been born in the Transvaal goldfields, where his father discovered the Barberton mineral deposits, and the youngster had already done a lot of moving around before he was brought up over the Limpopo to Southern Rhodesia at the age of 10. Now, like his father, he had the urge to travel, to get out far into the veld to hunt and prospect. His brother Eric recalls the two boys jumping a train one school holidays to the barren mining centre of Bindura, some 50 miles north east of Salisbury, and then travelling on foot to the trading post at Mount Darwin, named by the hunter and explorer Fredrick Courtney Selous after the British naturalist, thence on to Rusambo, 120 miles further where their uncle had a small house and ran a store. Each night they stopped at a village, sleeping in the traditional visitor's hut. At one remote village five lions prowled around their hut, growling and purring alternately. One, more hungry or determined than the rest, leaped up onto the frail cone of a roof and tried to pull the straw off. Rupert, normally mildly spoken, swore vociferously at the commotion above them and in due course the lions made off. They arrived at Rusambo and stayed for several days, living off maize meal and meat shot for the pot, before starting out on the long hike home.

For a while after leaving school Rupert worked on a mine amongst the Iron Mask range of hills near Mazoe, the name being a corruption of the indigenous word *manzou* meaning 'place of the elephants'. But he caught blackwater fever and, after a spell in a mission hospital, was forced to leave the area. It was the belief in those days that this step ensured that the disease did not return. He moved to Salisbury and served his apprenticeship as a fitter and turner.

Southern Rhodesia was the first country in the Empire to send troops beyond her borders when the Second World War broke out, and in 1939 the three Fothergill brothers joined up, managing to spend four of the five-year war in actual fighting. Eric Fothergill gives a most readable account of this part of their lives in *'Gunners'* by Tort (his pseudonym). All three brothers came through the war unscathed, although, like hundreds of others caught up in the same maelstrom, there were some close shaves. There was one occasion when all three brothers almost died together in the same incident during the Italian Campaign. All three were operating with the South African Division, with Rupert attached to the British Command Division in support of the main attack. By chance, his second youngest brother had bumped into him on the main highway south of Florence and after a quick chat and catching up of news, had continued on towards the area of the main attack. On one side of the Arno River were deployed the 1 Battery of 6 Regiment (Eric's unit) and he discovered that the medium guns of the South African Artillery (youngest brother William's outfit) had moved up on to the opposite side of the river. Thinking that there was very little chance of another reunion presenting itself in the foreseeable future, Eric Fothergill turned his jeep around and returned to collect Rupert. They crossed the river on foot and, after a few enquiries, discovered the location of young Bill Fothergill. They spotted him in a cherry orchard talking to a group of men and made their way across to him. They were still a few yards off when one of the men in the group stepped back on to a teller mine which exploded amongst them. The youngest Fothergill brother took a lot of shrapnel up his left side and had an ugly hole near his left ear. Rupert and Eric picked him up and carried him back to their jeep, themselves not entirely unscratched, then drove hell-for-leather for the main American Mobile Hospital in the rear. After an hour at the operating table, the two anxious brothers were assured that he would be fine and so returned to their respective units.

It is interesting to note that people who served with Rupert either during the war, or, many years later on the animal rescue operation on the newly forming Lake Kariba, were unanimous in one description of him - his complete lack of fear. One other episode during the war which helps illustrate this point has been related to the writer by three different people. This incident took place near a town called Sallem in the western desert. Rupert was a Staff Sergeant Artificer - guns, and his mobile tank recovery unit was being subjected to daily repeated Stuka dive bombing and machine gunning. He had been returning fire with a Bren gun at one particularly persistent Stuka and cursed when the machine gun ran out of ammunition. Grabbing a Boyes anti-tank rifle he stepped out from his cover behind a 'blitz wagon' and lined up on the incoming enemy fighter bomber. Before he could engage it, the weapon was shot out of his hands, a twisted mess. He was untouched.

Umtali is situated amongst the high, green mountains of the eastern border highlands which themselves appear to hover protectively over the collection of buildings and parks below them. It is here, through the Eastern Gateway, that travellers to the distant mosquito-plagued coasts of Portuguese East Africa gained their access to that wild, unsettled country. Here it was that Rupert settled after the war. He went into partnership in an engineering company, hoarding his money and his leave spells to embark on his beloved bush trips. He was 36 now and, if not in his own mind, then certainly in the opinion of his circle of friends, he was a confirmed bachelor, a 'dagga boy' in the making. Whilst not being a ladies' man he had, over the couple of years since his return from the war, squired almost all of the single ladies of Umtali, but seldom seeing any of them more than once. He was a busy man, with his engineering business partnership and his therapeutic trips off into the bush. There were long bets amongst his bachelor cronies that Rupert would never get married; not old, tough, lean, slow-talking Rupert with the mountain precipice of a nose and the direct stare.

In the suicidally hot month of October in 1948 a new nurse reported for duty at the Umtali Hospital. She was petite, pretty, blonde and English, and had come out to the country under the auspices of the Southern Rhodesian Nursing Services. She anticipated spending about nine months in this beautiful, rugged, carefree country before moving on elsewhere in the world. She had typical English country looks, rosy cheeks and a ready infectious laugh, and had been resident in the nurses' home for little over a week when a crisis invaded her life. One of her new girl friends had double-dated and, shortly to appear in the foyer downstairs would be two rather rugged, individualistic males. The girl was in a hopeless tizz. She begged Christine, who had just washed her hair, to join her in a foursome. She would do all the explaining. Christine was reluctant. Since her arrival in the small British colony, life had been a trifle hectic, very social, and she was, or had been, revelling in her evening of solitude. Her friend pleaded. One of the men had a successful business and had a reputation as a hunter and a 'sort of man about town'. He was really very nice! Eventually the newly arrived English nurse capitulated. One of her main objectives in coming out to Southern Rhodesia was to see some wildlife. And so far she hadn't seen a thing.

When Rupert heard that the new girl had not yet seen any of the wildlife of the country, and that this fact obviously perturbed her, he promised there and then that she soon would. Breaking from his previous pattern completely, he took her out three and then four times. A year and a half later, on 1 July 1950, they were married. For their honeymoon he took her first up to the chilly, windswept, bracken-covered expanses of the Inyanga mountains. Then they travelled clear across the country to where the Zambezi River formed a common border between the two Rhodesias. Down in the wild, hot Zambezi Valley he taught her how to hunt buffalo and lion, and they fished from a dugout canoe amongst hippos and crocodiles. At night they slept beneath the stars, the call of hyenas and lions mingling with the raucous chortling of hippos, lulling them to sleep.

Their first child, a boy whom they christened Martin, was born in April 1951. Rupert was still enmeshed in his engineering partnership. It was less satisfying now, and the wanderlust was there, a deep current, tugging strongly. Possibly the restlessness was simply because he was not a businessman. He was happiest when he was out prospecting - for that bug was never to leave him - or just wandering in the bush. Their second child, a daughter this time, Hilary, was born in November 1953. And Rupert became even more restless, the business more a millstone than ever. In the newspaper he had read of the formation of the new Game Section. He had wondered about it. However, the children were babies, and his business was more troublesome than ever.

Then, in April 1955, he saw the advertisement in the paper telling of a new post in the embryonic Game Department of Southern Rhodesia. He discussed it with his wife, and Christine, reading him well, agreed that he should apply.
A letter to Salisbury got him an interview.
Two, three weeks passed. And he held his breath.

Then they told him that, subject to a medical examination, seeing as he was in fact 43, the job was his.

Two days later he sent a telegram .....

CHAPTER 2

FIRST PATROLS

Within a week of joining the Game Department, Rupert Fothergill was out on patrol, and from this time on he would see very little of his family. Fleeting visits between trips around the country would be their only contact, his only opportunity to see the changes in his children as they grew older. In later years Christine would comment that she and her children had very soon become used to him being away for most of the time ... it was part of his life and she would never have changed him; and in a way it kept their marriage fresh and both of them young. Nevertheless, the life of a bush widow is seldom easy.

Rupert's first patrol was a round trip of 1 500 miles, up to the slowly rearing Kariba Dam wall and the surrounding bush areas of the Vuti and the Sanyati rivers. He accompanied his new boss, Archie Fraser, on this expedition. It was almost a full day's journey from Makuti ('the place of wet mist', in the local dialect), on the Zambezi escarpment, down the twisting, tortuous ribbons of dirt track that had been carved out of the steep, rugged sides of the valley, following the ancient elephant trails. Down on to the flat, ravine-studded expanses of *jesse* bush on the valley floor and, eventually, to Kariba gorge. At the dam site he was to meet Ian Nyschens for the first time, temporarily relieving the only other game ranger in the department in the duties particular to this area. From their first meeting there was an undercurrent: an antipathy between the two men, between the tough, mercurial ivory hunter and the quiet, controlled, almost dour newcomer to the Game Department. It was a state of affairs that would continue until Nyschen's departure from government service some three years later. It developed from their differing philosophies, and their opposite attitudes to hunting and bush tactics.

One of the principal tasks of the Game Section in this era of its evolution was to provide rations for the hundreds of staff involved with the construction of the giant mass of concrete that would stop the Zambezi in Kariba gorge. The food supply was not only destined for the countless black workers employed on this Herculean task, but also the many foreigners who were now living, and sometimes dying, in this remote part of Africa. Government policy had resulted in a designated quota of elephants being destroyed as part of the meat ration programme that would feed the masses working on the dam. The decision was dual-purpose. It was hoped that the hunting of the elephants would serve as an inducement to move the animals gradually out of the area, which, in the near future would be forever under water. In 1955 a total of 18 elephants were shot as part of the ration programme, the wary, survival-conscious beasts quickly abandoning the immediate Kariba area. They went far sooner than expected.

With this new, intensive persecution, the resident elephant population was soon to become aggressive and would attack at the least provocation. Ian

Nyschens had already had his hunting prowess tested when, on shooting one of a herd, the whole herd turned on him. In a critical situation he was forced to make a lone stand amidst the *mopane* and shoot 10 more that pushed home attacks on him. It was this task, to date, that had kept both Nyschens and Fraser in close touch with the building of Kariba dam. Now Rupert joined the team, and for the next month his days were spent travelling the bush routes of the area, hunting with his trackers, casting last, long glances at an Eden that would soon be gone, drowned, forever. And with the arrival on this once peaceful scene of mankind in force, he quickly saw that poaching activities were already under way.

In southern Africa the months of June, July and August are probably the best months to cure biltong. This sun-dried meat, taken off wild or domestic herbivore animals provides, when properly doctored, fine bush cuisine. It is also cheap protein. And where cold storage is limited, it is the most practical way of supplying food *en masse*. Thus, it was biltong that made up the principal item in the rations supplied by the men of the Game Section.

On this first patrol, Rupert shot two elephants. Their carcasses provided one thousand and fifty pounds of dried meat, delivered on demand to the Irrigation Department of Kariba Dam. This hunting of elephants, far in excess of anything the animals had ever experienced before, when the wild animals and the Tonga people lived in relative harmony in this patch of wilderness, soon caused a pattern to emerge. More and more the elephant tracks led out of the area. Away from the Kariba gorge. Away from man and mayhem and destruction. Across the Naodsa and Sanyati rivers, into the Sebungwe region. And quieter haunts.

The game section camp on the banks of the Nyanyana River, a few miles from the dam site, was a busy place. Especially at night. For it was here that the 'meat storeroom' had been established. The often large amounts of meat kept here made the camp the centre of attraction for all the predators and scavengers in the area. A gilt-edged invitation wafting on the valley breeze. It became a full time occupation keeping away lions and hyenas, jackals and the smaller cats, and especially leopards. One night, attracted by more disturbance than usual, Rupert investigated with a hunting lamp. Festooned in a silent ballet in the trees around where the meat was hanging, frozen in the light of his beam, he counted 13 leopards.

At the Nyanyana camp Rupert witnessed elephant behaviour that in those days had been almost unchronicled - and which makes the elephant so unique amongst its fellow inhabitants of the wild. Their presence in and around the camp was common enough and he enjoyed it. But on one particular evening their actions gave the game ranger a rare insight into their emotions. He had just bathed, using the water that seeped into the series of holes dug into the sandy river bed, and was making his way back to his tent when the first shrill trumpeting of an elephant split the evening stillness, drowning the relaxing, pleasant noise of roosting francolin. More screams and throaty rumblings followed. He hastened his step and, collecting his rifle, picked his way through the scrub towards the noise. In the last moments of daylight, he saw a family unit of some 10 elephants milling restlessly and grouping protectively. He stopped, studying the scene, wondering what had upset the animals. The furore continued. Predators, he reflected. Lions maybe? It's not us, they know we're camped here, there's man smell all around the place! Even as he evaluated the situation, with the light rapidly fading, the trumpeting died. Silence, an echoing quiet, broken only by the flapping of their great sail-like ears and muted growls. Then one elephant, the lead cow, wielded something aloft in her trunk. It was one of the poles the workers had cut a few days previously, to use as stretcher racks for carrying the piles of meat from an elephant carcass back to camp. Even as he stared, Rupert saw more of the herd picking up the poles from where they had been discarded. They picked them up gingerly, delicately, as though with great respect. In the last light they bustled away, hurrying after the lead cow, all of them, even the half-grown calves, taking away the poles with the scent of their brothers thick upon them. Rupert searched the area for a long time the next day, following their tracks. Of the poles, there was no sign.

Rupert returned to headquarters in Salisbury for a brief spell, broken only by a journey out to the Chishawasha mission, 12 miles along the Mtoko road, to investigate the report of a leopard that had forced its way out of a jaw-trap set by a priest. Rough, hilly country and high grass prevented any successful spooring of the beast to ascertain whether it was badly hurt, although Rupert scoured the area for two days. In early August Rupert returned to the Kariba gorge where he spent a week patrolling the area, checking on the game concentrations and keeping vigilant about the increased poaching activities in which both black and white men were involved. He travelled westwards as far as the Bumi River at its confluence with the great Zambezi, where it was over a hundred yards wide between sandy banks. There was an abundance of fresh elephant spoor, mainly young bulls, and at night elephants fed close alongside his camp. Throughout the night the African drums echoed as the people tried to keep the hippos and elephants out of their maize. There was much sign too, of trapping by the local tribespeople, as evidenced by the snares and pits he encountered. At Chitondo's kraal the locals complained bitterly about elephant damage and the baboons raiding their maize. They were most persuasive that the game ranger should shoot some of them, or any animals come to that, to keep them away. One man recounted how his wife was often troubled by baboons on her way back to the village from the maize lands. She would carry the maize cobs in a dish balanced on her head in the usual rural fashion and the baboons were apparently prepared to attack her to get at the maize she carried. To appease them she would throw the odd maize cobs to them as she walked on her homeward journey, and by the time she reached her destination the dish would be almost empty. The situation, complained the villagers, was becoming impossible. Never, reflected the game ranger, had he heard of baboons that would go to all that trouble as opposed to simply raiding the maize field. Indignant, the husband insisted that he would fetch his wife and give the game ranger a demonstration! However, his wife was nowhere to be found.

Rupert retraced his route to Kariba gorge and then took the game section truck up across the escarpment and down back into the Nemana Pools. During subsequent years this area, then the Urungwe Non-Hunting Reserve, was designated the Mana Pools Game Reserve. *En route* he spent the night at the deserted Rukometje mission, built by American missionaries years before and already given back to the wild, uncompromising Zambezi Valley; continuing early the next morning down through the last habitation of Dandawa's village, arriving at the pools at midday. During the midday break here, while Rupert inspected the spoor around the waterholes, a lone figure materialised out of the bush from the direction of the Zambezi. Mr Pat Bromfield, operating one of the earliest photographic safari businesses in the country, had come to meet a party of tourists whom he had contracted to escort and show over this area of unspoiled, unpolluted wilderness. When the party had not arrived by late afternoon, he drove with Rupert and his trackers in his vehicle back towards the river. Constant elephant usage had made the bush track badly rutted and almost impassable in places, and the speedometer never went over five miles per hour. Walking seemed a quicker mode of travel.

With the sun sinking closer to the horizon and still a mile of tortuous track to be negotiated, they stopped for a small herd of eight elephants that were browsing on the faint line of track. The animals were in no hurry. Soon the red orb of the sun teetered on the horizon. Rupert banged his fist against the vehicle door while the trackers knocked on the nearby tree trunks. It was the usual procedure. They had done it before. The elephants invariably moved off, keen to put distance between themselves and the noisy intruders. *En masse*, this herd turned and charged. Hastily, Rupert, his passenger and one of the trackers grabbed their rifles and clambered up a tree. The four other Africans disappeared into the dusk. The elephants stopped at the pick-up truck, milling and trumpeting their anger, and for a while Rupert was afraid that they would damage the vehicle. He considered firing a shot over their heads, but desisted due to his almost fanatical preoccupation with observing the rules to the last degree, in this case the ban on firing a weapon in a non-hunting area. The sun had gone now and Mr Bromfield was concerned about other clients that were already established at his camp on the Zambezi. The elephants, their anger dissipated, had moved a short way off, so he slipped down the tree to cover the rest of the journey on foot.

Rupert at the same time left the haven of the tree and eased cautiously back up the road with his tracker, keeping a weather eye on the still truculent elephants. There was no sign of the rest of his crew, and he moved on further. Whistling. Calling. Guessing that they had not slowed down until they reached the pools at Nemana, he returned to his vehicle and, finding the elephants no longer in attendance, called it a day. He moved the truck close to a substantial, climbable tree and camped for the night.

It was almost full moon and the night sounds of the valley increased. Lions kept up a steady chorus, in tandem with the hyenas. Several species of owl were calling. Once, there was the sawing rasp of a patrolling leopard. The elephants came back. Trumpeting and aggressive. Rupert and his tracker again retreated up the tree. Watching the elephants milling around the vehicle below, Rupert kept wondering what on earth was the cause for their behaviour. Uncommonly irritable and only too ready to charge, they did not present a picture of normal elephant behaviour. During his previous night at the mission the elephants had been plentiful, and the locals had told him that there too, the great animals were prone to attacking at the least provocation. Indeed, the situation had deteriorated to the point where no-one ventured on to that stretch of track until afternoon, when the elephants had dispersed and it was safe to move. Throughout the night Rupert wondered. In the morning as he ate breakfast, Mr Bromfield re-appeared with his missing team. They had preceded the safari operator to his camp the previous afternoon. Had been more than happy to see the night out there.

Over the next few days, during his patrols of the area, Rupert was charged often and determinedly by different herds of elephants. He studied animal after animal through his binoculars, searching for signs of injury or wounds. As time passed he grew ever more concerned. An occasional bull in musth was one thing, but this was something else again. The other game he came across was also nervous and wary. This included a huge herd of buffalo that frequented the area between the pools and the river. Twice, of a night, elephants feeding close to his camp suddenly became irritated and hostile, forcing his African crew to head for the trees, and even Rupert, eventually, moved his bedroll on top of his Bedford in order to get a reasonable night's sleep. Mr Bromfield had also been chased during his wanderings in the area and reported that he had seen one bull that looked wounded, it having a large lump on its left side near its hindquarters. He also reported seeing a dwarf bull elephant, with heavy ivory and standing no more than seven feet in height, always moving with three other normal-sized bulls. So Rupert, apart from searching for any signs of poaching that might give a reason for the truculence of the elephants in the area, looked eagerly for this dwarf, but to no avail.
He left the area nine days later and, as if to make sure he had got the picture properly, in one final display of temper, 12 out of a herd of some 30 elephants that he was circuitously passing, chased his vehicle for over two hundred yards. Discussing the situation down on the area of the valley floor with Archie Fraser, they could only surmise that an influx of elephants from the highveld and from the areas of tsetse operations that had bordered the west, east and south of the Urungwe Non-Hunting Reserve had made the rest of the population more nervous of humans. This, coupled with the fact that five miles either side of the twin strips of tar that joined Chirundu and Marongora was tsetse eradication area, plus the area north of the deserted Rukometje mission, plus the incidents of illegal hunting which undoubtedly did occur, had resulted in the elephant population of the area becoming more than ever distrustful of man ... to the point of hatred.

CHAPTER 3

EAST - SOUTH - WEST

Even during this early stage of the evolution of the country's game conservation body, the emphasis of the Game Section was on control. Wherever the conflicts between human settlement and wildlife came to a head, invariably it was the wildlife that came off second-best. It was a civilised, progressive, 20th century fact of life. Elephants and hippos were irreconcilable with wheat and maize fields. Lions and leopards were not conducive to well stocked cattle or sheep paddocks. Not to mention the baboons and the hyenas and the foot-and-mouth and the herds of buffalo. As human settlement increased, so the migration routes of animals such as the elephant were taken from it. As the antelope were slowly encroached upon and were forced to move further afield, the carnivores did not always follow their natural prey. After all, cows were a slower, easier prey and not all that different from an eland or buffalo. And the baboons - well, they too increased their numbers, as their natural enemy was destroyed, and the maize fields increased in acreage over the country. Until the poisons were brought into the war against them, and more and more people had access to guns.

Rupert's tasks took him to the flatlands that snuggled against the barrier of the Eastern Highlands. Today, in a modern car on tarmacadam roads that are still amongst the best in Africa, it is but a four-hour journey to the irrigation project of Nyanyadzi. The oasis of greenery lies halfway between the hot sulphur springs of Hot Springs and the graceful curve of Birchenough Bridge, within whose structure lies buried Sir Henry Birchenough, the water in its drainage ditches coming from the wide sandy expanses of the Sabi River. Here, in the second week of September 1955, was the last time in this area that elephants would ever be seen. Seven bulls had been plundering the wheat, and making short work of the paw paw and banana trees.

Pour encourager les autres. This summed up Rupert's latest mandate. To discourage the elephants, and encourage them to leave. To move on! To keep on moving. The fact that to the east lay white-owned farming areas, to the south the vast kingdoms of the Humani and Devuli ranches and, to the rest of the points of the compass, the subsistence areas of the tribal folk, simply was someone else's problem.

Rupert made a long reconnaissance of the area, finding spoor in the long evening shadows of that first day which was old. The following day, close to the Sabi River, he located the elephants in a wide expanse of tall, razor-edged reeds. They were hard to see. Occasionally he would see a grey back, a trunk upraised as it tested the breeze. He moved down into the river bed, keeping pace with the animals' slow meanderings. He knew that, sometime, they would come down out of the reeds, to cross the sand to the shallow, slow-moving ribbon of water.

It was hot. Sabi Valley heat. The slight breeze, occasional, almost imperceptible, eddied and changed direction mischievously. From somewhere downstream came the grunting of hippos. The mournful call of an emerald spotted wood dove tremored on the hot, still air. A pair of large raptors circled, high up. An elephant, a cow, followed by a juvenile, suddenly materialised out of the reeds. Followed immediately by two bulls. Only their heads and shoulders were clear of the reeds and Rupert took a brain shot at the nearest animal. It went down, into the obscurity of the greenery, and Rupert lined up on the second bull which was wheeling away. Rupert aimed for another brain shot, judging the angles of the moving elephant. He had already decided that two out of the small herd would do. Sufficient. Enough to get the message across. The panic and fear he caused amongst their ranks would, he hoped fervently, drive the rest of them south. With luck, they would keep going and not cause any trouble on the big ranches they had to cross and maybe, *hopefully,* they would reach the relative safety of the Chipinda Pools area. But the pools were a long way away.

As these thoughts flickered through his mind, the first elephant reappeared from the reeds, standing tall above the obscurity. He switched targets and fired rapidly twice at its head. It kept moving, turning, and in seconds it had disappeared. Mortified, Rupert went after them, running now in the sand, razor edges of reeds cutting him as he tried to keep up with their fear-induced long strides. Within 40 minutes, when they had slowed, he caught up with them again. Just their sounds, the swishing of reeds and the occasional rumble. Nothing visible. He moved position, deliberately allowing them to get his scent. One of two things could happen: either they would move again, possibly on into less dense bush; or they would come up-wind in a furious, pushed-too-far, red-eyed charge ... They ran again, panicked by the man scent. Out of the reeds at last, but now into thick scrub. Rupert shook his head and signalled to one of his trackers to climb a tree and see what was going on. Kosiah, his senior tracker, even from the elevation of a tree, could see only the dust of the elephants' passing. They continued in the wake of the herd, the pungent, musty smell of the pachyderms strong in their nostrils, the elephants' droppings loose with fear.

It was well after noon, with the sun at its zenith, when Rupert saw them again. He'd climbed an anthill and found them feeding close to the opposite side of the bush-entangled mound. He and his trackers counted 22 elephants, amongst them the seven bulls. The closest animal was little over 15 paces away and they checked carefully, searching for signs of the wounded bull. Nothing. It was virtually impossible as the elephants were showering themselves with dust, effectively covering any wound marks. Nor was there any sign of blood on the foliage. The wind veered and their scent was picked up by the alert animals; again they shrilled and bustled off, now breaking away towards the river. Again Rupert and his trackers trotted after them, sweat pouring, rifles trebling in weight, lungs sucking in the furnace-like heat of midday. On the banks of the Sabi they almost ran into six bulls. Rupert swept the binoculars over them. One had what might have been a bullet hole, so he aimed carefully and fired. The elephant dropped, but within a minute was struggling to his feet. Rapidly he banged another two rounds into its head and it fell again. As Rupert loaded his fourth cartridge into the breach it jammed: he freed it, pushed it home ... and then the bolt would not close. The remaining bulls were milling around close to their fallen companion, alternately sifting for the scent of their enemy and then nudging the animal that lay motionless. Rupert grabbed the spare rifle from one of the trackers, just as the remaining elephants turned and ran off. As the noise of their passage subsided, silence enveloped the bush. He warily inspected the dead elephant and then backtracked to where he had first fired. In his mind he was certain that they would find the carcass hidden somewhere in the reeds. But there was no elephant. They searched methodically to and fro. To no avail. Bitter with himself, he called a halt.

They rested in the meagre shade of a patch of scrub. Rupert went back over the morning's events, brain working, eyes habitually roving over his surroundings. His gaze rested on the foresight of his rifle, newly issued at the beginning of this patrol. The sights were out of line. He touched it with one finger and it moved freely across. He shook his head, cursing. The next day, while his trackers guided the irrigation scheme's tractor and trailer to the elephant carcass, he used the facilities of the nearby C.M.E.D. camp and reset the sights, zeroing the rifle afterwards to his satisfaction. In these early years problems with weapons were a constant concern and it was only due to a mingling of luck and skill that one or more of the game rangers was not badly hurt. He'd instructed the staff of the scheme to drag the entrails and guts of the elephant around the lands and to hang pieces on fence posts. The death smell of one of their kind would, he hoped, keep other elephants away in the future. In which case he would not be forced to destroy more of the big, wonderful beasts. At least, not in this area.

For the next six days Rupert hunted in vain for the wounded elephant. Around the confluence of the Devuli and Sabi rivers he picked up spoor of another herd of some 15 animals and tracked them. Within sight of the silver span of Birchenough Bridge he contacted them in the shade of a copse of mahogany. None appeared wounded. He fired a shot in the air to get them moving to see if any were limping or lagging behind. All of them rushed nervously away at high speed, tails high. Coupled with his anxiety over the last wounded elephant was his concern over his rifle jamming. Hunting any of the dangerous game, in thick cover particularly, was always a serious business, even without complications caused by your weapon.

Eventually he left the Nyanyadzi area, reluctantly, to visit Chipinga. There in the small, isolated agricultural village he was informed by the native commissioner that in the coming months more African resettlement would be taking place along the hitherto untouched wilderness of the Changadzi River. Any resident elephants in the area would, in all probability, have to be wiped out as they would be unlikely to leave and would become a 'nuisance'. Furthermore, even if one or two were shot and the rest *did* move on, they would only be moving into other areas where human settlement was planned. So Rupert, in the coming months, would be serving as reluctant executioner once again. For the sake of progress.

As part of his task on his first patrol in this area Rupert had instructions to visit the Sabi Tanganda estate, situated on the eastern bank of the Sabi River, a few miles south of Birchenough Bridge. Previous visits by both Archie Fraser and Ian Nyschens had been prompted by increasing wild animal problems cropping up here. More particularly, there was a small resident herd of 20 buffalo residing in the vast expanses of reed beds which occurred along the river. The manager of the estates wanted the animals destroyed because he maintained that they carried the tick which infected cattle with thielieriosis and were also a danger to people who lived in the area. A further reason was that a major irrigation furrow would be constructed in the near future through the most inhospitable area of bush which the buffalos often frequented. Rupert noted it as a 'pending' matter, not relishing the combination of buffalos in thick bush with a rifle that tended to jam.
As it was, a further 'problem' needed immediate attention. Hippos, residents too of the Sabi reed beds and the succession of deep pools that formed during the dry months, were taking their toll of the estate's wheat and lucerne crops. The manager, as well as several local farmers, had spent some time attempting to shoot the animals, without success. Rupert went out that night into the lucerne with rifle and hunting lamp. He came upon two hippos which, as soon as the lamp light pinned them in its beam, went trotting off into the reeds at high speed, with much raucous grunting. It was as if they'd played the game before! The next morning Rupert tried again. While his trackers probed with a long pole in the deep, dark areas under the reed banks, he waited thigh deep in the shallow water of midstream. Eventually a hippo surfaced with a whoosh of air and Rupert shot it behind the ear. It slid slowly back into the deep water and disappeared. Two days later it would re-surface as its body gases expanded, and sent it balloon-like to float in the pool.

Rupert moved across the river to the giant horizon-to-horizon spread of Devuli Ranch. Here too he met hippo and elephant problems. To some degree the manager, a Mr Rawl, had solved his own problems as far as the 'river horses' were concerned. He had fenced, with strategically placed large rocks, the irrigation section of the ranch. But elephants were another story, and he was sympathetic. Yet progress was progress. He explained to Rupert that he considered the shooting of one or two elephants at a time as no answer to the problem of the invading herds found around the Sabi/Devuli confluence, and that the Game Section should formulate a plan of some sort to ease the problem. Permanently. It was no small request! At the time of Rupert's visit the situation was complicated further. The Tsetse Department was shooting on the Sabi and Lundi rivers, which resulted more than ever in the frightened, confused elephant herds being driven back into the farming and irrigation areas of Humani, Devuli and Nyanyadzi. In short, whichever way the problem was approached, the elephant (or any other animal that interfered with progress) was a loser.

Paragraph two of the diary entry took up all of two lines:

'Objective: To observe elephants' movements, determine numbers, and destroy them in the control area.'

This objective was a task lasting nearly a month. It was November. Suicide month had passed, but it left the heat and the oppressive humidity that comes before the first rains of the season sweep across the country, cleansing it. Together with Archie Fraser, Rupert travelled south west to Bulawayo and then eastward through Gwanda to the rugged, uncompromising scrubland near the confluence of the Umzingwane and Limpopo rivers. On the banks of a smaller river, the Tongwe, they made a rendezvous with Ian Nyschens and a new, fourth member of the Game Section, where a camp was already established.

The new man, the third game ranger, was Tommy Orford. He was from a farming background and was only just 21 years old. From the age of 16 he had been pestering the Game Officer for a position, any position, in the Game Section. Even at this time of writing, Tom Orford looks an easy 10 years younger than his actual age, so one can perhaps understand Archie Fraser's reluctance at taking on the young man with the baby face and even younger voice. Finally, after continual badgering, Fraser, in the hope that time would find some other whim for the young enthusiast, told him to stop bothering him until he had turned twenty-one. When he was approached one day after the due date by the young man, Archie Fraser was forced to admit to himself that he had, whether he liked it or not, a new game ranger. Time would provide the test.

The first adventure that the field men were to face together proved to be out of the run of the ordinary hunting experience. They were an interesting threesome: the extremely self-assured ex-ivory hunter, the silent, introverted prospector-cum-naturalist, and the young novice, determined to prove himself in the presence of old hands. On the sidelines, their superior watched carefuly.
They drove their Land Rover along one of the bush tracks in an effort to cut fresh spoor of elephants. It was still relatively cool when they found the tracks of a herd and left the vehicle to follow up. In a short space of time they had made contact with a solitary bull, browsing away from the herd. The three men, trackers following up several paces behind, approached to within 30 paces of the elephant. While Rupert covered him with a Double, Ian Nyschens shot the animal cleanly with a Westley Richards .425 Magnum. The elephant collapsed, its trunk caught in the fork of the tree off which it had been browsing. At this embryonic stage of his career, Tom Orford was an observer, allowed only the armament of a box camera! The men continued on the tracks of the main herd. From the spoor it looked as if the strength of the herd was in the region of 40 animals.

On the banks of a dry river bed they came upon three cows, browsing on the far bank. Rupert shot one cow, which dropped in her tracks, while Ian Nyschens took the second, which dropped and then regained her feet and started lurching away. The ivory hunter, followed by the babyfaced newcomer clutching his camera, moved after the wounded animal. At this stage events began to telescope at top speed. Rupert, some two dozen paces behind, watching the bush where the third cow had disappeared, was suddenly aware of another cow elephant coming at him. Already in full charge. At the same time he saw another group of about a dozen cows and sub-adults starting an attack on his companions. The trackers, with spare weapons, were nowhere to be seen. Rupert sprinted for his comrades so that they could make a concentrated stand against the elephants which by now were well on their way in. The scene was a tapestry of scrub bush with massive grey bodies appearing out of the swirling dust in jerking, savage charges, coming from all directions, squealing and screaming their anger and hatred. Rupert's attacker had joined the other group and now the two men were stopped, feet solid, forcing their breathing steady, taking aim on the horrifyingly close elephants. Rupert dropped the leading cow at fifteen paces with a brain shot and almost immediately Ian Nyschens killed another. The herd turned, their charge broken, sweeping past on either side. Suddenly, out of the dust on the elephants' heels, appeared the trackers, running hard. On their heels was another group of elephants, gaining fast. Later it transpired that they had departed rapidly from the scene of the second encounter and, whilst running away, had bumped into another section of the herd ... which was now chasing them. As Nyschens and Fothergill manoeuvred themselves into a position where they could shoot their trackers' pursuers without also harming the men, the elephants wheeled away into the scrub. The dust settled. The sound of the fleeing elephants became softer. The men took a deep breath. A morning's total of five elephants - three bulls and two cows. Where would the herd go to next? Where was it allowed to go?

Once again the weapons, government issue, were a cause for concern. During this particular interlude there had been two jams, but tragedy had been averted by team work. As with all other aspects of their section and, perhaps, a forerunner of problems encountered even today, there was very little government expenditure on weapons. Out of a dozen second-hand magazine-supplied 0.425s it was soon established that only three worked satisfactorily. The three Wesley Richards double 0.500s were the only rifles the rangers felt safe with and Fraser had his own 0.450 Rigby. Despite repeated complaints to the relevant authorities in Salisbury, it was a long time before an inspector from the Public Services Board was detailed to investigate. He accompanied Ian Nyschens on an elephant control task, almost openly contemptuous of the complaints outlined to him. Two jams later in thick *jesse* bush with an irritated cow elephant almost in his lap, he was grateful for the presence of Nyschens' personal 0.450 double. Only in the last few years have some of those initial issue weapons been withdrawn, and adapted to drug-darting work.

The team then split up. Ian Nyschens left for the Limpopo ranches; Archie Fraser departed to check the Bubye area; and Rupert and Tom established a camp on the Umzingwane River near Umgulumbi Hill. The Umzingwane, its literal local meaning being 'a river with small beginnings' is one of the largest rivers in the south west of the country, rising in the granite studded Matopos and flowing south to the Limpopo. It is notorious for its sudden flash floods. The heat and the humidity had built up until one late afternoon the first rains fell. Slowly at first, great, heavy, fat drops, making miniature explosions in the dust. Then the storm became heavier, the wind gone now, with the rain sluicing straight down, washing the veld clean. The two men scoured the west bank of the Umzingwane for elephant signs. They observed lions and giraffes and numerous herds of impala, zebra and wildebeest. After the initial storm the rain had ceased and the sky cleared. But the rain clouds were still there on the horizon, a blue indigo mass illuminated occasionally by flickering sheet lightning.

Archie Fraser rejoined them four days later and they continued to search the area. It was a far cry from the form of elephant control that was to be developed some 10 years later in 1966 in Wankie, when a highly mechanised team of hunters, aided by spotter planes, would move in to decimate a whole family unit of elephants. Of adults that were 60 years old (traversing a time span that saw the arrival of the first settler columns in the country) and middle-aged animals, right down to week-old stumbling, floppy calves (if there was no current demand from the zoos of the world). There was no doubt the men involved in the killing hated it, dreaded it. But it had to be done. In the name of progress! The humans needed more land. To plant and excavate, and erode and pollute. Meanwhile, the areas set aside for the wildlife, ostensibly vast and fertile, now have to feed more and more animals. Slowly the ecosystem crumbles. The plants and trees can no longer feed the elephants, and the impala and the sable. Yet still the humans need more land.

On the fifth day, not far from camp, they saw a goshawk attack a dove in flight. It dropped from above like a stone and a trickle of feathers floated down. It was over in seconds, but then, inexplicably, the raptor released its prey. At first the dove just fell earthwards, fluttering feebly. Then it found strength and wheeled erratically, finding its balance, before flying off. Each of the men smiled quietly to himself as they walked on. After two hours they crossed the spoor of seven bulls. The dung was still warm and olive green. The sun had been up a little over two hours. They followed the spoor, noting where it joined a herd of cows and calves. Gradually, in the scrub *mopane*, they lost the spoor of the bulls, and kept on the smaller spoor. At noon the men heard sounds of feeding elephants, and they moved carefully, studying the wind. Ahead of them two cows and a calf appeared. Fraser and Fothergill shot the first cow and then the game officer put down the second cow which had taken up a defensive position in front of the calf, although the youngster's own mother was dead.

They continued hunting in the area, walking over 23 miles on one day. The rains had gone now. The heat was back with them. Hotter than before the rains, with the force of the sun an almost physical entity, sucking the sweat from a man's pores and swelling his tongue. For another week they hunted, killing three more elephants. But the herds were wary now and travelled long distances, some even crossing into South Africa. They would stay scattered now, for a while, and move into other areas. Seeking peace and quiet. They would find it, maybe, until the next attack.

CHAPTER 4
PERSPECTIVE

Now might be a good time to take a closer look at Fothergill, in the context of his role with the relatively new government body formed to work in conjunction with its sister Tsetse Department. The headlines of the historic game rescue task of Operation Noah are still three years away, when his image would be seized upon by the news media of the world. In these first years with the Game Section, the primary work involved control, that innocuous diplomatic word which was the synonym for the destruction of wild animals whose existence interfered with that of humans. Rupert had been, in one form or another, in the bush all his life. He had been hunting since he was a youngster and had shot more than his share of game of all types before he joined the Game Section. Now, in his middle forties he had tired of the hunt as such, but it was a task which, in the name of progress, still had to be carried out. And he would much rather have it carried out by men of ability, with the minimum of suffering, than by all and sundry in an open season-type debacle.

At this stage of the country's development, when elephant herds were 'causing trouble' it was usually sufficient for two or three of the guilty party to be destroyed, resulting in the remainder fleeing to quieter parts. It was, nevertheless, a short-term strategy and in the annual report of the Game Section in 1956 it was noted that *"the land available to the elephant population of the colony as permanent or temporary habitat is fast diminishing, and with problems of control rapidly increasing, it is evident that even greater numbers will have to be destroyed each year. Natural increase is accepted as 7% of the population and, on current numbers, it is necessary to destroy about 700 per annum to maintain numbers, at their present level."*

That was forty years ago!

In the same report, dealing with the subject of elephant control it was stated that *"rather more"* than 426 elephants had been destroyed that year and it gave the breakdown as being:

Game Section	129
Tsetse fly operations	90
National Park Game Wardens	30
Native Commissioners	35
Amateur Hunters and Deputies	102
Under Royal Game licence and on private land	40 (estimate)
	426 (a decrease of 91 from 1955)

During that year too, control work involved the killing of 48 hippos on the fast developing Triangle Sugar Estates. Also destroyed were baboons, lions and leopards that were killing stock, and, on the Liebigs Ranch in West Nicholson and the Lazy Y Ranch in Beit Bridge, zebras and wildebeest were culled commercially in an experimental operation that supplied 60 909 lbs of biltong to butchers and other agents.

So this, then, was the scenario when Rupert first joined. While control was certainly the major task of the Department, it was done as judiciously as possible and with the least amount of interference to other animals or the ecosystem. And with initially only three game rangers and the game officer covering the entire country, everyone had a busy time. The visits to head office in Salisbury were but brief interludes devoted to the upkeep and maintenance of the few vehicles, the resupply of basic provisions and ammunition and the constant intense detail to weapons, rectifying malfunctions that had occurred in the field. There was also the chance of eating a few home-cooked meals and seeing how fast one's children were growing.

Then it was back to the control and patrol work. Journeys were not as swift and as predictable as they are today. Once off the basic network of 'main roads' connecting the major centres, with most of these highways being no more than two parallel tarred strips, necessitating a fair amount of juggling when one met another vehicle coming the other way, dirt tracks were the order of the day. Once the rains had set in, these were not always functional, even to the modern four wheel drive vehicles, and anyone who travelled in Africa during those years, when rainy seasons were real, usually spent an occasional night in a car that was irrevocably bogged down to its axles in mud. On these long stretches of road and bush track, fellow travellers were not always common, so if one's truck broke down or one got stuck at the bottom of a dry, sandy river bed, some initiative and mechanical knowledge were essential. Apart from the largely undeveloped communications systems that existed then, particularly in the areas frequented by the game rangers, there were other normal existing facts of life which made it essential for one to know what one was about, and be adept at improvisation. There were no deep-freeze facilities, so rations had to be planned accordingly for the ranger and his field team. A non-hunting area meant just that, and it being part of Rupert's make-up to observe laws and carry out instructions to the last degree, it was often a pretty lean and hungry team which left such an area.

The upkeep of one's health was of fundamental importance. A dose of malaria, blackwater fever or some other tropical malaise, miles from anywhere, had its inherent problems. So it was that the actual physical aspect of the game ranger's patrol work and control duties was really a small part of the day-to-day events in his chosen way of life. For a salary of £62 a month before deductions, Rupert considered he had got a bargain of a job.

A person is weighed up and evaluated in such a variety of ways by his fellows: he is either frail or strong, schooled or unschooled, meek or aggressive. No one person categorises him the same way. It was absorbing for this writer, over long months and in a variety of environments, talking to people having at least one thing in common ... their association with Rupert, in one context or another. It was not all sweetness and light. There were those amongst the wide spectrum of people who knew him who were critical of one or another of his characteristics, or his approaches to situations. One of his early colleagues was unimpressed with Rupert's hunting ability, while another described him as being an uneducated, unambitious civil servant. Taken in the appropriate context there is probably some truth in both opinions. His hunting critic, a noted elephant hunter, has himself been described by several people as a butcher with none of the quiet controlled approach that Rupert displayed. Rupert was very methodical, almost irritatingly so, and his method of hunting reflected this. No shot was hurried, unless the situation demanded it, and he thought everything out as much as possible in advance. The nickname given to him in those early days, which is used even now by the surviving African game scouts from that era, was *'Katasvora'* - 'the one who shoots through the eye'. Archie Fraser, to whom he was directly responsible for several years, including the first year of Operation Noah, describes him as an outstanding naturalist, very reliable and totally committed to his job and to wildlife.

Rupert, by his own admission, was no scholar, and made no pretence that he was. The bane of his life was the field diary that game rangers were obliged to keep, but which he religiously wrote up every night, whatever was happening. Yet he was a scholar in other respects. His knowledge of the veld and its inhabitants was endless, and he was a ready, if somewhat harsh, teacher of it. Tommy Orford, newly arrived in the ranks of the Game Section, was to become Rupert's protegé and in the following years regarded him almost as a father. Orford recalls the pair of them being despatched to the Sabi Tanganda junction shortly after he had joined the section ...

"Even then the buffalos in the reedbeds were notorious and a few people had come to grief trying to shoot them. The attempts had just made the animals more wary and aggressive. Rupert and I were sent down to have a look at the situation. I was very new then and on the first day he went off to check an area of reeds where some local farmer had apparently wounded one of the buffalos, leaving me with strict instructions not to leave the camp and go off hunting. It never did take me long to get bored and I took my rifle and tracker and went off to do a little reconnaissance of my own. It was very hot and the reeds were incredibly thick and I was crawling along a tunnel when I saw just the feet of several buffalos ahead of me. You can imagine how the adrenalin was working as I manoeuvred my rifle up through the reeds. Suddenly I received a terrific jolt from behind which sent me skidding forward on my face. I desperately turned, juggling with the rifle, and there was Rupert, puffing his old pipe, his size nine shoe still poised from the kick. After a few seconds he spoke, telling me in his slow steady way that if I was going to hunt buffalos I had better do it properly like a man, on my two feet instead of my belly ... and that it was just as well the feet I had been looking at were cows belonging to a local farmer. There was still a twinkle in his eye. Behind that dour, almost grim expression of his, he had a great sense of humour, and you could tell from his eyes when he was pulling your leg."

He was not loquacious, not a chatty type at all, and tended to be wary of people who were. His austere features masked a good sense of humour,

and he was not uncomfortable telling anecdotes against himself. His reputation as a totally honest, down-to-earth person whose word was his bond, was parallelled by his reputation as a tough, stubborn individual whose quiet, unflamboyant dedication almost bordered on the fanatical. His attention to detail and imperturbable single-mindedness when it came to a specific task has more than once earned him the title of 'an old granny'. These characteristics lent themselves to his other love. Prospecting. He was an intelligent and avid prospector from his youth to his years of retirement, and it was an interest he certainly inherited from his father, whose life was governed by the quest for metals. His father who, when dangerously ill and in an ambulance being rushed to hospital, had diverted the ambulance to the government Geology Department with his latest batch of ore samples. Father and son prospected a lot in the beginning and they staked many claims: for nickel in Mtoko, gold near Karoi and Selukwe, and diamonds near the Shangani River. Chrome beckoned from deep in the heart of the Wankie National Park. As seems so often to be the case, there were nearly always third parties involved, the silent partners, and for both Rupert and his father whose handshake signified a bond, the prospecting never yielded much. Perhaps the search was enough. That and the solitary life.
Throughout 1956 and 1957 normal control and patrol duties were carried out. In February 1956, whilst Rupert and Tom Orford were south, hunting crop-raiding elephant, the Game Section was expanded by one man. An ex-policeman who for a long time had tried, ironically, to catch up with Ian Nyschens during the latter's pre-government days hunting ivory, Barry Ball had hankered after a change of commitment. He became, in due course, one of the senior men in the Department of National Parks and Wildlife Management.

Since January the rains had set in with a vengeance. In Gwanda and the Liebigs Ranch area, scattered herds of elephants were destroying crops. The native commissioner, who normally dealt with any routine game problems in his area, had been unsuccessful in tracking the raiders. It was raining daily, the bush was impenetrable and the ground saturated. Extensive foot work brought the two men no closer to the elephants and they were forced to move camp several times, seeking more stable ground. Their Bedford bogged down repeatedly and one stretch of 12 miles took eight hours to cover. Their trackers fell sick. Standard kit issue did not extend to raincoats or great-coats and the men were perpetually wet. They hunted in the rain and rain-sodden bush for a month, only once getting within seven paces of three bulls but not being able to see them in the thick greenery. The elephants migrated regularly across the border into Bechuanaland and the main contingent had not yet returned. Prior to Rupert's arrival a herd of 250 plus animals had been observed leaving the country.

Apart from the elephants, lions were killing stock in the Nuanetsi-Bubye district and Rupert and Tom spent nights around cattle enclosures with hunting lamps, hunting the raiders. It was an impossible task, the beam of the lamp fuzzy in the pounding rain, the noise drowning every other sound. Sometimes they wondered if it would ever stop. They returned to Salisbury with colds, 1 824 miles added to the speedometer of their Bedford truck, and three of their four issue .425 magnum rifles defective.

The journeys to the different parts of the country and the innumerable hunts, mostly for elephants, became a single vast tapestry in their minds. Baboon control in the Lomagundi District, wild dog control in the Chipinga area, hippo problems in the sprawling, green uniformity of the new Hippo Valley Estates, leopard-baiting in the Mtoko African farming areas ... and all this time poaching was on the increase. In their hunts the game rangers found more and more snares and a spiralling amount of wounded or dead animals. It was a problem which, in the years ahead, would become ever more critical. It would become increasingly organised and would expand from the basic need for meat at subsistence level to commercial, opportunist slaughter.

Occasionally there arose duties of a different kind, that of tour guide.

It was a task which did not sit easily on Rupert's shoulders. Then, as today, the Game Section staff were from time-to-time called upon to chaperon certain dignitaries who expressed the desire to visit remote areas of the country. So it was in October 1956 when the Southern Rhodesian Prime Minister, the Honourable Garfield Todd, the Acting Governor General, Sir Robert Tredgold, and his public relations officer, Mr Playfair, visited Nemana Pools. Rupert and Ian Nyschens were allocated the task of 'nursemaid', driving down onto the Zambezi Valley floor to set up camp. As on previous trips, the elephant population was as conspicuous and restless as ever. At night the camp was the focal point of their attention and they wandered through at will, often less than a few feet from the rangers' camp beds. Their trumpeting competed with the nightly grunting of lions, who were also frequent visitors, and it promised to be an interesting trip for a group of V.I.Ps. In due course, Rupert departed for Kariba airstrip to collect them and Archie Fraser. There followed four days of general lazing for the visitors, who fished and filmed and game-viewed. The only real excitement that showed potential for getting out of hand was a nocturnal invasion. The elephants routed the trackers from their camp, forcing them to retreat at speed through the main camp area. The screams of the pursued trackers, the trumpeting of the angry elephants, and the general mayhem there in the flickering firelight had Rupert and his comrades with their hands full for a while. Career prospects were definitely dim if any of the politicians got an elephant in his lap, or his tent flattened, or if his nightcap was spilt.

CHAPTER 5

THE MKWASINE EPISODE

The herd of zebra milled restlessly, hooves pawing at the parched earth, nostrils flaring. The noon day sun, burning out of the faded, blue sky, picked out the black and white stripes of their hides with miniature reflecting highlights. The sun reflected brightly too off the six-foot high, eight-strand fence. The barrier! The water was in their nostrils and they snorted and fidgeted. True, there was water, small isolated pockets of it, on their side of the wire, on the western side, but it was very brackish. Undrinkable. And they were dying of thirst. A hundred yards away lay the rotting carcass of an eland. It had died with the smell of water in its nostrils, tormented and confused. The lead stallion moved away from the herd, towards the fence some 100 paces away. The others stood there waiting, turning to watch him. Dust spurted up in small explosions as his hooves touched the ground. Over the group of 15 animals the dust hung in a smudged pall. The stallion kept moving and when he was about 30 yards from the fence, broke into a fast trot. The fence held, throwing him back off its wires and he rejoined his herd.

Within minutes he was retracing his steps, at a faster pace now, rushing the barrier that kept his herd from the life-sustaining fluid. Again he hit the wire and again he bounced off the fence, almost losing his footing. He stood for some moments and shook his head and snorted. Then trotted back purposefully, again. It was as if he had tested the strength of the wire and now knew what he would have to do to break it. He wheeled and charged at full speed, head-long at the slender threads of steel that stretched away interminably into the distance. This time he was supported by a stallion on either side of him and slightly to the rear and, in their wake, the herd followed at full gallop. This time the fence snapped and the herd passed through, their black and white stripes forming a surrealistic kaleidoscope in the form-obscuring clouds of dust. The lead stallion faltered and then fell, chest heaving and big horse eyes rolling. One of his front legs was broken and pink frothy blood bubbled from his nostrils. He was still alive, barely, when Rupert found him. He never moved when the game ranger moved up to him. One eye swivelled to follow the man's progress, his breathing shallow now. The rest of the herd had gone. They had found the water he could still smell. Rupert shook his head softly and shucked a cartridge into the breech of his rifle. He was murmuring gently to the animal.

Prior to World War II very little development had occurred in the southern and south eastern lowveld and large tracts of land were unoccupied. Occupied land, in the south, took such forms as the vast 2 000 000 acre Nuanetsi Ranch and the 1 650 000-acre Liebigs Ranch. The African population was relatively small and scattered. Communications, apart from 'main roads' were bad or non-existent, and as yet, the four-wheeled vehicle had not evolved. The Land Rover would appear on the scene only

in 1948. Vast areas were out of reach for all but the most intrepid of hunters, and in these wild, remote parts the animals found sanctuary, harassed only occasionally by man. The Sabi Valley was noted then for large game concentrations, while stories of vast herds on the Mkwasine and Lundi rivers were legendary. It is interesting to note that as early as 1934 land had been set aside for the Gona Re Zhou Game Reserve.

During the Second World War years, young men were in far-off lands as part of the allied war machine and the inherent shortages of petrol and ammunition kept most would-be hunters out of the thickly concentrated game areas. There is no doubt, although no records are available for this period, that the fauna of the colony increased considerably. Post-war years saw great progress and development in Southern Rhodesia. The large increase in population, both black and white, created such a demand for essential protein foods that new land was inevitably opened up. Ranching land in the lowveld began to be developed to its maximum capacity, and irrigation projects were established on the fertile alluvial soils bordering lowveld rivers. The future would see thousands of acres under intensive agriculture and close settlement. The land which was once free for wild animals to roam over at will was gradually fenced. The fencing would continue and increase and the animals would have less and less land on which to live and hunt and breed, and to avoid the guns.

The increased lowveld development pushed land prices upwards. Larger ranches were subdivided. In many cases the smaller land units became 'hunting boxes' and it was not uncommon for the new land owners to destroy every wild animal that crossed their path. This indiscriminate killing led to the introduction of the Game and Fish Preservation Act which was passed in June 1957. Coupled with this surge of development came the implementation of the Land Apportionment Act, and in many areas the resettlement of Africans pushed the resident wildlife out, to search for safer, wilder country. The search for minerals increased and intensified, and prospectors scoured the country, leaving their marks in remote areas that before had seen little, if any, indication of modern man. In those post-war months areas that had been inaccessible were now within the sphere of influence of the magic words: progress and development.

And so, in the lowveld, at least, this era introduced considerable upheaval to the lives of the game concentrations that had lived there since time immemorial. There were more radical and final pressures that paralleled this progress. The spread of the tsetse fly in Portuguese East Africa had increased, alarmingly so, in the context of the vast lowveld development and settlement. The fly had become established on the west bank of the Sabi River, constituting immediate danger to the domestic stock in the Bikita, Ndanga and Chipinga areas. The Department of Tsetse Control and Reclamation worked strenuously to counter the movement of the fly. Which meant more barriers and fences, the destruction of large areas of vegetation affording the vital shade needed by the tsetse fly, and the destruction of wild animals that attracted the tsetse fly. By the hundreds and thousands. Foot and mouth disease, the cattleman's ogre that is still with us today, and various other tick-borne diseases to which domestic stock is susceptible, were taking their toll. Veterinary authorities believed then, although they had not proved, that these diseases were attributed to wild animals and their movements. The result? More destruction of wildlife!

And so the wild animals made way for progress. On the Liebigs and Nuanetsi ranches zebras and wildebeest were shot to make way for cattle. On the three vast Limpopo River ranches, irrigation projects and ranching development saw the beginning of the permanent elimination of elephants, zebras and wildebeest.

In the Gwanda and Beit Bridge areas campaigns were mounted against elephants migrating from Bechuanaland. The railway line linking the Portuguese East African capital of Lourenço Marques with Southern

Rhodesia disrupted the migration of elephants and zebras moving to the Nuanetsi River area. On the blossoming lowveld ranches lions and leopards adapted very easily to stock-killing, and consequently became hunted themselves. There was also poaching for the game to contend with. The poaching increased, season after season, year after year. But there wasn't an awful lot that three game rangers could do about it, covering the whole of the British colony as they did.

This then, was the background, briefly penned, to what became known as the Mkwasine Tragedy, culminating in September 1957. It was at this stage that the press gave publicity to the deaths of 'thousands' of animals, along the game fence in the Ndanga and Bikita districts, due to lack of water. It was publicity that, quite erroneously, brought severe criticism of the Game Department.

Since mid-1930, when the rapidly spreading menace of tsetse fly had been noted in Portuguese East Africa, the Department of Tsetse Fly Control and Reclamation had been fighting a losing battle in the checking of the advance of the fly. By 1955 the insect was well established within the lowveld areas of Southern Rhodesia, its furthermost incursion occurring on the west bank of the Sabi River, not very far from Buffalo Range. In view of this deteriorating situation, a decision was made to erect a fence, 80 miles long, from a point on the Sabi River, running in a south-westerly and southerly direction to below the Lundi River. The object of the fence was to demarcate the westernmost boundary of a cattle-and-game-free belt five miles in breadth at its narrowest point, so that contact between infected game and cattle on the east and non-infected game and cattle on the west could, as far as possible, be prevented. This decision conformed with the established policy that shooting operations would now be restricted and that game west of the proposed fence would be left undisturbed. As a member of the committee that had been formed to study the feasibility of the fence, Archie Fraser supported its erection, convinced that in the long run it would save the lives of many wild animals that would otherwise be destroyed in the course of tsetse control operations.

In the middle months of 1956 a start was made on the building of a fence. It began near an artesian well on the Lone Star Ranch, owned by Ray Sparrow, an ardent conservationist and pioneer of the lowveld. In three months it had travelled 14 miles, to the banks of the Mkwasine River where, a year later, the drama of this drought-stricken part of the country would unfold. The work on the fence continued in stages over the next year. It was backbreaking, sweat-pouring, time-consuming labour, in one of the most inaccessible and inhospitable parts of the colony. Between June and September 1957, 15 miles of game fence north of the Mkwasine River was erected; for several months the actual bed of the river was left unfenced, allowing some access from east to west. On August 25, that too was barriered. Since the last rains in March, Rupert and Ian Nyschens had been keeping a weather eye on the game in the area, the surface water situation, and the effect of the fence on the wild denizens. In this area and continuing on southwards to the wilder Gona Re Zhou (which in the local dialect means 'horn of the elephant'), the game concentrations were varied. Elephants, buffalos, kudu, impala, zebras, Lichtenstein's hartebeest, bushbuck, nyala, sable, roan and the smaller antelope were all well represented. And, as part of mother nature's set of scales, so too were lions, leopards, cheetah and other predators. All wildlife to the east of the game fence was earmarked for liquidation.

As the year progressed into the winter dry months, with its biting, cold, star-studded nights and uncompromising, hot, windless days, the flow of the smaller rivers dwindled and the levels of the scattered waterholes receded a little more each day. Rupert watched these signs with misgivings. The previous rainy season had not been a good one and the rivers and general water table of the countryside had not received their usual seasonal boost. Another poor rainy season, or even late rains, would leave this part of the lowveld in dire straits, and the long tendrils of wire stretching from horizon to heat-hazed horizon would only add to any problems, hindering the wild animals of all species in their search for water.

Added to this concern he had another worry. Poaching! Slaughter! With the game fence itself playing its part in the killing. Tribespeople from the Ndanga and Sangwe areas were stealing lengths of wire from the fence and making snares. And with their packs of dogs they were driving the antelope into the fence. Around the dwindling water holes and isolated pools in the river bed, the animals ran a gauntlet of traps. Cunningly concealed loops of strong new government-supplied wire surrounded each and every water point, fastened to a part of the undergrowth. They brought a slow, agonising, terrifying death to the luckless beast that they snared. Never was it a quick merciful end, for the people seldom checked their snare lines regularly. A week could pass. Depending on what species of animal fell foul of the circle of death, any part of its anatomy could be trapped. Around its neck, on any one of its legs, around a muzzle, wherever, it meant a lingering horrific end. There, with life-giving water only a few yards away it would be caught. Puzzled, perhaps, at first, by this alien, human-tainted thing that gripped it. Then, quickly, panic set in as it bucked and fought against the restriction, and the noose slipped tighter against its neck, or around its back leg, and it felt the first spasms of pain as the wire bit into its flesh. Then came terror. Terror and more pain as it struggled violently, uselessly, against this thing that trapped it. And the wire now would be cutting deep into it, into its neck muscles or its leg tendons and the animal would be screaming now with the agony. Weakened soon by its crazed, desperate attempts to break loose, and by thirst, it would collapse motionless on the game trail, reviving occasionally to kick and struggle against the snare. And the wire would cut in a little deeper, sawing through living, tormented flesh and eventually, after endless, timeless hours, it would come up against bone, or against the jugular vein. If the animal was lucky it would be discovered by hyenas or lions and then its suffering would be terminated. Not quickly, for the meat eaters might not kill the helpless beast before feasting. But certainly it would be spared more long agonizing hours.

There was always an outside chance that the person who had set the snare line would return to check it within a couple of days and the ordeal would be ended with a hunting knife across the animal's throat.

Nor were the increased poaching activities confined to the tribespeople of the lowveld. With the blossoming of the region and more and more of the veld falling to the plough and domestic stock, so too the white man added his attentions to the lives of the wildlife population. In some cases a shroud of legality was sewn over some of the killings. Triangle Sugar Estates had made it a practice to offer 30/- for every zebra and £3 for every buffalo destroyed. That this resulted in many animals being wounded, with no attempt made to follow them up and despatch them, seemed to cause little concern. With buffalo, whose penchant for revenge when wounded is legendary, this was an ignorant, indeed murderous, policy. It was common knowledge amongst the farmers in the area that there were at that stage more wounded than fit buffalos roving the rugged lowveld bush.

Rupert found abundant signs of the increased killing. Apart from the carcasses, he was frequently coming across wounded game which he was forced to put out of its misery. The victims were not restricted to the ubiquitous zebras and buffalos; elephants were being shot often, for no reason other than to satisfy the ego of some pseudo hunter. In one herd of 24 elephants of varying ages, Rupert observed three wounded beasts, the fact clearly evidenced by the blood patches on the heads and bodies of the animals. A doctor resident in the area openly bragged about shooting 25 impala in one night, mesmerising the animals with the strong beam of a hunting lamp, which allowed a casual approach to within a few yards of the victim. Other people travelled from further afield, from Fort Victoria and Bulawayo, to have their share of the shooting, the news of which had filtered far and wide. Fothergill steadily collated evidence against one such visitor over several months, finally catching the man after he had just shot three members of a family of cheetahs.

Not everyone was kill-crazy. Some of the early lowveld ranchers, who would become doyens of controlled scientific game ranching, were ardent conservationists and from these people Rupert received much ready assistance. People like the Styles family, headed by George Styles, and Ray Sparrow, and Starling and Hein contributed much to the welfare of the game. And so Rupert had his own special intelligence network and he worked quietly, persevering, listening much and saying little, until gradually he could put water-tight cases together. He was always grimly triumphant when he hit the jackpot. But many were never caught. The country was too big. Too big and wild and unheeding of the dramas on its surface. Catching the mechanised, modernised poacher was not the same as catching the local poacher. With the latter a different kind of planning had to be initiated, and it was much more affected by luck, patience and quick reactions.

★ ★ ★ ★ ★ ★ ★ ★

Rupert walked slowly around the patch of water in the barren river bed. The spoor was of impala, zebras and buffalos, and was several hours old. They had probably watered around first light, he surmised. It was mid-morning now and he and his two trackers had also been on the move since dawn. Checking the water holes, and the accompanying snares. He'd collected over 200 so far today. He was about to move away when another indentation in the sand caught his attention. His eyes narrowed and he grunted, jutting his chin at the spoor. His chief tracker, Langton, also grunted his interpretation. Dog. Ordinary, domestic, local mongrel. Here, in the middle of nowhere. The spoor was fresh, water still seeping back into the imprint. Rupert motioned for the second tracker to dump the snares they'd collected, his eyes roving across the river bank. As he watched, a small dog crept up the bank and disappeared from view. They followed. Once they caught a glimpse of it as it paused to look back. Its tracks led towards a small densely-bushed hillock. The three Game Section men walked on warily. From the skeleton-like branches of a large baobab some vultures launched themselves heavily into flight. Rupert moved away from the dog's tracks towards the tree, simultaneously catching the faint smell of woodsmoke. The Shangaan poachers' camp was empty. Tracks of eight men led out of the camp, southwards. The slow fires burning under the network of meat racks were well established, and the meat racks were in turn cunningly camouflaged with fresh-cut greenery and leaves. Rupert surveyed the hidden base bitterly, noting the carcasses of warthogs, zebras, impala, duikers and a young kudu calf. He didn't touch any of the contents and murmured instructions to his companions. Langton he posted in some thick shrub above the camp and took the other tracker with him south of the camp, ambushing the existing set of tracks. With some luck they'd return from the same direction. The sun rose higher in the belljar sky. At noon it was at its zenith and the heat beat remorselessly down. The bush was still and silent. Nothing would move in this heat. Only the vultures, drifting high up on the thermal currents in their endless vigil. After two hours Rupert moved his position. Back to where Langton waited in some meagre shade. The game ranger felt parched. Barely five minutes later they heard the first sounds of the returning poachers, already close. They were coming up the kopje behind their position; from the direction Rupert had least anticipated. The three men crouched lower in the brush. The first two poachers appeared on the fringe of the camp, carrying the freshly killed carcass of a buffalo calf. Warily they moved into the camp area, followed by the rest of the gang. Rupert noted the bows and the quivers of arrows and one old Martini Henry rifle. Behind him a dog barked and he cursed silently, moving, jumping, pounding at the group of poachers. But they too were moving, with the first sound of the bark. Scattering, yelling, dropping the carcass. Rupert went after the one with the rifle, his trackers abreast of him, selecting their quarry. It was a confused, blurred chase amidst the boulders and scrubby lowveld bush under the relentless midday sun. Rupert caught a fleeting glimpse of his quarry as the man appeared from below the lip of a dry river bed and he heard the report of the Martini Henry. He heard the heavy load slug crack through the underbrush and hoped it hadn't hit one of his trackers. And he ran harder, gasping, sweat pouring, tripping, thinking: 'Right chum, that was your shot and you missed. Now you're empty. And it's attempted murder, as well as poaching, so you'll be out of the way for a long while'.

But they lost them, there amidst the barren river courses and rocks and patches of thorn bush. They razed the camp and confiscated the meat and rolls of wire and other tools of the trade and piled it into the Land Rover which Rupert had walked back seven miles to collect. But they didn't get *them*, the killers themselves; and tomorrow they'd be setting new snares and there'd be scarcely a pause in their killing.

He quartered the area again. The five pools he knew east of the fence were dry now, the surface pockmarked with the countless hooves of game, and dried hard solid into a sort of miniature, barren, lunar landscape. He went back to the Mkwasine River, high up, close to where it entered the tribal settlement area, and walked back along its winding, sandy course to its confluence with the great Sabi River. There was no surface water now save for Ndongo Pool on the settlement boundary. This water hole was surrounded with snares. Patrolling southwards, the once reliable pools of Chikwarakwara and Sinuku were dry, although, when he dug down, he found water at around six feet below Sinuku. Only when he approached the Sabi-Mkwasine confluence on the east of the game fence did the water cover the river bed. He retraced his steps two days later and, helped by labourers loaned to him by a rancher, dug out eight watering points where he'd observed animals digging. He drove along the game fence, studying the scattered, nervous herds of sable and zebra, kudu and eland. There were no signs of obvious distress. They were still finding isolated pockets of water somewhere. And there they would be finding the snares as well. Throughout August and into September Rupert hunted poachers, setting ambushes on known tracks and around discovered camps concealed in the bush, finding snare line after snare line. Always the water supplies dwindled more. Every day, before the sun had climbed above the horizon it was stiflingly hot, airless, still; and long after dusk had fallen the earth was still hot.

In the first days of September the game began to congregate along the fence. The water was practically finished. And now, for the last week, the only break in the fence occurring in the bed of the Mkwasine River was sealed; effectively blocking off the permanent water of the Sabi and lower Mkwasine in the east from the game concentrations on the western side. The water holes dried up. And there was no sign of rain. Meanwhile, the poachers' attentions continued unabated. On the fourth day of that month Rupert counted 309 zebras in 14 miles, restlessly patrolling the wire. Other species of game were also congregating; nervous, wary, thirsty. Buffalo, eland, impala, warthog, sable, kudu, all overcoming their distrust of the man smell of the fence and the open cleared ground, as the instinct for water drew them closer. Rupert discovered the first carcasses on that day; 19 zebras and 3 buffalos.

The days that followed blended into one long sweat-soaked, toiling, heartbreaking blur. He contacted headquarters in Salisbury to advise them of the predicament. The game officer, barely back from a patrol in the northern part of the country, immediately took the step of advising the relevant government minister. The wheels began to move, almost imperceptibly at first. Rupert went straight up the Mkwasine to the dry Chikwarakwara Pool and started digging. Seven feet below the surface of the scalding hot sand he located water. It was just a dampness at first, barely discernible, then wetter, and cooler, with the sand darker from the moisture. Then came the first squelching trickle. Soon began the widening and enlarging of the hole. With the sun hammering down and his throat parched, lips caked dry, he and his trackers took turns in the open river bed - digging, digging.

And that was just the first step. Just the start of it. Just the start of the dying. Back near the start of the fence, near the artesian well on Lone Star Ranch, Rupert started digging a small dam. Ray Sparrow gave him the pick of his labour force and the task progressed well; soon the water from the trough was channelled into it. A little more water. A couple of puddles that weren't there before. But for some of the game it was too late. Every day Rupert was the witness to new tragedy and drama. One zebra made two attempts at rushing the fence, breaking its jaw in the process. He found numerous zebras and buffalos collapsed beside the fence, no longer strong enough to search for water.

Parallel with the fence a track was being scoured by the endless pacing of the game searching for a break. At one of the water points he saw nature breaking down its normal waterhole etiquette when a thin, emaciated buffalo gored a zebra that attempted to drink from the same pool. At another water point he saw a lioness with two cubs kill five zebras in a spasm of wanton destruction. The committee dealing with the fence construction called a meeting to discuss the drought tragedy. By now the press had learned of the unfolding drama and had visited the area, calling for the breaching of the fence. The committee vetoed the idea.

All Rupert wanted was more help. More pairs of hands. Help came slowly. The contractors building the fence made available a tractor and scoop, which Rupert detailed to the river bed to establish more water points. A pump unit was despatched from Fort Victoria and Rupert assembled it at one of the points that had been scooped out by the contractors and the first large pool formed. Local ranchers lent labour and equipment. Fraser and Orford arrived on the scene and the efforts began, very slowly, to have a result. But it was still early days, and there was no sign of rain. Some of the animals were managing to get through the fence, fatally injuring themselves in some cases; but others could be seen weakly staggering off into the bush on the east side. Rupert made a patrol of this side to check what surface water still existed between the fence and the life-saving blue-green waters of the Sabi, several miles away. The waterholes that he had monitored over the year were in need of maintenance. Countless wild animals visiting them were churning the pools into muddy quagmires. He set to work on this task. Further inland he discovered newly erected extensive snare lines. And there was a camp with meat racks festooned with zebra meat, sun drying. He left his trackers to ambush the camp, and dismantle the snares and continued his reconnoitre. Later in the day he saw through his binoculars three zebras trailing wire snares. The animals were in poor condition, continually stepping on the trailing section of the snare and so tightening the nooses around their necks. Bleakly he stalked them and put them out of their misery. When he finally returned to the fence and the Land Rover it was almost midnight. Standing in the moonlight beside the fence, their sunken flanks silver against the shadows of their ribs, three buffalo bulls barely shifted their heavy, bossed heads to look at him.

By mid-September small dams and pools had been constructed by the small nucleus of men weathering the drought and scorching sun alongside the wild animals. Rupert kept up an endless cycle of patrolling, checking water points, studying any game for serious injuries and snares, searching for snare lines and hunting parties. At every water point the pattern of spoor bore mute testimony to the animals that were congregating in their quest for the life sustaining fluid. Lions, kudu, leopards, baboons, sable, zebras, duikers, buffalos, elephants - all running the gauntlet of the poachers' attentions. He noted that many zebras and eland had 'slipped' their calves, but saw no signs of abortion in other species of game. Some of the animals had jumped the six-foot fence with little difficulty, eland and kudu especially. But he also found many which had fallen heavily or injured themselves and he mercifully and sadly shot them. Impala and smaller antelope often manoeuvered themselves between the strands, while buffalos were shy of using their strength and breaking through, often plodding along for considerable distances, stopping occasionally to test the strain of the wire with their horns. Elephants, those true kings of beasts, also did not break the fence, although they were seen to approach it on a number of occasions and tentatively test the wire with probing trunks. In other instances, however, their intelligence caused Rupert and his comrades some irritation. When the great beasts found the troughs that had been sunk into river beds, it did not take long for their gargantuan thirsts to empty them. Whereupon they would proceed to remove the trough and start to search for more water beneath it, damaging the carefully-constructed water trap and muddying the water for other inhabitants of the bush. Shortly after sunrise one morning, Rupert was visiting one of these water points and discovered three elephants in the process of searching for more water, the abutments of the trough already crushed. Piqued at their destructiveness, he shouted at them, clapping his hands loudly, hoping to move them away. For a few seconds the three delinquents surveyed him silently, up on the lip of the river bank. Then, as one, they shook their great heads, flapped their ears, and with much harrumphing and squealing, came up the bank at speed. Muttering, Rupert retreated quickly. He knew it would be a morning's work to repair the trough.

There was one occasion when the actions of a particular animal brought a brief smile to the features of the haggard, weary game ranger. He watched an eland bull purposefully approach the game fence. The animal was in good condition, unlike many of his companions. With scarcely a pause, the eland put his horns between the wires and eased his forelegs and body through the gap. Then, with unhurried deliberation, he drew his rear legs through, pausing while he shook himself, then wandered off, seemingly most pleased with himself.

In the outside world, Harold McMillan was now established as the new prime minister of Britain. Russia's first satellite launch had been a success, and Sputnik One was orbiting according to plan. The pop star, Elvis Presley, had been called up for his military service.

Throughout the lowveld region of Southern Rhodesia the drought took its toll of wildlife, especially in the Nuanetsi area where young elephants and zebras and kudu were perishing. Here, bush fires and the use of locally-concocted fish poisons in the diminishing water supplies added to the toll of the wild game. By the end of September a sufficient number of water points had been constructed in the Mkwasine area and the situation had eased. However, the object of the tsetse fly fence had been defeated, with the game getting through the fence from the west now consorting with domestic stock at the water holes and on the Sabi River in the east. Thus the elected committee agreed to the breaching of the fence once it was definitely ascertained that sufficient water was available on the western side. Then game would be able to move freely or, if necessary, could be driven through the gaps in the fence. Accordingly Rupert, Tom Orford and their small band of helpers continued to maintain the water points and apprehend as many poachers as possible, and await the rains, whenever they came. Daily temperatures were in excess of 130°F and the game would alternate between massing against the barrier of the fence and the thick bush near the series of man-made water holes. Rupert had been on this assignment for over two months now and was beginning to feel the strain.

Rain fell in mid October. For days the clouds had massed on the eastern horizon: indistinct at first and then building up, thicker and heavier, from grey through wine-grape indigo to black. Then came the rumbling, like distant artillery duels, coming closer and louder and the thunder reverberating across the heavens, preceeded by jagged, crackling lightning forking earthwards. And the air was heavy and suffocating and charged with desperate anticipation. The animals became more restless. Then came the first drops, blown sideways by a sudden, gusting wind, big and fat and coolly wet, patterning the dust. For just a few minutes it was like that, and then it petered out. Now there was only the rushing of the wind and the sound of the trees being buffeted. The clouds swept closer, lower, blacker, and then there was the gale. Roaring, gusting, bullying its way across the veld, drowned only by the thunder. And it brought with it the rain. A solid, grey, hissing curtain of it, advancing on the dry, dusty camp on the banks of the Mkwasine. At last it was on them and they laughed and jigged about in the downpour, relishing the needle points of the rain that saturated them and cleansed their pores of the ingrained dust and sweat. And the game too stood in the rain.

For two days the rain fell. Then it was gone. The clouds vanished and the furnace heat came back. Now Rupert found game massing on the east of the fence, trying to break through to the west. He discovered the carcasses of several antelope that had killed themselves in the process. It was time the fence was breached. They cut the fence in four places, where the animals had massed heavily, on the north bank of the Mkwasine, and removed all the wire and poles in each of the 400 yard openings. At first they left the poles in place, but still the animals did not move through. Only when the men removed the poles did the game cross over, as though only then acknowledging the removal of the barrier. While some animals were quick to utilize the new gaps, others, further along the fence had to be driven. Using vehicles and on foot they shepherded the animals towards the openings. At this late stage in the drama this exercise was not without its dangers. Perversely, now, zebras and buffalos reacted against the drives, and the game rangers and their assistants were often forced to seek the safety of trees. Again the clouds massed, and in early November the rains fell again. The season was here in earnest now and within three weeks the vegetation had flushed, transforming the almost desert conditions to a panorama of lush, green grasses and rain-soaked vegetation. For this year, the crisis was over. By Rupert's observations 300 zebras, 12 buffalos and 6 eland had perished; it was a tragic tally, involving terrible hardships, but nowhere near the press estimate of thousands.

CHAPTER 6

RECOLLECTIONS FROM THE DAILY DIARY

It had taken Rupert two days to reach Tswiza from Salisbury, in the aged government one-ton Bedford. In the heat of October the small cluster of drab railway buildings shimmered in the sun light, even in late afternoon. The railway line stretched away in twin, bright ribbons of reflecting rays, disappearing into a hazy mirage on the far side of the water tower. There was not a breath of air, and no sign of movement, as Rupert climbed out of the truck. His shirt was saturated with sweat and he stood for a moment flexing cramped muscles and enjoying the momentary coolness across his exposed back. On the other side of the vehicle his bush companion and chief tracker, Langton, also unkinked himself. Rupert wandered over to the hut nearest the railway line, his gaze sweeping the area methodically as he lit a pipe. Somewhere around was the line ganger, he supposed. He paused. Around the small cottage were the embers of several separate fires, and beside the door a large pile of wood had been stacked. Rupert squinted into the haze, looking eastward along the line to where it disappeared in the silvery, watery mirage, long before it crossed the border on its way to the busy trading port of Lourenço Marques. It looked as if the ganger was out of camp, so the ranger inspected the surroundings, looking for a suitable place to pitch camp.

At Rutenga, on the main road to neighbouring South Africa, he had checked the latest situation with the station foreman. It was unchanged. Herds of elephant were crowding the railway line, on the eastern side. Patrolling the line endlessly, yet not crossing it. The water in the wild hostile bushland on that side of the line was almost finished. Evaporated, baked dry, sucked out of the soil. And the elephants wanted to travel westwards, towards the Nuanetsi River and other water. But the railway line was there. Two ribbons of steel, little more than 10 inches in height, stretching from horizon to horizon, was spooking them. Halting their journey so that now they continuously searched along its length for a break. They were becoming desperate with thirst, crazed and irritable and aggressive, even taking to uprooting telephone poles in their frustration. Further down the line, Rupert had been told, survey parties were being harassed daily by the elephants. And so Ranger Fothergill had been sent down country to sort out the problem.

"They're bleddy dangerous, man, those bleddy elephants. Every bleddy night they're around my cottage, swearing and trumpeting. That's why I started building those fires ... they were right outside. Why, one night I looked out ... I saw two of the bleddy things put their heads up against one of the pillars of the water tower and push it ..." The sweat on the ganger's forehead glistened in the light of the tilley lamp and he brushed at it with a grimy paw. Rupert listened impassively for a while longer, before bidding the railwayman goodnight. He stepped around one of the piles of wood that stood in preparation for lighting if the elephants visited again tonight. Strolling across to his tent he listened to the gentle, lilting call of a fiery-necked nightjar as he considered the facts he had. Why weren't they crossing? The line had been down for almost a year now, and there were no other instances of this happening. So ... why now? In the distance he heard the shrill, banshee trumpeting of upset elephants, as if they too wanted an answer.

By vehicle, and on foot patrol, he inspected the line, north to Chikombedzi, and south-east to Nyala. There was plenty of elephant spoor to be seen, though with the rising of the sun the animals themselves were back in the thicker bush, seeking shade and whatever food and moisture they could find. But there were the carcasses. He found several that first day, one a calf no more than a few days old. All had died of thirst and were near the railway line. Rupert inspected their remains, tight lipped and worried.

In some places he found where elephants had scooped away some of the ballast of the embankment, using their trunks to brush away the chipped gravel. In other places the spoor indicated that some of the elephants would place an exploratory foot on the ballast, but then back off in apparent distrust of the shifting, loose surface of the granite. He kept moving, checking all the signs carefully. A look at the balls of dung showed that the animals were surviving on dead leaves and tree bark only, indicating that lack of water was only one of the problems.

Rupert went inland from the line, to a dam he knew of some 23 miles east of Chikombedzi. There was some water still, but no sign of elephants visiting. The zebras he came across were in very weak condition, and would trot off only a few yards before stopping. He found 10 zebra carcasses, the attendant vultures and marabou storks giving way to him reluctantly. In the parched bush near the dam he discovered a large ground hornbill lying still on the hot earth. At first he thought the bird was dead, perhaps bitten by a snake. Then its head swivelled as it turned to watch his approach. And he saw the jaw trap and he winced. The steel was

rusted and the cruelly sharp, serrated teeth of the trap were clasped on one of the bird's legs. It was the kind of trap used for lions and leopards, or any other hapless beast that used that trail. Rupert wondered how the thing had got there. He put his rifle down and knelt beside the hornbill, mildly wary of its big beak. But the bird remained unmoving, merely watching the human intently, long black eyelashes blinking as if in reproach. Painstakingly Rupert eased open the jaws, all the while murmuring softly to the bird. Gently he inspected it, aware of the fixed stare of the victim. The leg wasn't broken. He massaged it tenderly and then eased the hornbill onto its feet. Kneeling as he was, the bird now stood higher than him. For a while Rupert and the freed hornbill eyed each other, the bird showing no sign of unease. Long, curving eyelashes blinking, it studied the game ranger with what seemed like frank curiosity. Finally Rupert stood up, murmuring to the bird. "Well, go on then, the leg is okay. Beat it. *Hamba.* Go ..." The bird blinked once more and turned and limped away, head swivelling as it kept its rescuer in its sight.
Other game seemed to be more successful at resisting the lack of water, even buffalos. Giraffes and wildebeest were in fair condition, as were eland and kudu. Shade was scarce. Veld fires had ravished large tracts of bush, often starting across the Portuguese border and sweeping westwards. The roaring, crackling infernos would add their heat to the already furnace-like conditions that prevailed, eating their way through the dry grey moisture-starved bush, driving all before them. And, Rupert knew, there on the other side of the border the indiscriminate hunting went on unabated. No animal, regardless of size, sex or age, was immune from the killing that went on there.

Rupert soon built up a picture, and planned accordingly. The elephants crowding the railway line numbered something over 300, and they had split into smaller groups. They were newcomers to the area. He was certain they had come from Portuguese East Africa, driven here by the fires and the killing. The railway line across their path was a new thing to them, confusing and unsettling them. Other elephants residing in that part of Southern Rhodesia were crossing the line to and fro with no problems. So Rupert started building crossing points.

It was a long, hot task. Rupert and Langton, aided by a few labourers from the railway camp, started by building several causeways at strategic points along the line. The causeways, about the width of a normal road, consisted of sand banked up to the rails, and spaded over to cover the loose ballast between the rails. It took three days of work under the high, bright sun, digging out the sand, carting it to a selected position, unloading it, and then building it up around the line. At the end of the third day, with the sun gone and the blue-grey of twilight fast enveloping the land, Rupert stood and surveyed their work with satisfaction. This would be the test. Tonight. Tomorrow they would return and check the spoor and see if any elephants had used the causeways, crossing to the Nuanetsi River, and water.

Nothing. Not one had crossed. Rupert studied the ground carefully, eyes narrowed in the new day's sunlight. They had been there all right, in the night, plenty of them. Their spoor was milled all over the place, right up to the edge of the newly constructed sand ramps. But there they had stopped. The humped causeways stood unmarked, pristine, almost mocking in their undisturbed newness. Rupert squatted on his haunches and took out his pipe, sucking on it reflectively as he tried to think it out. Langton squatted also and carefully scattered some tobacco into a twist of old newspaper. Together they went over the problem yet again. The sun, only just above the horizon, was already hot. The ranger's glance dropped to the methodical toiling of a dung beetle, drawn by the scattering of giant mounds that had been deposited in the night. Already it had built a ball the size of a cricket ball and was manoeuvring it along in its characteristic head-down, legs-up backwards moving gait. As he noted distractedly that the insect was out and about far too early in the season, an idea began to form in his mind.

It did not take long to scatter the causeway liberally with elephant dung.

Then they moved off to a patch of meagre shade and waited. They had heard the distant snapping of branches and other elephant sounds while they had been at the causeway. Two hours later, Rupert's eyelids were succumbing to the heat and monotony, when a small group of elephants emerged from the bush and made their way over to the line. They were in poor condition, ribs and cranial bones protruding from the shapeless, wrinkled, grey hides as they shuffled purposefully yet resignedly towards the barrier of steel. It was as if they knew their search was going to be fruitless. Occasionally, when a barely discernible breeze ruffled the leaves above them, Rupert caught a whiff of one of the carcasses.

The leading elephant reached the railway line, pausing for a few seconds as its trunk inspected the gravel. Then it turned and walked slowly along the embankment, and Rupert's heart went out to the poor thirsty great beast. Other elephants were now emerging from the bush into the open space beside the line. The first elephant stopped at the causeway and stood silently, big bulk swaying gently as its trunk carefully tested the sandy breach. Rupert could see the tip of the trunk moving to and fro, discovering, interpreting, brain being fed the information that other animals, other elephants, had crossed already. Their scent was thick here. Then, slowly, tentatively, this first animal of the herd went up and over the railway line. It kept on going, following the smell of the water that had slowly been driving them crazy. The other elephants began milling at the causeway, and Rupert could hear the throat rumblings and other elephant talk and the whooshing of expelled air as they tested the breeze. Great, grey, sail ears flapped in the heat-filled silence. And the game ranger held his breath as the next elephant crossed, plodding up and over the tracks. And the others followed. He felt like yelling with happiness.

Whilst elephant control formed a major part of the game rangers' tasks in those early days, it was not always that 'an elephant problem' ended in death and destruction. Rupert has been accused of being almost critically judicial in his summing up of control tasks. Of not carrying through orders to the final degree in the destruction of a particular herd, or segment

SOUTHERN RHODESIA
(ZIMBABWE)

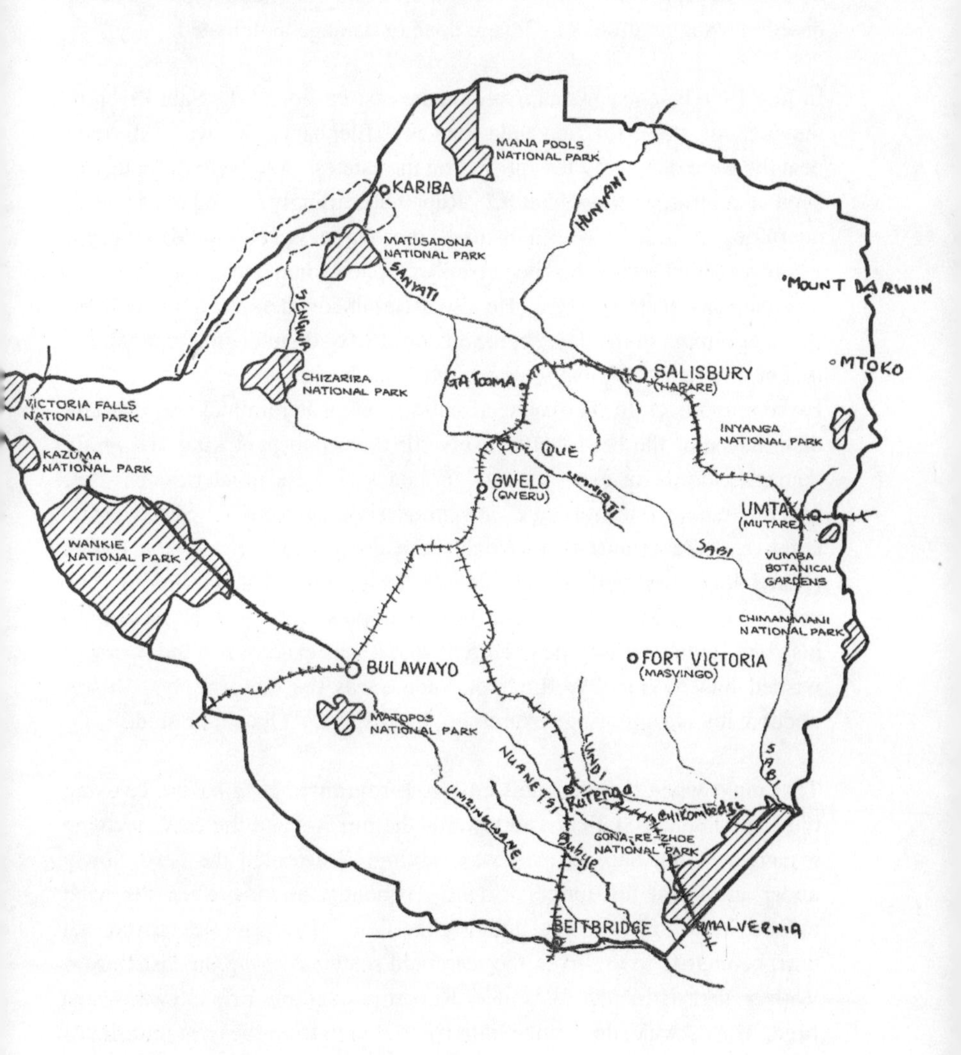

of it. Certainly, if he felt he could achieve the necessary results by shooting only one or two of the members of a bothersome herd, he would do so. Especially if a summons to an area had been, deliberately or not, based on exaggerations of damage done or damage anticipated.

In July 1956 he once again arrived on the eastern side of the Sabi River, in the area of the Sabi-Tanganda estates. Elephants, he was informed heavily, were damaging the furrows on the estates. And were definitely in need of control, with a capital 'C'. Rupert accordingly carried out a patrol, quartering the said area with his usual thoroughness. He found one place where a cement furrow had been barely chipped when one of the elephants had quenched its thirst there. He also ascertained where the animals spent the hotter hours of the day, approximately 100 of them dozing contentedly in a large patch of almost impenetrable *jesse* bush.
He reported back to the manager that damage was minimal and that any disturbance of the herd would likely stir them into panicking and *really* damaging crops, or even humans, in their search for quieter areas. But, said the manager, what if they *did* start causing real trouble? Surely a pre-emptive strike against them would be a good idea? Don't you think? Hmm? Rupert studied the man intently, the always direct, unblinking gaze across the rock-precipice nose drifting unimpressively over the farmer. In his slow, deliberate way he enquired what it was exactly that the manager wished him to do. "Well, shoot some", was the quick reply. Rupert nodded, his craggy visage expressing his disgust. "Okay", he said.

That night when the elephants emerged from their *jesse* haven, crossing the Experimental Station road towards the furrows and the cool, reviving expanses of the Sabi, Rupert was waiting. He trailed the herd slowly under an almost full moon. Silently, patiently, moving when the wind moved, he followed them. Judging the time. The herd was strung out now, here close to the river, the rearguard scattered along the last furrow. With a sure, deliberate movement Rupert pointed his rifle skywards and fired. Once, twice, the orange flame blossoming from the twin muzzles of the 500 Express. And the night was suddenly filled with the trumpeting of

100 elephants as they took fright, squealing, screaming, roaring, bustling away in their long, baggy-trousered strides. Into the river and across it, the cacophony bouncing back off the sides of the valley. Rupert waited until the night became silent again before retracing his steps.

He was in camp cleaning his rifle when the manager arrived the next morning. Rupert watched him calmly as he came striding over to his tent. "You see", he fumed, "I knew it would happen. What were you doing last night?" Rupert took out his pipe and spoke slowly, letting the surprise diffuse into his reply. "Hunting", he replied. "Your elephants. Easier at night in the moonlight than the *jesse* in daylight. Not much luck though. Only had two chances of a reasonable shot and missed both times. Must be getting old. Anyhow, your problem's solved ... They're across the river now, on the Devuli side. Got a heck of a fright, they did. I'll move camp today and see what they're doing".

The manager let rip a string of oaths. And the furrows? What about the .... furrows? Rupert inclined his head, looking up curiously from under the brim of his shapeless bush hat. Taking his cue from the game ranger's silence, the farm manager raved on. Yes, the .... furrows. The .... elephants broke the furrow closest to the river in eight places. It's the worst damage they've caused yet!
Rupert shook his head sympathetically.

★ ★ ★ ★ ★ ★ ★ ★

With the first dawn chorus of the birds the kraal stirred into life. The first wisps of smoke curled upwards as the cooking fires were rekindled, and the ever-present, motley crew of dogs scratched and stretched. In summer in central Africa the days start early. It is light at half past four and the cockerels have long been crowing. For rural Africans, well out of the mainstream of civilisation, it is time to start with the daily chores, working until the sun has reached its scorching zenith, whereupon they retreat to the cool of their village until the cooler hours and the lengthening shadows make the idea of work less daunting.
The tribesman and his youngest wife wound their way down the

hard-baked surface of the path to the stream, where they stopped briefly to wash. Then they picked their way across the rocks and up the opposite bank. In the riverside greenery everything was dim and still, with the rays of the newly-risen sun throwing splashes of sunlight on the upper leaves of the trees. As the path levelled out, the man glanced ahead along the track and suddenly halted. His wife bumped into him and peered over his shoulder. On the edge of the thick vegetation that fringed the course of the stream, before it gave way to open scrubland, a vast, black mass blocked their way. Tall, immobile, with not a sound coming from it. The woman instinctively murmured fearfully, while the man moved a few steps closer, curiosity winning over apprehension. In this region they had never been visited by elephants before, and now, for the first time in his life, he was looking at one. And, in his ignorance, he couldn't read the signs. He picked up a stone and threw it, berating the mass to be off.

With a short squeal of anger, the elephant charged. Ears pinned back, trunk curled, head down, the young bull covered the 20 paces before either human had moved. With his trunk he grasped the man in one sweeping motion, lifting him and smashing him against the ground. The woman too was sent reeling against a tree. Stunned and limp, she disappeared over the edge of the river bank. The elephant now beat the man against a tree, and after that knelt down, crushing his great grey wrinkled forehead into the inert form, pulping and pulverising the man. Then he whirled, tail twirled on high now in sudden fear, and was gone.

Rupert studied the tracks. They weren't large, by elephant standards. And they weren't making much sense. From the native commissioner in Gutu, the closest administration centre to the killing, he'd learned the details. The woman was still alive, with some broken bones, and had recounted the story. Now Rupert had spoored the elephant over the Devuli River and the tracks were becoming erratic. The animal appeared confused. Its spoor led off in three different directions and then the tracks would return, as the young bull retraced his steps to the original point. To Rupert it really appeared as if the elephant was lost. He stayed on the trail for the rest of the day.

By nightfall he was no closer to the animal. There was no set pattern to the spoor. It meandered through the *msasa* scrub and maize fields, and Rupert was now convinced that the young elephant had become separated from its herd and was lost and confused. And, he mused, just what the heck do you do with a lost and frightened elephant? An elephant that, like most of its species, desires above all to be left alone and in peace, and because that is seldom the case, develops a self-protective aggressiveness, which ultimately must be its undoing.
He found the animal the next day, standing in a belt of *msasa* scrub that fringed cultivated land. Less than half a mile away was a farm homestead with its attendant village complex of workers. Rupert worked his way to within 20 paces of the unsuspecting animal. On its left, stubby, undeveloped tusk he could see dried blood. Methodically and unhappily he aimed for the side brain shot, reflecting that at least the animal wouldn't know anything about it.

Another summons. A year had passed, almost to the day, since Rupert had joined the Game Section. The season of winter had come again in central Africa, with its broiling hot days and uncompromisingly cold, teeth-chattering nights. Together with Archie Fraser, Rupert was in the Jombe Crown Land in the Midlands. Again the object of the exercise was elephants. The animals had been raiding the pumpkin and groundnut fields of the tribespeople. The locals told the two trouble shooters that one elephant in particular was the root of all the ills befalling them. The reaping period was almost over, but still the one animal was proving to be incorrigible. Nothing could keep the elephants out of their lands. The evidence was plentiful. Grain storage bins were demolished, and spoor was abundant. On their first night, camped close to the village that had suffered most, Rupert and Archie watched four elephants in the half moonlight through field glasses, totally absorbed in their plundering of a pumpkin field. With the dew still bending the grasses and the sun's newly-risen warmth not yet penetrating their bush jackets, the two men were on the tracks early. The way was clear enough and their trackers made fair passage.

Less than three hours of tracking had gone by when they heard the elephants in the bush ahead. From the restless behaviour it was obvious that the crop raiders were aware of the pursuit, and soon afterwards they broke cover, bustling noisily away. Neither man was able to line up a reliable clean shot. The tracking continued. The sun climbed higher and the earlier seeping chill of the morning became a memory. They caught up with the four elephants again, and again the animals bolted, allowing no clear shots to be taken. This time the men called a short break. They had been moving non-stop for over five hours. A 10-minute rest would rejuvenate the senses. It would turn out to be a fortuitous decision.

A few minutes later, as the trackers retook the spoor, a low rumble floated out from a patch of dense bush a few score paces away. Archie and Rupert traded enquiring glances. They had guessed the elephants were by now some long way off, putting as much bushveld as possible between themselves and the pursuing humans. Warily they moved up on the thick *jesse.* Safety catches were eased off. A gut feel, more than anything more positive, made both men sure that at least one elephant was close. For long minutes there was a vacuum. No noise, no movement, as man and elephant waited things out. Archie shook his head briefly at Rupert, who nodded his agreement. An interesting situation. Thick bush, a fickle breeze, and smartypants elephants were reason enough for the adrenalin to bubble a little faster through the system. Somewhere close by, a grey lourie told them all to go away.

A tall anthill protruded through the tangle of undergrowth, its nearest side not quite in the jumbled screen of *jesse.* Archie motioned silently for his chief tracker to climb it, moving into position behind the African. Rupert followed, a pace or two to the side. Slowly, with infinite care, they eased their way up the slope of the large termite mound. At the top the tracker suddenly ducked down, and his expression told the story long before his right hand gave the silent signal. Stealthily the two game rangers peered over the crest of the mound. Two pairs of eyes narrowed as they observed the situation. An elephant stood immobile behind a tangle of thorn scrub, eyes rivetted on the patch of bush it had just passed through, ears outstretched to catch the slightest sound. It was disquietingly obvious that the elephant was waiting in ambush. Long seconds passed, becoming longer minutes. Men and elephant remained motionless, in limbo. Finally, eventually, the animal moved. Slowly, silently, back along its track towards the bush it had traversed. For the first time in the hunt the two men were presented with a clean target and a shot from each man dropped the elephant. As the reports of the rifles boomed and crashed through the confines of the bush the three other elephants, which were hidden and waiting also, broke cover and ran.

When they inspected the dead elephant, the tribesman who had accompanied them was adamant that the beast was the one which had led the crop raiders. It was a big animal, and a broken tusk made it easily identifiable. Rupert and the game officer inspected the carcass slowly, searching for some clue as to the animal's actions. They found three old gunshot wounds, and saw that its tail had been cut off, only now healing. Also in its rear they discovered where a charge from a shotgun had left several pellets embedded just below the skin.

Less than a month later both men found themselves outnumbered against a group of elephants which were raiding the gardens of local tribespeople. It was in the Sebungwe District, on the flat, featureless expanse of the Zambezi Valley floor. It was the usual story. Maize fields and grain bins were being raided almost nightly, and no longer were the drums and fires keeping the elephants at bay. And, as usual, where elephants and crops were involved, something had to give.

The tracking was difficult. Again the terrain consisted mainly of *jesse* bush, that dense, tangled impenetrable barrier of combretum that favours only the elephants and the rhinos. Add to the *jesse* the unceasing attentions of the tsetse flies, their red-hot, needle bites piercing the thickest bush jacket without warning. Then, add to the *jesse* and tsetse the *mopane* flies, small, tiny, a couple of pinheads in size only, but hundreds of them.

Not biting, but there in front of one, a vague, shimmering blur over one's rifle sights, and in one's eyes, one's ears, up one's nostrils, squeezing ticklingly in between the watch strap and the skin, anywhere there is moisture, anywhere there is sweat. Blend with the heat of the Zambezi Valley, and stir well.

There were four of them. Archie and his personal tracker, Manweri. And Rupert and a new tracker for whom this would be a test trip, named Kosiah. Today they were on the spoor of six animals. It was a slow, labouring pursuit, there in the claustrophobic game trails that weaved through the *jesse*. The only way of negotiating them was in single file, the men taking turns at walking point, and if you met with a rhino or buffalo, or elephant coming the other way, well, then life became interesting. There was no room for manoeuvring in those grey bush corridors. Things had to be dealt with very much off the cuff.

The elephant spoor was leading southwards, up into the first folds of the escarpment, and the hunters were starting to catch up. Rupert was spelling at lead when a crackling of the *jesse* ahead indicated some large animal approaching them. The group halted and Rupert waited, rifle ready. There wasn't much else to be done in the *jesse*. Paces away, an elephant emerged out of the miasma of bush. Even as the sight of humans registered with the animal, Rupert calmly and cleanly put it down. Before the echoes of the shot died away, there was bedlam. Quadraphonic chaos descended on the tableau. The shrill, enraged screams of elephants deafened the men, coming at them from every direction. With the mounting crescendo of trumpeting came the crashing in the bush surrounding them.

In those first seconds the squeals, growls and trumpeting and the crashing and smashing of the bush became one cacophonic roar in the four men's senses. Then an elephant appeared out of the bush, already in full charge, only a few feet away, followed by another and another. Ploughing through the *jesse* in full terrifying stride, red-eyed hatred blazing, deep growling screams reverberating off the dense thorn scrub. Rupert and Archie shot instinctively, knowing there was no room or time for second shots, switching targets as soon as one bullet had been fired at the closest attacking elephant. The animals were appearing out of the vegetation like pheasants, great, grey masses materialising out of the dim, grey obscurity of the valley bush. Rupert whirled as he heard a scream behind him and saw Archie shoot a cow elephant that had been steamrolling in on his back. She fell at his feet, trunk flailing, the earth shaking.

And still they came, charging, screaming, and the two men stood back to back, trackers crouched at their feet out of rifle level, driving them back. For perhaps two minutes, a lifetime, the battle raged. And then there were no more great, grey giants hurtling at them out of the bush. Around them seven bodies lay where they had fallen, the closest within touching distance. But it wasn't over yet. The screaming still ripped the air and the bush crackled menacingly around them. Not so close now, but still there. Very much still there. Fraser pointed at a slender tree a few feet away and Manweri scrambled up it. The three men below saw him shake his head in disbelief. They stared up at him silently as he tried to count. The seconds crawled by. Finally he slid down the tree and whispered his report in shaky breaths. He had counted over 60 elephants, not more than 50 paces off. Grouping and facing the humans in what looked like a prelude to a massed charge. Rupert and Archie had reloaded. Now they moved up behind one of the dead animals and waited, all senses screaming alert for the first indications of the attack. There was no point in retreating. With your back to the danger you cut your chances to nil. Zero. Better to face it and do the best you can. But the attack never came. The screams and squeals were more muted now, the elephants holding off, retreating into the security of the deeper *jesse*. Eventually there was silence. Deafening, almost.

★ ★ ★ ★ ★ ★ ★ ★

In the late summer of 1958 Rupert was once again tasked with investigating the report of crop-raiding elephants amongst the African villages along the Mushowe River in the Zambezi Valley. Two bulls, he learned, were the culprits. The rainy season was still very much with them. Rupert stood on the banks of the swollen Tengwe, which prevented any further progress along the ribbon of track that wound down onto the valley floor. There was nothing for it but to wait for the river to subside. By evening it had dropped all of three inches and Rupert made temporary camp. At daybreak it had dropped but a little more and he decided to complete the remaining 15 miles on foot. Through both the Tengwe and Mushowe he waded waist high, he and his tracker balancing the limited gear aloft. In due course he inspected the damage to the crops, and studied the spoor of a lone bull. According to the tribesmen, the elephants had split up and now only this one was raiding. Rupert followed up then and there. The extract from his daily diary probably gives the best description.

REPORT ON RIFLE No. 43012 .425 MAGNUM WESLEY RICHARDS

The rifle was carried with the safety catch on the safe position. On sighting the elephant, the safety catch was turned over to the Off position; the elephant was approaching to within 25 to 30 yards, the elephant standing broadside on.

A careful aim for the brain shot was taken and the trigger squeezed; the trigger is a single pull, but was absolutely rigid and would not move; two more hard tugs at it had no effect; by now the elephant had seen us and started to turn towards us. I reloaded quickly, ejecting the live round; the next round went off, hitting the animal at the wrong angle for the brain.

The animal then bolted; I tried a snap shot behind the ear, but the trigger jammed again; reloading and ejecting the live round, the same thing happened on the fourth round. Quickly reloading with four new rounds of ammunition, my trackers and I ran after the elephant for approximately 100 yards, when the animal turned and charged. My first and second shots at the head (frontal shots) failed to go off. I yelled to my two trackers, Langton and Clever, who were carrying spare guns, to shoot; simultaneously my third round went off with theirs, and the animal dropped within a few yards of us. I had one live round left in the magazine; this I fired into the animal - the trigger worked perfectly.

If my two trackers had not been reliable, an accident may have occurred.

CHAPTER 7

RHINO HAVEN

The year of 1958 was to be a period of major change for the Game Section. The wheels of its evolution were gathering momentum. At the end of 1957, in November, the team of four game rangers had been increased by one. Danie Bredenkamp, a personal friend of the game officer, was appointed on contract for a period of two years. At his headquarters in Salisbury, Archie Fraser now had two clerks to deal with the ever-increasing paperwork. The trackers employed by the Game Section were now appointed game scouts, and with the new title came new regulation uniforms, replacing the tattered and torn cast-offs that had been the order of the day. By the new year of 1958 one other change had also occurred; in name. Now it became the Department of Game of the Division of Irrigation and Lands. In the annual report for the year ending 1957, the staff record for the newly named department took a little longer to read than it did in 1955.

Appendix 1.

DEPARTMENT OF GAME
STAFF, 1957

Game Officer:
A. D. FRASER

Clerks:
K. D. BROWN MRS. T. M. JONES

Game Rangers:
I. R. NYSCHENS R. B. FOTHERGILL L. B. BALL J. D. BREDENKAMP
T. P. ORFORD

Game Scouts:
KASAYA MANWERE TAWONEZWI TSORO
FURESI RAMBERITO SANDURIDZAI JAMKOKO

Nineteen fifty eight, the year of the flood, was to evoke even more changes, particularly with regard to personnel. Initially, life continued as normal, with the five game rangers and the game officer traversing the country on their control, anti-poaching and general wildlife observation tasks. As the end of the year approached, staff turnover set a new precedent, coinciding with the history being made in Southern Rhodesia. The history was *Kariwa*, or Kariba, as the anglicised name of the gorge on the mighty Zambezi River came to be known, where man and progress had halted that hitherto unchallenged, powerful waterway, the largest eastward-flowing river in Africa. The years and the lives were a thing of the past now. Soon the project would be completed, and the final steps taken in plugging the 1900 feet of curved wall that had reared up, despite the prophecies of doom and retribution for defying the river god, *Nyaminyami*. And the plugging of the wall, the final sentence in that particular period of engineering history, would open a new chapter of history. A totally new chapter of achievement for the hopeful new colony would emerge, which, in itself, would draw more attention to the country over the next year than the actual building of the dam itself. And it would happen that, in the world of wildlife conservation, the group of men who toiled on the five year long game rescue operation would put the name of Southern Rhodesia way ahead of that of any other country or body involved in wildlife preservation.

The ranks of the Game Department swelled. In March Brian Hughes joined the team. Like Barry Ball he had left England to join the British South Africa Police in the colony, and had also subsequently applied to Archie Fraser for a position in the department. Frank Junor, fresh from Rhodes University in Grahamstown on the South African coastal belt, joined in October, adding his Bachelor of Science degree to the pool of experience. Transferring across from the controversial Tsetse Department in December, six foot five inches tall, Fred Middleton Stokes, or Lofty Stokes, as he was universally known, found vast relief in leaving the endless killing that was the cornerstone of tsetse control policy. Leslie (Greg) Gregory became the most senior man in years in the department. On the other side of the coin, the departure from the ranks of Ian Nyschens in September deprived the Game Department of a considerable amount of bush experience.

Even though this new influx of men swelled the Game Department numbers to a level not previously experienced, the many tasks that were part of the job, and the inherent travelling that went with it, saw to it that it would be some time before the old and the new orders of the department would meet. Kariba, in the coming months, would be the catalyst. And the new additions were not only limited to personnel. Two vast new tracts of land were to be utilized for the resettlement of the wildlife displaced by the spreading waters of the new dam. The Matusadona range of the Zambezi escarpment, it was decided, had little agricultural potential and was of no value for the purpose of African resettlement. The department was invited to survey the area as a potential game sanctuary, and it was subsequently agreed that it should be developed as a game reserve. The serene, reed-fringed Bumi River formed the western boundary while the eastern demarcation was the wide, island-studded Sanyati River, which would begin at the hauntingly beautiful Sanyati Gorge when the dam reached its final stage of inundation. In the south, the border of the new national park would be lost amongst the wild, forbidding ridges and valleys of the escarpment. The rapidly-advancing shoreline of the forming inland lake would be the northern boundary of an eventual 543 square miles of new wildlife area. The second new game reserve, Chizarira, would be 3 500 square miles of wild, remote wilderness hidden behind the great Zambezi escarpment. The riverside administration centre of Binga, many miles distant, would become the closest settlement on the new dam to this latest of game areas. In the initial period of the formation of the lake, the access to Chizarira was from Chete where, 100 miles from the Kariba base camp, the game rangers would establish a second base for the animal rescue operation. Greg Gregory, with his mining, farming and welfare background would become the first custodian of Chizarira, with the task of developing this vast game-preservation area. And so it was that on 7 November 1958 these two non-hunting reserves were proclaimed, joining a handful of already established wildlife areas into which, in the future, the game of the country would compress and multiply and would have to be managed as human development advanced towards saturation point. The sanctuary areas already established occupied a variety of environments and perhaps it is worth listing them:

Wankie Game Reserve, formed in 1928
Matopos National Park, formed in 1926 (abandoned to squatters during the Second World War and redeveloped after 1945)
Kazuma Pan National Park, formed in 1949
Ewanrigg Botanical Gardens, formed in 1949
Inyanga National Park, formed in 1950
McIlwaine National Park, formed in 1952
Sinoia Caves National Park, formed in 1955
Ngezi National Park, formed in 1956

There was another sanctuary, which would only be officially promulgated as a Game Reserve in 1963: when the breakup of the Federation of Rhodesia and Nyasaland prompted an amalgamation of the game conservation bodies and the Department of National Parks and Wildlife Management was born. This sanctuary was the Urungwe Non-Hunting Reserve, known today as the Mana Pools National Park. It was regarded

then by nature lovers as a special and unique part of the colony. Even today, many years later, there are conservationists, ecologists and ordinary nature lovers who still consider this to be so. The story of Mana Pools provides an interesting insight into how progress does not heed past lessons. For a while, in the 1970s and early 1980s, this beautiful, wild, area was in jeopardy. Another Kariba was on the cards. Progress decreed that a dam, one of a choice of three, be established downriver from Mana Pools at Mupata Gorge. And Mana was doomed. Given the thumbs-down. The flood plain alongside the Zambezi, with its fertile alluvial soils providing food and forage for the vast concentrations of animals that congregate there in the dry months, would have been flooded. Lost forever. The vast herds of buffalo, the impala herds, elephants and waterbuck, eland and zebras, would have been forced permanently up into the hard, barren country of the escarpment. With them, joining the exodus, would have been the myriad of other animals that make up the tapestry of Mana. Up there in the high, dry rifts and thrusts of the escarpment it is not a pleasant place to be in the dry season.
An extract from the annual report of the Department of Game for the year ending 1958 reads ...

"In 1955 consideration was given to the possible effect of the flooding of the dam on the wild animal populations. It was thought that if hunting was permitted in that part of the Zambezi Valley which would ultimately become inundated, that the effect would be to push the larger animals back to the escarpment foothills. To this end the 'HUNTING OF GAME IN THE SEBUNGWE CONTROLLED SHOOTING AREA, REGULATIONS' were promulgated and hunting, under permit, commenced in August 1955. From observations made, however, it soon became apparent that big game animals had to rely on the riverine vegetation for their dry season food requirements, and that little short of a major hunting campaign would be likely to succeed."

It came to pass that this desecration was shelved, in favour of another dam site up-river, at a gorge called Batoka.

However, in September 1958, Rupert Fothergill had none of this dilemma. His immediate problem was a lot more simple. For another couple of days he had to make sure that His Excellency the Governor of Southern Rhodesia, and Lady William-Powlett were not stepped on by elephants or chased by rhinos or have their slippers stolen by hyenas. The party of dignitaries had been at Mana Pools for almost a week, relaxing in the idyllic surroundings of the Zambezi flood plain. Game viewing, photography and fishing were the order of the day. While this was not as arduous as many of his tasks, it was nevertheless one which Rupert did not relish very much. He and officialdom did not rub shoulders easily. He was glad Archie had come down with the party and that Danie Bredenkamp was also along for the picnic. The new game ranger had already had his wits tested when he'd taken the Governor's party out game viewing near the string of pools that gave the area its name. An irritable old elephant bull had made a determined beeline for the sightseers and he had had to lead the animal off in a different direction, away from the visitors. It had been a close run race.

Two days later the game rangers returned from Kariba where they had left the party and Archie Fraser to fly back to the capital. Rupert was relaxed and in good humour. Ahead lay two weeks of uninterrupted work at Mana before the duty of chaperon came up again. Then, the Governor General of the Federation, and the Countess Dalhousie would be visiting the area, which already had the reputation of offering more scope for photographing big game animals than any other in the colony. But that was two weeks away, and in the meantime Rupert and Danie Bredenkamp were going to explore eastward to the confluence of the Chewore and the Zambezi, blazing a new trail along the river. Darkness had long fallen. They had left Kariba late in the afternoon and now the beam of the Land Rover headlights led them over the last remaining miles of the flood plain. It was full moon and at one of the many scattered pans they stopped to watch a rhino drinking. The moonlight reflected off its flanks and long front horn.

Mana Pools is shining sand banks and a thousand yards of smooth-flowing, blue, reflecting water; reed-fringed islands, green and restful to the eye; steep, eroded river banks with elephants sliding clumsily-sedate downwards on their rumps; endless vistas of open, wild parkland with cool, inviting oases of shade under the great canopies of natal mahogany, wild fig and tamarind trees; tall slender mulala palms reflected in the still, clear waters of the pools with the baboons and warthogs rooting at their bases for the brown, shiny fruits: the raucous, contented grunting of hippos echoing across the floodplain stillness, and a dozen different species of animals drinking together at one pool; and away in the heat haze of distance, the Zambezi escarpment, blue-grey, immense, brooding.

Animals! Wherever the eye is cast, there is game. Staring, mildly curious, back, pausing briefly in their grazing and browsing to note the human intrusion. And there on the wide, flat, seemingly endless floodplain, is the sign of their passing, the churned, pockmarked spoor patterns and the dung and the fallen trees, forming a mosaic which continues inland into the old rhino paths among the *jesse* and *mopane* thickets and the dry, harsher landscape. Mana is wilderness. Never Never Land. Once remote, Mana had its own standards, as a pristine wildlife destination. Mana used to be fine therapy. Today the area is over-used. Abused even. An abundance of commercial operators, uncaring visitors in two-wheel-drive vehicles, and the beer-can brigade have left their mark on paradise. That fine balance between use and abuse, ever tenuous, of a wilderness region, has been tipped down there at Mana Pools.

It took only a day to manipulate a track from the pools to the confluence of the Sapi River with the Zambezi. Rupert was now in the habit of spending virtually half a month's salary on filming. Almost every great *Acacia albida* and sausage tree had its attendant elephant. Herds of buffalo, one herd on the Kachowe River, over 1 000 strong, formed a shifting, black mass against the greenery, the clicking of their horns echoing across the plain. Shaggy waterbuck, massive eland, aristocratic kudu, burnished gold impala, zebras, bushbuck, warthogs, indolent, satiated lions, restless curious wild dogs - it was God's own special zoo. Rupert guided the Land Rover across the 100 yards of the river bed up onto the more solid ground of the far bank. For most of the way they had merely followed an elephant path which had eventually petered out on the banks of the Zambezi opposite the long, green-fringed mass of Chikwenya Island. Tonight they would make temporary camp beneath the stars and compare the hyena chorus here to the regular serenade at their Pools base. Tomorrow a section of track would have to be hacked through the thick riverine growth of *jesse* and acacia and then it would be another day of slow travel between the leadwoods and acacias and nyala berry trees, skirting dongas and elephants, and absorbing the peace.

Their next camp was halfway between the Sapi and Chewore rivers. The bedrolls were spread beside the Land Rover under the spreading mass of the foliage of a mahogany. They were a few yards from the Zambezi and behind them were two large pans, still containing water, even as the suffocating, leaden heat of October approached. That evening Rupert and Danie Bredenkamp checked the churned morass of mud surrounding the pans. There was the usual kaleidoscope of spoor, but what was predominant was the shamrock-type prints of rhinos. Twice that night the great prehistoric beasts passed close to the makeshift camp.

The following morning a rhino temporarily halted their journey. They had seen it several hundred yards off, standing beneath an acacia. It looked as if it was already deep in siesta. The nature of the terrain made it necessary to veer in the rhino's direction and Rupert judged they would pass about 70 paces from the beast. Only at about 100 paces did the usually acute hearing of the animal pick up the soft murmur of the vehicle. It wheeled towards them with a snort of alarm. It was a magnificent specimen. Rupert stopped the Land Rover and switched off the engine. The rhino trotted towards them, head up as it tried to use its myopic vision to best

advantage, short explosive snorts coinciding with every purposeful step. It stopped 20 paces away and started to nibble at a thorn bush, watching the intruders unblinkingly. They watched it for half an hour and then Rupert eased the Land Rover around the placidly feeding animal. The rhino ignored them. Over the course of the day as they approached the Chewore River they saw seven more.
Rupert and his companion stayed for four days by the great sandbanks of the Chewore and the wide swirling Zambezi. They saw more rhinos than either game ranger had ever seen before. The place was swarming with them. Every patch of scrub seemed to house a rhino, every river bed produced rhinos, every thicket of *jesse* appeared to be a particular rhino's haven. And, in a rare display of uninhibited excitement, Rupert thought he'd hit the jackpot. For it appeared as if both species of African rhino were living side by side here in this forgotten corner of paradise. The great, bulky, square-lipped beast, known as the white rhino, was sharing the same stretch of valley as the smaller, aggressive, black species. Rupert's first incredulity returned. It just did not seem possible. To his knowledge there were two conflicting schools of thought on the last recorded sighting of the 'indigenous' white rhino. One was that the last of that species had been shot in the Midlands in 1896, whilst there were equally adamant people who maintained that the last known white rhino had been hunted and shot in the not-too-distant Makuti area of the escarpment in 1928. And now it looked as if he had discovered a new, unknown existence of the animal. He inspected midden after midden and, certainly, amongst the many scattered markers were dung deposits that consisted almost entirely of grass.

To add strength to this belief, a scattering of tribespeople living along a section of the Chewore under a headman named Tugwe were matter-of-fact in their agreement that two types of rhinos inhabited the area. The one kind, they said, was a grazer and the bigger of the two: they referred to it as *chipembere* or *furauswa.* The other type, the smaller one which they called *nhema,* was vicious and lived on thorn scrub. Furthermore, this smaller rhino lived mainly in the broken, hilly country of the escarpment, while the bigger grass-eating rhino was found only on the floodplain, especially around some sweetwater springs called Kaputuputu. These local folk, who survived by hunting, fishing, collecting honey and growing small pockets of millet, added that the bigger grass-eating rhinos had been seen by many of them across the Zambezi in what is now Zambia. Rupert and Danie Bredenkamp talked late into the night around the fire of the headman, and seldom did the subject shift from rhinos.

At first light the next day, the game rangers worked through the heavy, riverine bush and deep gullies as they headed south towards the springs. It was the first Saturday of October and already, with the sun still to emerge fully above the horizon, it was hot. As the day progressed the heat increased, and the ever-present tsetse flies were having a field day. Where a thick-boled sausage tree joined branches with a mahogany, forming a wide, deep tangled patch of shade across an upward-rearing termite mound whose tip was lost amongst the branches, they came upon some rhinos. Massive shapes merging into shadow and greenery. Rupert studied them intently. There seemed to be four animals half hidden in the vegetation. They were certainly all much bigger than average black rhino specimens, and their muscled shoulder humps seemed larger than was usual. Of course, Rupert mused, it would help if a person had actually seen a white rhino. In the flesh. But no chance of that, here in Southern Rhodesia. Not for a very long time. He shook his head in frustration.

One of the shadowed shapes looked to be a calf. The first young animal encountered on this patrol. He wondered how to get the rhinos up and running. Depending on where the calf took up position in relation to its dam - at the front, or at station in the rear - he would know what type of rhino he was seeing. Plus of course, he would probably get a clear view of the mouthparts. He edged the Land Rover closer to the hidden tableau of beasts. They fidgeted and moved deeper into the obscurity. Rupert grunted. The rhinos could disappear completely behind the mound and then down into a thickly-bushed gulley behind it. And be away. He wasn't winning. He let the vehicle purr softly closer. Thirty paces. Twenty.

Fifteen. At the same time he changed direction slightly. And there, at the new angle, in a bright-pooled splash of sunlight behind the termite mound was the somnolent backside of a rhino. Motionless. Fast asleep, in spite of its edgy companions and the close-by intruders. He eased the Land Rover a few feet further, hearing one of the rhinos suddenly chuff off through the vegetation in retreat. That left two, and the sleeping animal that he could now see in full repose. It was snoring even, puffs of dust blown up at each exhalation. Rupert grinned as he studied the rhino. Even if it wasn't the jackpot. Because he was definitely old *Diceros bicornis* alright. Black rhino, oh yes. Not a white rhino. He was definitely the thorn-eating type, the browser. The prehensile lip was obvious. He glanced back into the deep shade. Mother and calf were still there, half-hidden by the anthill, poised for flight - or maybe an angry, mother-protecting-child raging charge.

Everything was still. Motionless. The vehicle, the humans and the rhinos. There was just the stentorian breathing of the sleeping rhino and the rhythmical heaving of its flanks. Well, thought Rupert, let's get things going. Can't sit here all day. He sounded the hooter, the alien, strident squawk loud in the bush stillness. Mother and calf bolted. Away behind the anthill and down into the *jesse*-thronged gulley. Rupert caught a glimpse of grey, lumbering hide. He thought it was the rear end of the mother, behind her calf. The remaining rhino had not so much as twitched. He sounded the horn again, hand held down this time, counting the seconds. At 50 the rhino was suddenly awake, ears erect, swivelling, little pig's eyes startled. Snorting, grunting, he scrambled to his feet. Almost in the same moment he was running straight at them, into full stride and there was nothing but the huge, grey, fast-approaching rhino. Rupert gripped the steering wheel and braced himself, gaze fixed to the oncoming animal. At the last possible instant the rhino swerved around the strange, motionless hulk of metal, his right haunch grazing the fender. Dust swirling, ground thudding, he continued at an angle away from the game rangers. Rupert let his breath out, exchanging thoughtful looks with his companion. Danie Bredenkamp glanced past Rupert, his grin disappearing rapidly. Rupert turned. The rhino had stopped, 100 yards or so away. Now it turned and faced them again. For seconds time froze. Rupert shook his head again, glancing instinctively in the rear view mirror at the reflection of his racked rifle. In the same instant the reflex was dismissed. There was no danger to them. To the Land Rover, yes. But not to them. Unless the horn came through the side of the door. Anyhow, this was a 'no shooting' area. And it was their country. He had had enough of shooting. He glanced back at the rhino and his eyes widened.

The animal was urinating. Copiously and purposefully. And at length. The stream finally stopped, and the rhino started towards them in characteristic, short, erratic, charges. Wrinkled folds of armoured, grey hide, the too-small myopic eyes, horn smooth and shiny, almost two tons of irritated, rudely-awakened rhino. Rupert had his 16 mm. camera out, resting on the edge of the half door, and the animal filled the view finder. Rush forward; stop; rush menacingly forward; halt. Closer the rhino came. Within 50 paces now as it paused yet again. Then another short, intimidating charge. At 30 paces the standoff continued. Rupert was still filming. The rhino snorted, weaving his massive head to and fro, and came on. Danie Bredenkamp, now standing on the furthest side of the Land Rover, was taking still pictures. The rhino was into full stride again, within 20 paces. Rupert braced again, eye to the view finder. And the film ran out. He cursed bitterly, at the same time as his companion slammed the door. The rhino jerked to a halt. Silence. Dust. Breathing stilled. Then the animal was off. Head high. Trotting fast. Putting as much distance as possible between himself and the intruders.

In the days that followed they took more film, endlessly checked spoor and the many scatters of rhino dung, taking samples for further inspection back in Salisbury. They saw many more rhinos, but all black browsers, there on the Chewore. Rupert counted 19 individuals. But they never saw another calf. He was no longer convinced about there being two species. Yes, maybe. Africa always had surprises up her sleeve. But not convinced. Maybe once the films had been developed, the boffins back in Salisbury could tell *him.* Undoubtedly, there was a large variation in the habits of rhinos down here; in size, food source, the methods of scattering their droppings. Even the local people believed they were two different kinds of rhinos. Rupert made plans to return soon to this part of the valley. To give himself more time to study the situation in depth. Maybe come down here on his next annual leave. He was not to know, however, of the toil that lay ahead, just around the corner, which would keep him busy for the next five years. In a subsequent report to his headquarters, Rupert recommended that the area around the junction of the Zambezi and Chewore rivers be declared a rhino sanctuary.

Their journey back to Mana Pools was made in one day, following the route they had blazed on the way up. Before dawn they were on the trail, driving west with the sun, and throughout the day they drove slowly through this beautiful, remote portion of Africa, pausing often to observe the vistarama of game. At nightfall they were still several miles from their main base near the pools. As a *finale* to the trip, they were treated to the sight of a big-maned lion a few yards ahead of the Land Rover. They were travelling slowly along the game-rutted track when the animal stepped out into the beam of their lights, barely 20 yards away. Without a glance at the vehicle it walked up the track, in the same direction as they were moving. Rupert slowed down, adjusting his speed to that of the lion. The small convoy continued, Land Rover and lion, the predator seemingly oblivious to them. Rupert wondered at the animal's lack of concern. The breeze off the river was blowing their scent straight at him. But still he walked. Lithe, powerful, arrogant, shaggy, thorn-ripped mane gleaming in the lights. Rupert wondered where the rest of his pride were. Still the lion padded along, his attention riveted ahead. Rupert peered over him. Perhaps the cat could scent some quarry. Maybe there was another male, a potential usurper of territory. But the head moved to and fro, absorbed with something closer. The game ranger puzzled some more. The track took a bend to the right. The lion stopped abruptly, head turned also. Gradually it dawned on Rupert. The lion was totally involved in the bushes being lit up in the glare of the headlights. Rupert grinned and reached for his hunting lamp. Switching it on, he played its beam off the track, moving it tantalisingly away. With a grunt the lion leaped after it, stalking the illusive, scentless patch of sunshine. They accelerated past him, leaving the animal to stalk the ghostly scrub.

That night they were awakened by a loud crash. Both Rupert and his companion leaped from beneath their mosquito nets, Rupert playing his lamplight across the camp. Eyes. Two, three pairs, green, gleaming back at him. Then more. At least a dozen. A table turned over. Rupert slipped across to the Land Rover and fumbled for the light switch. The beam flooded the camp with light. Hyenas. One more slinking away into the darkness. Rupert threw a rock after the scavengers and the two men inspected the upheaval. The story was plain. A hyena had grabbed at some bait left on the hook of Danie Bredenkamp's fishing rod, and run with it. The rod jammed against a chair and the hyena, after a few tugs, had let go ... and fallen against the camp table, turning it over with the assorted camp crockery atop. In the morning they discovered that more items were missing. They found the cast iron lid of their stew pot in the shrub below the camp. A small scrap of leather was all they found of Rupert's right shoe. He muttered unkindly under his breath and then, catching the suppressed laughter of Danie Bredenkamp and the game scouts, laughed aloud.
For that was Mana Pools.

PART TWO

THE FLOOD YEARS

CHAPTER 8

TRIAL AND ERROR

There had been no rain now for almost two weeks. Not since the first torrential downpours had swept their grey sluicing veil over the Zambezi Valley, driving away the oppressive, leaden heat that had built up as the clouds accumulated over the massifs of the distant escarpment. Cleansing the valley. Washing it clean and bringing forth the new flush of greenery, filling the hidden pans and seeps with new water. These rains had fallen hard, had been sucked up by the barren earth, rejuvenating the grasses and the foliage of the moisture-starved valley.

The animals roved further afield now, away from the permanent shade and food of the riverine growth along the wide Zambezi. There would be more rains. Soon. The wild animals could feel it in their very fibres. And they would move further from the life- sustaining river, because the rains made the river bigger, wider, and the animals of the Zambezi Valley were flood wise. It was an instinct deep within their systems. Rains, water, flooding. A yearly cycle. They would move naturally, unworried, inland, up onto the higher ground of hillocks and kopjes. To wait out the rise of the water. Afterwards there would be more forage, greener and thicker, and food and water would not be a problem. Animals like elephants and buffalos welcomed this period of the flood even more. For they would swim and wade from high point to high point, across stretches of shallows, seeking new succulent pastures.

The old bull was in his sixtieth year. Still tall and in fair health, although the folds of skin were more wrinkled and looser now, and he took longer to chew on the grasses and bark as his last set of molars wore down. He carried good ivory for this day and age, with man's depredations more intensive than ever. His tusks, creamy-yellow lined logs, were both a little over 63 pounds apiece, with his left working tusk having a large chunk worn out of one tip.

For a long time he had lived with two younger bulls always in attendance. Companions, and two extra senses to help warn of danger, which was only man. But they were gone now, to other haunts, seeking mates and new elephant relationships. So he lived alone, here in this stretch of the valley, and he was coping adequately with his age and isolation. Now, in this fourth month of the rainy season, he paused at the edge of the widening river. Today it was much further to the other side of the expanse of spreading flooding water, to the island he could not see but knew was there, several hundred yards away. And after the island was a little more river, and then the other mainland, spreading away into the haze of the distant northern escarpment. He did not often visit the northern side of the river because in the past he had always encountered the human things there. Far more so than on this side of the river, which was his home. But today he was going there again. For no special reason. It was just a thing in the mind of the old elephant.

He stood at the edge of the sheet of water which had already seeped a little more around his great feet, huge bulk swaying slightly as he ruminated. For a long while he was unmoving, as if deep in thought. Then he walked into the wideness of the river, shallow at first, for a long way, the waters splashing, swirling around his knees, forming a bow wave out away behind him. Then the water was deeper, reaching up to his lower chest now, and he carried his trunk resting across his tusks. The water puzzled him slightly, for he could not remember the other times with the water spreading this far. But he loved the water. Water was life. It was coolness from the furnace valley heat. Playfulness in its simplest form. Mudbaths and protection from the insects and sunburn. Finally he reached the island and here too was something new. For the patch of land was smaller, much smaller, and a lot of the thick, green shrubbery was below the water.

The old bull browsed on the small island for several hours, content and unworried as he worked his way slowly through the bush. Once he trumpeted and shook his great head, ears slapping noisily, when a solitary, irritated, huffing rhino mistakenly lumbered close by him. Then both giants of the valley resumed their own tasks of feeding. Finally the elephant moved off the solid ground of the island, straight away into chest-deep water, and he aimed for the far shore.

It was midday now, and the sun bounced off the sargasso-like sea and the horizon melted into the sepia of the endless panorama of water. The water very soon deepened and the old elephant began swimming, the tip of his trunk held aloft like a periscope. Occasionally, when the waters were not so deep over the high thrust of a submerged hill, his feet would touch bottom again and he would think that at last he had reached the far mainland. But then the water was deep again and he was swimming. He was becoming tired, and a little confused. Never before had it taken so long to cross the river. By now he should be on the other bank among the acacias and baobabs. The many trees he encountered jutting above the water forming a quilted labyrinth of drowned bush, confused him more. But the old elephant swam doggedly on, tired from the weight of his tusks, but pushing purposefully forward towards the far bank. In his fatigue and confusion he could not know that he was swimming aimlessly in circles.

For five hours he had been swimming, and he was a long way from any land now. And he became frightened. The aching tiredness brought fear, for it was becoming almost impossible to keep his head up and the tip of his trunk clear of the water. The tip had taken on a pale, almost bluish pallor. And the old bull began to flounder, the confusion and fear amalgamating into panic. His tusks were pulling him down.

That was how the game rangers found him, there in the spreading waters of this new man-made lake in the Zambezi Valley. Far out in the expanse of blueness, close to drowning, alone and afraid, and totally confused. It was hard work, getting the ropes around his trunk and head, to keep his head up, and avoiding the tusks that could splinter their small boat like matchwood.

At first the old bull fought, smelling the man smell, desperate against this new enemy as well as the water. But he was exhausted and his struggles diminished. The rangers improved their initial rope supports around the huge head, manoeuvring their launch so that the elephant was up beside the bow, tusks pointing ahead, away. The trunk was held aloft so that he could breath. And slowly, very slowly so as not to create too much of a bow wave, they guided the elephant back across the flooded country to dry land.

Much was written about Operation Noah. Especially in that first, cataclysmic year of 1959 when the world news media flocked to the Kariba Dam site, everyone searching for the story that would give them the edge on the competition. They descended on Kariba in ever increasing hordes. Journalists, film crews, television teams, writers, members of a wide variety of international wildlife bodies, politicians and personalities - all seeking the time and attention of the small team of rangers who were toiling against impossible odds to rescue the game. Before the end of 1959, emanating from the first story by a locally-based journalist in the *Sunday Mail* in mid-February, books had been published on the rescue operation, as well as full-length films, television episodes, and major articles in such prestigious magazines as *Life*. The game rangers became celebrities overnight, as the attention of the media brought their endeavours into the limelight of world attention.

To a large degree this media influx served to hamper and inhibit the game rescue operations. Camera equipment and personnel, often totally out of their normal environment and not coping too well with the rigours of rescue life, took up valuable boat space. The never-ending stream of journalists and photographers took up a lot of time as each newcomer in turn tried to learn the up-to-date achievements of the team. Endlessly the rangers answered questions that had been asked a hundred times already, and patiently they weathered the rude and ignorant characters who are sometimes a part of it. Some journalists even felt that the rangers should be grateful and flattered by the prospect of publicity.
Rupert and his team did their best to help the visitors and, certainly, there were amongst them some genuine caring people. Moreover, these very multitudes were undoubtedly responsible for much of the forthcoming assistance, and the valuable attention that was to be concentrated on this greatest ever animal rescue operation. The world learned about Operation Noah.

It had already learned of the building of this massive dam, deep in the wild, hot heartland of southern Africa, that would provide hydro electric power to the burgeoning industry of the three colonies that made up the Federation of Rhodesia and Nyasaland. For several years the newsreels had showed the building of this, the biggest man-made dam in the world. The world had already heard of the millions of pounds spent on the bush-clearing for future commercial fishing operations, had heard the gameplans for the future tourist industry. They had even been told something, just a little, of the tragedy of the 50 000 Tonga tribespeople who were being made to move out of their ancestral river home, and their controversial resettlement in pastures new ... and often barren.
But world opinion was quite unaware of the lack of finance in the Game Department, of the lack of equipment and back-up of the men, the small band of brothers, black and white, who had, since December 1958, been working hard on the rising waters of the new lake.

For months prior to the final plugging of the dam wall, a lot of guesswork and speculation had been taking place. There was no precedent on which to work, concerning the extent and swiftness of the pattern of flooding. Nor on the reactions of the animals that would be faced with the greatest inundation since Genesis. Archie Fraser and his men had studied maps endlessly, trying to work out in advance areas that would be affected first by the rising waters. But it was very evident that even this planning had severe limitations. Boats and equipment were scarce and untried, techniques had still to be developed and, as even today seems the case, finance for the Game Department was not high on any list of priorities.

The whole prospect, Archie Fraser was to confess at a much later stage, was rather awful. And so, in those months before the media learned of the drama unfolding in the Zambezi Valley, a handful of men were already driving themselves to the edge of collapse from exhaustion and hunger every day. A few hours' sleep every night, a hurriedly eaten meal snatched sometime during the day. Always gnawing in the back of their minds was the frustrating knowledge that the waters were spreading faster than their small team could cope with. Their efforts were unknown and unrewarded and their successes never seemed indicative of the amount of toil involved.

But they pushed on, the three game rangers and their gang of helpers and temporary assistants. On the Northern Rhodesian side the wheels were turning even more slowly, and it would be some months before the rescue operation mounted by that territory would be launched, carried out by an equally undermanned and unprovisioned team of dedicated men.

As the year progressed and the drama and persevering courage of Operation Noah was watched by the world, there were people who were cynical of the rescue attempts. In all fairness, some of the criticisms levelled at the operation, particularly when paralleled with the devastation of the ongoing tsetse control operations, may have had some justification. When one considers that, up to 1958, in the name of progress and development, ***six hundred and fifty nine thousand, six hundred and four*** wild animals were destroyed in tsetse fly control areas, it is understandable that a cynic may question the almost superhuman attempts by a handful of men to save the eventual total of a little over 6 000 animals. Toiling over five long, hard years. It's a sobering comparison. Food for thought, indeed. And perhaps summed up in the words on the simple grave of that doyen of conservationists, Bernhard Grzimek, high up on the cloud misted rim of his beloved Ngorongoro Crater.

"It is better to light a candle, than to curse the darkness."

However, on that day in December 1958 (Tuesday 2, at 7.00am) the final sealing of the massive Kariba Dam wall occurred, and the first hectic, frustrating, courageous chapters of Operation Noah began to unfold. For Rupert and Frank Junor and Greg Gregory, the period of waiting was over. Their brief from the headquarters in Salisbury was to make observations and *"take such measures as they thought necessary to save animals which were endangered by the rising water."*

The year that was to follow was challenge enough, and would be well-chronicled by the media. But after that, when the initial glamour and novelty of the drama had faded, would be four more long, arduous, repetitive years of game rescue on the ever-expanding waters of the lake. And Rupert would still be there, right to the end, in mid-1963, to see it through.

In those first few days after the plugging of the wall that reared across the gorge, nature began to struggle to come to grips with this new phenomenon. The waters of the Zambezi began to back up the smaller river beds, and although there was no spill-over as yet, the rangers found it eerie to witness the river reversing its course. Blocked by the mammoth man-made structure the river backed up, flowing back against itself in the opposite direction to its natural course. On that day the river climbed six feet up the wall in nine hours. Amongst the rangers there was a feeling of tenseness and restlessness. Even sadness. With them in these initial days of anticipation and river monitoring were a variety of representatives from different organisations. Museum staff, personnel from the Department of National Parks (which then was a different department from the Game

Department), and even a woman scholar from the British Colonial Office expanded the team. In a week the Zambezi had started overflowing its banks and soon the level of water would outstrip the area of water covered by the previous years' annual floods.

Rupert, Frank Junor and Danie Bredenkamp patrolled the river ceaselessly. The first pandemonium began to erupt. Insects, millions upon millions of insects, were being flushed out of their underground colonies. Driven to the surface by the seeping, unrelenting waters invading their nests. Crickets, ants, scorpions, spiders and many other species emerged into the light of day and the birds blackened the skies in swarms as they gorged themselves on this unexpected harvest. The noise of birds and insects blended into one shrill, ceaseless cacophony, echoing over the implacably rising waters. And then there were the reptiles, and the rodents. The snakes and lizards and leguaans and rats and moles had all been forced out of their hidden nooks and crannies by the flood, searching for escape from the invading water.

The men inspected the floating islands of matted debris, awed at the crawling, seething mass of life that swarmed on these small temporary sanctuaries. Tiger fish were rising near the brushwood islands and gorging themselves with insects. Subsequent inspections of these and barbel that were found floating dead on the surface showed their bellies full to bursting point. They had died from overeating and possibly the poisonous insects they had gorged. From one partly submerged tree a python slid down into the water. On the protruding branches of another drowned tree a giant eagle owl blinked in the daylight as it studied the countless rats scurrying on the floating islands. Spiders were spinning their webs higher in the trees, as the water followed them. In another tree the rangers saw a hyrax climbing into the topmost branches. Suddenly it fell down into the water, convulsing. They guided the boat over and plucked the little animal from the lake. It died in Frank Junor's hands. Puzzled, the rangers scanned the tree. Realisation dawned. Coiled in the branches was seven feet of black mamba. In some places columns of air or gases rose from the recently covered valley floor, and more than once they caught the

offensive smell of sulphur.
The days blended into one long search for trapped pockets of game. Little more than a week had passed and already it was obvious that the two boats they had, the launch *Hilda Mary,* and a smaller, green 13-footer, were inadequate for the task ahead.

They were summoned to the airfield. It seemed that their presence was needed to greet the arrival of the Governor General, Lord Dalhousie, on the coming Friday. Rupert begrudged the time away from the lake and obeyed the summons with reluctance. But the summons was not without reason. Once he had descended the ramp from the Air Force Dakota, the Governor General excused himself from the throng of dignitaries and made his way over to the trio of bush-worn rangers trying to be inconspicuous in this unfamiliar environment. He knew Rupert from his visits to Mana Pools and, stutteringly self-consciously under the curious gaze of onlookers, the game ranger introduced his companions. The tall, affable representative of the Queen offered the Dakota to the rangers for an aerial reconnaissance of the area, while he was busy in Kariba. It was a gesture that was typical of this keen conservationist, and the rangers accepted it readily. The crew followed their directions at low level. Up the Sanyati and then along the Matusadona range as far as the Sengwa River, and then back along the Zambezi, with its tentacles of water spreading everywhere, to the Kariba airstrip. The Governor General was waiting. Eyeing the men as he climbed aboard, he asked whether they were feeding themselves properly.

The first animals to be cut off from the mainland were the species which were most at home in the riverine vegetation. Bushbuck, baboons, warthogs, monkeys, genets, monitor lizards and numerous varieties of snakes were encountered, and the rescue team gradually developed techniques for their capture, care and release on safe ground.

As the end of December approached, numerous members of these species were captured and taken to safety while others were driven from islands onto the mainland. A lone male duiker had the distinction of being the first mammal actually caught by the team of rangers and transported to safety. They had driven several bushbuck off the scattered islands onto the mainland. Already the habits of the various animals when confronted with humans and the widening expanses of water were being noted. It became the anticipated habit of bushbuck to break through the line of beaters and take cover in the water under bushy outgrowths overhanging the water's edge. There was uncontained excitement among the rangers on the day they discovered that vervet monkeys were competent swimmers. Prior to this they had discovered a few trees, isolated and nowhere near any mainland, festooned with vervets. Each time they had approached a tree to study the rescue problem from a closer viewpoint, the monkeys had systematically dived into the water and had immediately sunk, without reappearing. The men had unhappily decided that, as the monkeys seemed impossible to rescue, and to save them from a slow death by drowning, they would have to shoot any more they found too far from the mainland. And then Frank Junor pursued one female vervet that had jumped into the water and paddled rapidly away. When he increased his speed the monkey dived. He followed. And could see her swimming determinedly, some six feet down. After several dives, when she repeatedly swam 15 to 20 yards, he eventually caught her when she surfaced among the half submerged branches of a tree.

Baboons also indicated their knowledge of flood sense. One troop, discovered clambering amongst the branches of a submerged tree, were unconcerned at the water around them. Rupert and Frank drove them off the tree so that they could swim to the mainland some 40 paces away. The baboons scolded and swore as they fell over each other, climbing onto the biggest branch so they could dive off into the water, splashing happily off for land. A day later they were all back on the same tree, presumably expecting that this early flood would soon subside.

By now the many rafts and islands of driftwood, maize stalks and reeds had accumulated against the shore of the mainland, especially in the Sampakaruma area. Jacanas, egrets, ducks, geese, marabou storks, francolins, lilac breasted rollers and many other birds were now in permanent attendance at the always advancing water's edge, partaking of the easy feast. Snakes were an everyday acquaintance and every member of the team had their share of close shaves with cobras, mambas, boomslangs and other poisonous reptiles. The very usual task of negotiating the ever-expanding labyrinth of half submerged trees brought the men consistently face to face with scorpions, centipedes and stranded reptiles. In Frank Junor's case the danger was even more extreme. He was allergic to snake bite serum.

Rescue was not confined to wild animals. A couple of days before Christmas the rangers were checking over the large island that split the Sanyati River at its confluence with the Zambezi. The team had split up and soon Frank heard distant cries for help. Nonplussed at first, he returned to the water's edge where they had left the launch. He could still hear the faint cries, but way off in a direction that none of the other rangers had used. Soon after, two men appeared in a dugout canoe. They looked fairly burned and bristly. They were from one of the bush clearing gangs, they said, and four more of their party were still stranded in a leaking boat some five miles up the Zambezi. They had been travelling from Bumi to Kariba and the engine had given up. For three days they had been stranded out on the lake, with no river flow to carry them to Kariba. Frank headed upriver in the launch to tow the castaways back. Today a grin still creases the Noah stalwart's features as he recalls the incident. When he reached the boat he was amused to see only a hand, in which was firmly clutched a bottle of beer, dangling over the side. They had long since run out of food, but there was case upon case of beer ...

Christmas 1958 in Kariba was sweltering heat, servicing the Land Rover, and dinner up at the only hotel on the heights, with some of the contractors working on the dam. Across the dry sere hills and valleys of this new mountain town, the bells of the Catholic Church of St Barbara echoed, temporarily drowning the Italian workers' homeland songs that floated so often from the peaks. In the hot, humid night air of the rainy season the people gathered for Mass.

And the waters spread.

For a few days over the eve of the New Year, Rupert and most of his team returned to Salisbury and their families. When they returned they were surprised and alarmed at the rapid transformation of the enlarging lake. The Sanyati, at its confluence with the Zambezi, was no longer a river but a lake. The aerodrome was already partly under water. And back on the lake they discovered that it was easier than ever to get lost. Familiar landmarks and islands disappeared daily, and under an overcast sky or on a moonless night it was difficult not to lose one's bearings. Rupert requested compasses and, with little hope of success, a weekly flight over the area to take aerial photographs so that marooned game could be more quickly pinpointed and rescued.

On 11 January they found the first corpse floating on the water. It was a large bushbuck ram whose horns had become entangled in a bush while swimming.

Today, Peter's Point, just a couple of bays from the dam wall, is a well-established National Parks base surrounded by luxurious, well-tended greenery and tall, cool, shading trees. A succession of department personnel have developed it thus and the warden's house is a cool, relaxing oasis after hours spent on the lake under a broiling sun. It is a far cry from the motley collection of scrounged tents and Nissen huts that sweltered on the bare, treeless ridge 200 feet above the advancing water's edge during Operation Noah. Some of the offspring of the paw paw trees that Rupert planted then, thirty odd years ago, are still growing. And so is the baobab he planted.
And the lake is still there of course. Timeless. Ageless.

The rescue base was the focal point, then, of the daily operations. The huts and tents on the baking, rocky ridge were a world away from the Impresit Club further up in the hills and the air-conditioned Kariba Heights Hotel, perched on almost the highest peak available. Later, as the islands were more scattered and distant, the members of the rescue teams would spend days and weeks away from the base, living in makeshift bush camps, sharing the islands with the antelope and rhinos, lions and elephants. They would be supplied by boat, skippered by a succession of open-space, bush-loving individuals, and the moods and idiosyncrasies of the lake would govern their lives.

Already they had established techniques for capturing, with the least amount of panic and harm, the variety of species of wild animals that lived in this part of the valley. For the first time ever the game rangers had the opportunity of observing many of the animals at close quarters, of learning more about the wild creatures they loved. They began adapting their own tactics and approach as much as possible to their new discoveries. Every single day involved something new. Long after the day's captures had been completed, there were still the diaries to write up, technical data to record, weak or abandoned birds and animals to feed and look after, and the never-ending repairs to the boat motors to be carried out. Every day brought new quandaries. How do you feed a pair of three-day-old fish eagles whose parents have at last deserted them with the lake waters lapping at the nest? How do you catch a porcupine bare-handed, without damaging it or you? Where did the flock of 56 flamingos come from that they saw yesterday in the shallows near the Naodsa River? What made the crocodile attack the baboon that Rupert was swimming after, a half dozen strokes behind, instead of the game ranger? How on earth were four game rangers and 20 assistants going to be able to scour every island and pull off every living thing to safety?

And this was just the beginning. Just the tip of the iceberg. They had more than they could cope with already, saving the smaller animals. The bushbuck, duikers, steinbuck, porcupines, antbears, grysbok, baboons, monkeys, warthogs, hyraxes, squirrels, pythons and leguaans. And the snakes. The snakes had to be saved to get at the other animals. And the birds. The nests and the fledglings. Instinctively building their nests above normal flood limits, the birds were unprepared for this new, man-made flood. The water crept up the tree trunks, each day a little higher. Each week higher still.

Month after month. As the nests were washed away and the eggs destroyed, or the chicks drowned, the parents would build again. Higher this time. The fish eagles, herons, storks, cormorants and innumerable other species would start again. And they kept on building, and mating, and laying eggs with incredible perseverance, as this new phenomenon sought to destroy them. Higher. Standing guard in the higher branches of the trees, the parent birds would fly off with echoing cries of alarm as the rangers' boats approached. As late as June, the nests clustered on the branches barely above the water line would contain eggs or naked, helpless chicks. It was a race against time, whether *some* of the young would learn to fly before the nests disappeared below the surface of this man-made death trap.
Invariably the water won. And the adult birds would begin their desperate preserving cycle all over again.

And this was just the beginning. As yet, the forming islands were too large to beat. On the islands were impala by the hundred, sable, kudu, waterbuck, zebras, lions, leopards, buffalos ... and rhinos and elephants. Most of the elephants and buffalos, like the carnivores, were flood-wise and had gravitated away from the encroaching waters towards the lower escarpment. But not all of them had gone. And certainly not the stubborn, irascible, black rhinos. Rupert wondered often, then in those early months of 1959, before immobilising drugs were a tested and proven fact of life, just how he and his men would get almost 2 000 pounds of irritated, prehistoric leftovers off the diminishing islands.

CHAPTER 9
FIRST CASUALTIES

Sunday 8.3.59　　　　　*Frank gored by buffalo*

The innocuous one line entry in the daily diary, a bare 14 weeks after the start of the rescue operation, shows the matter-of-factness with which the rangers faced the challenges of each day. There was, in fact, quite a prelude to this casualty, the first serious one experienced since the start of Operation Noah.

It started four days earlier. Frank Junor and a short, powerful African game scout called California landed on an island to check the spoor patterns, which would tell them what and roughly how many species of game were stranded on the heavily thicketed island. It had been a large island, but now it was slightly diminished, with the waters invading it by the minute and, since their last visit it had been sub-divided at its lowest point by the lake. A stretch of 25 yards of shallows, about two feet deep, bisected the land. The two men stepped ashore, Frank carrying a single-barrelled 12-bore shotgun. The spoor was plentiful - numerous impala and warthogs, bushbuck, duiker, steenbuck, three zebras and three buffalos. Because of its size it had been too big to beat before. Now Frank wanted to check it again. They inspected the first part of the island and then crossed the new stretch of shallows. The shotgun was for destroying any badly injured game they might discover. Self protection certainly wasn't its role and couldn't have been further from Frank's mind. California had the cartridge belt slung over a shoulder. They were about 30 paces from the water, when a loud snort stopped them in their tracks.

The buffalo was in full charge, 10 paces off, when they looked around. The big, black, heavy-bossed bull had broken cover from one of the dense thickets. The two men instantly split-up, California sprinting one way towards the shallow channel and Frank aiming for a tree. The buffalo swung after him, closing, leaving him no time to climb the slender *mopane* tree close by. He dodged behind it, mind and body instinctively trying to make the human torso thinner, much thinner. A branch sticking out, just a small, stunted one, gave that much more cover. The buffalo wheeled around the tree, lunging at the game ranger as he pirouetted desperately away. Then the attacking buffalo's gaze caught the still-running game scout and it went after him. Something like five seconds had elapsed. Gasping, Frank stepped away from the tree ... and his eyes widened disbelievingly. Two more buffalos were charging at him. With the speed that only flooding adrenalin can cause, he shinned up the tree. They thundered past, towards California.

The last he saw of the game scout was with the buffalos a yard behind him, splashing through the shallows in an explosion of spray. His back was arched like a bow as he anticipated the horns' ripping lunge and his legs were lifting high as he attempted to gain speed through the hindering water. Then he was gone ... and the buffalos too were through the shallows, disappearing into the *mopane* scrub of the other island. Teeth gritted, Frank waited for the screams. Seconds passed. He noticed a swirl of water in the shallows. And California, a wet, muddy, bedraggled California, clambered out of the mud. White teeth flashed in a sheepish grin as Frank gaped. He had waited until the last possible instant and then flung himself sideways, wriggling along the mud of the shallows like a barbel. One of the buffalos' hooves had grazed his shoulder.

They postponed any further reconnaissance. Now they had to return to their boat, and it was in the same direction in which the buffalos had disappeared. Gingerly they retraced their steps, keeping close to the water's edge. Once a warthog broke cover, almost sending them into the lake. But there was no sign of the buffalos.
A few days later Frank returned to this part of the lake. There were other slowly-vanishing islands close to the one he'd visited earlier. Already these were very different in shape. This time the reconnaissance party was bigger. And better armed. His companions were newcomers to the operation, although all were men of reliable bush experience. Barry Ball had been called from his base on the Limpopo on the southern border with South Africa, temporarily to relieve Rupert, whose wife was ill in Salisbury. His flair for organisation, and the fact that he was the most senior field man after Rupert, made him an obvious choice. Also along for the ride were Boyd Reese, an American ex-missionary who was an enthusiastic volunteer and who manned the main launch of the slowly expanding rescue fleet, and Len Harvey. Another bush veteran, Harvey paralleled Rupert with his almost fanatical love of animals and addiction for hard work. In the months ahead this quiet, introverted man would prove to be one of the mainstays of the team. In a tragic set of circumstances, Len Harvey would be killed by a lioness in 1972 whilst trying to save his new wife on their honeymoon, in Wankie National Park.

Frank and Barry Ball carried 0,425 rifles, while Len Harvey carried his personal 0.500 double. They had already checked two islands and had returned to another when everything started happening. The spoor of various animals had been noted, and several waterbuck, impala, warthogs and two porcupines had been seen. Buffalo droppings were fresh. Frank had drifted off on his own. The next couple of seconds were a virtual replay of the previous encounter. There was a snort and crashing of undergrowth ... and the buffalo was already in head-high full charge, just yards away. Frank lifted his rifle to fire at the massive animal. He was conscious of pulling the trigger, and nothing happening, and thinking ... the safety, the bloody safety catch is still on ...

And then the buffalo hit him. Its left horn ripped into the back of his left leg as it swung its head. It tossed Frank skywards, high, like a rag doll, and it was there waiting when he came down. It smashed him and tossed the game ranger a second time and this time Frank screamed Barry Ball's name. He landed again and the buffalo was there, head down, horns missing him by inches as it buffeted the man into the ground. Frank was shoved along, kicking at the mass of hatred trying to kill him. A shot sliced through the pandemonium and the buffalo turned away. Wheeling, searching for its new enemy. It took five shots to kill it.

Barry Ball ripped away what was left of the injured ranger's trouser leg. Blood poured over his hands. He caught a glimpse of torn ligaments and nerves and the white of the bone at the back of the knee. Using his shirt, newly-bought the day before, as a makeshift field dressing for the wound, he staunched the flow of blood. The party carried Frank down to the launch, the ranger tight-lipped and pale. The base they were using at the moment, dubbed 'petrol island', was on the way to Kariba. They stopped briefly and collected a stretcher and Frank's shaving gear, and then, with Barry Ball at the helm and Boyd Reese supplying the injured man with whisky and cigarettes, aimed the prow at the distant smudge of land on the horizon that was Kariba.

Every day the lake presented a new side to its character. Storms and squalls came out of nowhere, whipping the waters of the inland sea to a foaming, rolling maelstrom. Getting lost was only too easy. The everchanging islands and shoreline, fringed with an almost impenetrable barrier of submerged trees and foliage, were a constant, irritating problem. There were more islands now. And the lake was bigger, a relentlessly spreading monster that swallowed up the land. The rescue teams found many carcasses floating on the water, mute testimony that for some animals they were too late. From before dawn until well after the sun had set, they worked. But sometimes it wasn't enough. There were daily problems quite divorced from the question of removing 60 impala from an island, or 30 sable, or driving off a pride of lion before the proper rescue could start. Food supplies, petrol, medical equipment - all of it had to be transported from Kariba which, as the weeks passed and became months, slipped further and further away. Capriciousness and contrariness managed, on occasion, to percolate all the way into this stretch of wild, waterlogged wilderness. For a time, petrol supplies closer to hand on the Northern Rhodesian shore of the lake than the increasingly distant Kariba base, were denied the rescue team. Simply because the new native commissioner for the area, fresh out from England's green vales and flexing bureaucratic muscle, said no. North was north, it appeared, and south was south, and the twain simply could not meet ... A constant source of frustration and delay was the breaking down of the boat engines. There was not a motor on earth that could stand up indefinitely to the rigours of the operation. And of course, there was the never-ending stream of visitors, the media people, senior governmental people, foreign dignitaries like Lord Mountbatten, wildlife celebrities like Armand and Michaela Denis, and scores of others. All wanting to see Operation Noah, to *experience* Operation Noah.

It wasn't all one-sided. Things were improving, very slowly. Initial teething problems were ironed out. Techniques and methods of capture were streamlined. With world attention now focused on this remote part of the colony, the Government moved with a little more alacrity to aid the rescue teams. And the teams themselves were expanding. The handful of men was a bigger handful. Tom Orford was now working on the lake, once again working with the man he so respected. Rex Bean and his wife Gwen, long resident in this part of the country and pioneers of the building of the dam, were seconded to the team. With his own craft and knowledge of the area, coupled with his wife's catering experience at the stark Kariba base, they were a welcome addition. And there were other men, from varying walks of life, drawn to the life-saving venture on the new lake. Stuart Klaasen, Peter Jones, Brain Hughes, 'Tinky' Haslam - who subsequently courted and married a strikingly dark-haired, very blue-eyed nurse on contract at the hospital ... and over the coming months there would be many more. Some would stay on and make their own reputations, and others would be short-term visitors; disillusioned and unable to adapt to the endless, backbreaking toil that was not so romantic after all. Doctor John Condy, who was to become very involved in the experimental drugging of the bigger game and whose name would become synonymous with the lake, recalls one such prospective 'Noah' sending himself a telegram within 24 hours of his arrival, conveying the news that his mother had died. Others simply melted out of the lives of the men on the lake.

Many years later there are people who say that any one of the men in the rescue teams could have led the operation. That may be the case. But the fact is that it was Rupert Fothergill who was there, from beginning to end. Through the first desperate, frustrating months, when the world news media first seized on his image - making him the figurehead, he personified the breed of men out there, sweating their guts out. Then, and on through the long, tedious, bone-wearing years ahead. Unavoidably, in the environment in which the rescue teams were working; with the relevant strain and tension and frustrations boiling out of their concern for the animals; and with the continued coming and going of members at the scattered makeshift bush bases which brought into close association a wide variety of tough individuals who were often loners, set in their own ways - there were clashes of character. And in the raw, wild remoteness of the drowning valley the results could be violent. Very rarely, however, did things go that far. An exhausting day under the baking, pitiless African sun, hauling, chasing, dodging, sweating, swimming, calming, *rescuing* terrified wild animals who could not know that the humans were trying to save their lives, made sleep a long-anticipated luxury. And Rupert, a couple of years off 50, the oldest of the rangers, and arguably the most stubborn and dedicated, who would never instruct someone to carry out a chore that he would himself not undertake, was still handy with his fists. There were few of the younger men who could outstare the impassive, level gaze of the leader of the operation. At twice the age of many of his contemporaries it was seldom that the quiet, imperturbable game ranger was caught lagging.

And so 1959 slipped by. Island after island. Animal after animal. Summer into winter into summer. There were more casualties, though none would be as serious as that of Frank Junor. There was no man who did not have scars of one kind or another. Warthogs were the main cause. One sideways scythe of those tusks could disembowel a man or rip a leg to the bone. And they are brave, undaunted animals. A big dog baboon can rip an Alsatian apart, so that one slip could have disastrous results. An official tally of 268 baboons were rescued; and 585 warthogs. Even a terrified kick from one of the smaller antelope, or a stab from its horns could, and did, cause ugly wounds. And such undramatic animals as hyraxes, and monkeys, squirrels and mongooses could bite painfully and give tetanus. There were the snakes. The sweeping scimitar horns of the sable antelope have killed lions. That's before one considers the bigger dramatic game. In Africa, wild, unpolluted Africa, anything can kill, if one is a little careless. Disease, compliments of the mosquito and the tsetse fly, for example, does its fair share of human 'management'.

And there was the other side of the coin. Apart from the animals that it was too late to save, other casualties were incurred. Some animals died of shock, their systems unable to cope with their capture and the proximity

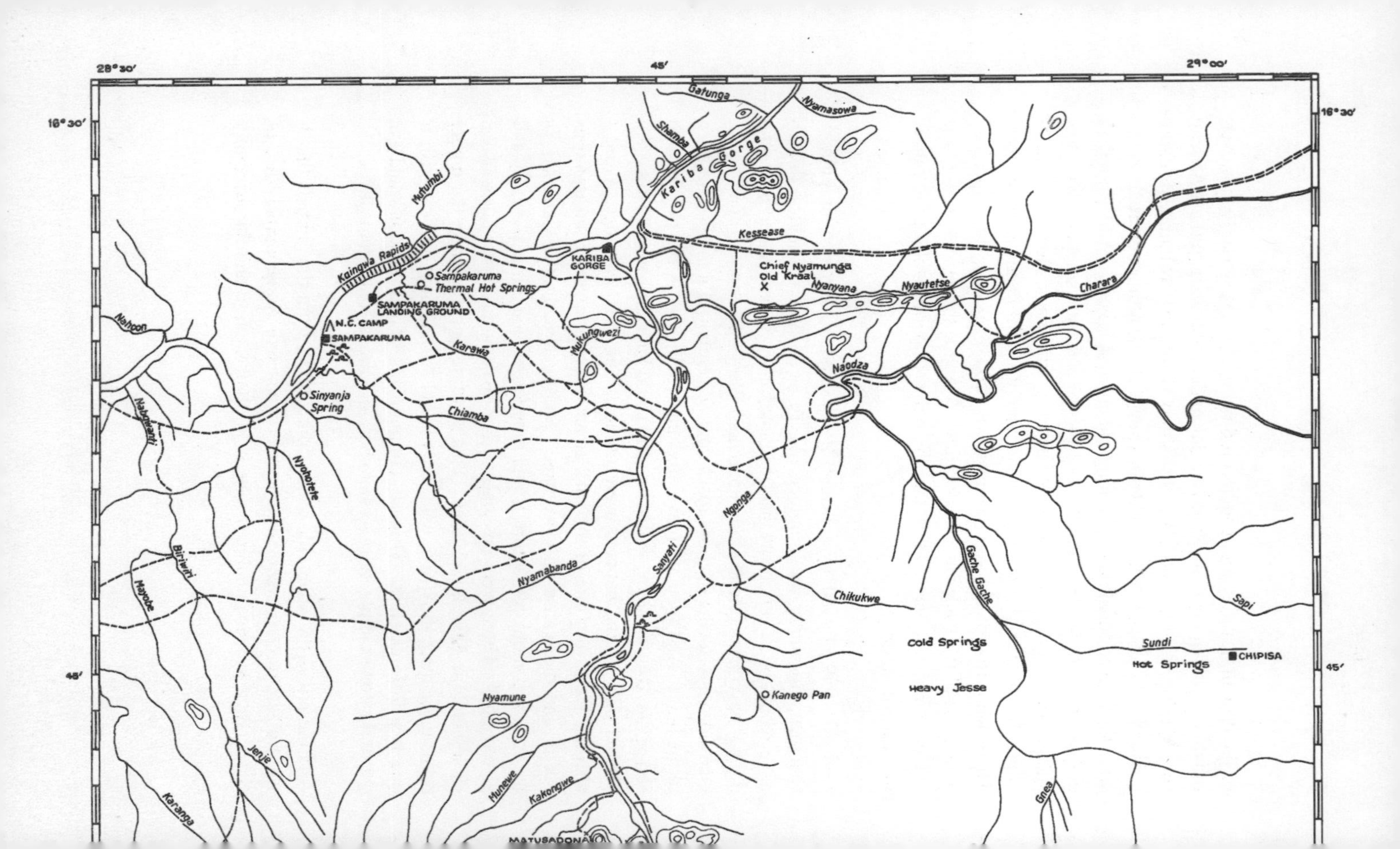
28°30′
45′
29°00′
16°30′
16°30′
45′
45′
Gatunga
Nyamasowa
Shamba
Kariba Gorge
Mutumbi
Kessease
Kaingwa Rapids
KARIBA GORGE
Chief Nyamunga Old Kraal
Nyanyana
Nyautetse
Charara
Sampakaruma
Thermal Hot Springs
SAMPAKARUMA LANDING GROUND
N.C. CAMP
SAMPAKARUMA
Nahoon
Karawa
Mukungwezi
Naodza
Sinyanja Spring
Nabgwanti
Chiamba
Nyohotete
Ngonga
Biriwiri
Mayobe
Nyamabanda
Sanyati
Gache Gache
Chikukwe
Sapi
Cold Springs
Sundi
CHIPISA
Hot Springs
Heavy Jesse
Kanego Pan
Nyamune
Jenje
Munewe
Kakongwe
Karanga
Gnea
MATUSADONA

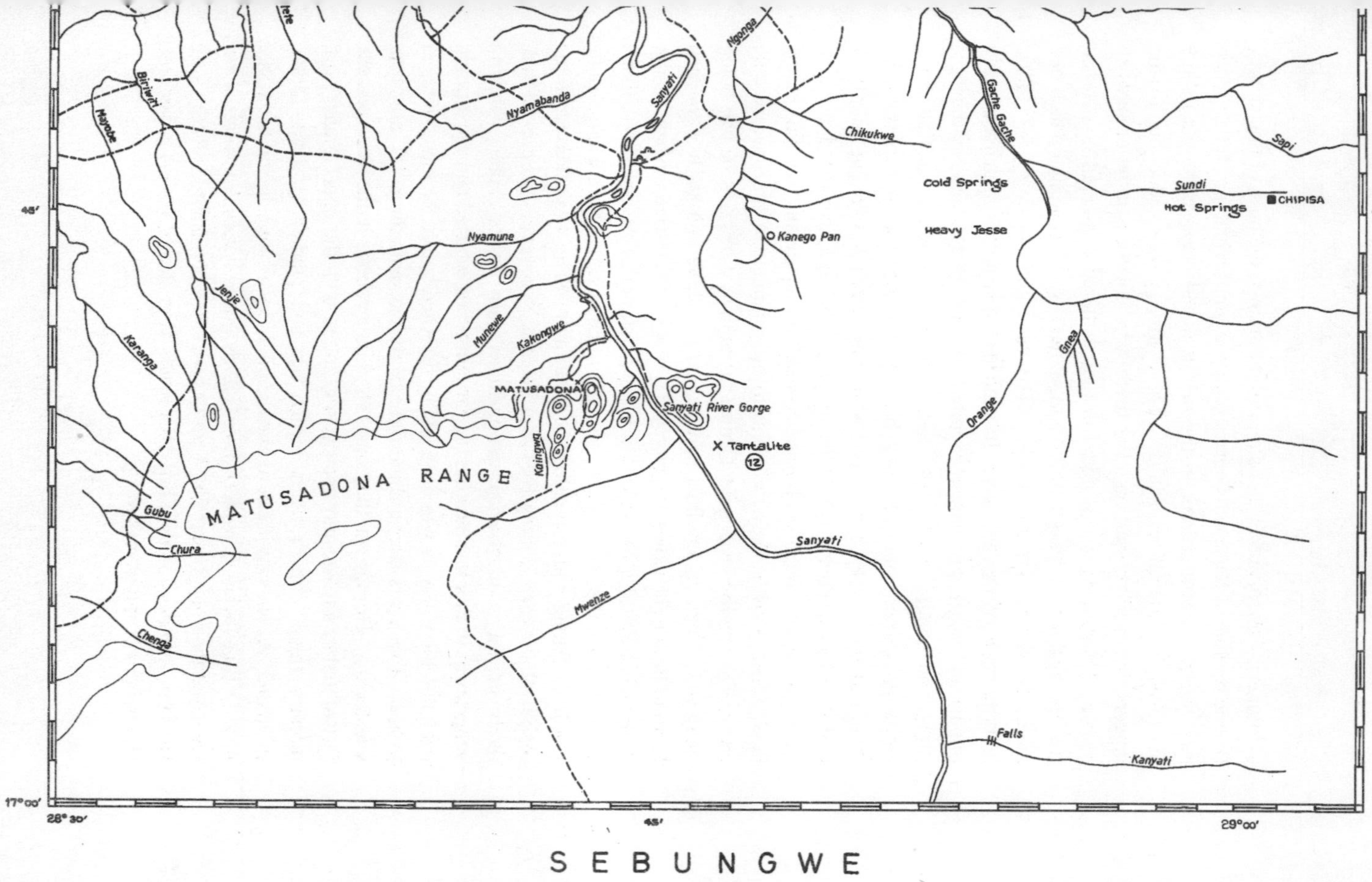

Tete
Ngonga
Biriwiri
Mayobe
Nyamabanda
Sanyati
Chikukwe
Gache Gache
Sapi
Cold Springs
Sundi
CHIPISA
Hot Springs
Heavy Jesse
O Kanego Pan
Nyamune
Jenje
Muneve
Kakongwe
Karanga
MATUSADONA
Sanyati River Gorge
Gnea
Orange
X Tantalite
12
Kaingwa
MATUSADONA RANGE
Gubu
Chura
Sanyati
Mwenze
Chenga
Falls
Kanyati
45'
45'
17°00'
28°30'
45'
29°00'
SEBUNGWE

to humans. Others in their headlong flight through the bush of the islands, fleeing the line of noise and beaters, snapped limbs when they fell or when they struggled, fear-crazed, in the nets that had been strung across the narrowest section of an island. These losses were saddening to the rangers, but they pressed on. For there were countless more animals to rescue. Every animal was noted in their battered dog-eared notebooks: species, age, sex, and tag number and, in the case of an animal which had died, the reason for its death. The tag numbers were for future identification of the animals. It happened that some animals, notably impala and warthogs, were recaptured two and three times, as they got caught on another pocket of land. The rangers felt it most when a particular animal, one they had battled to rescue and transport to the mainland, was lost to them at the last minute. Such was the big waterbuck bull they had discovered floundering out in the lake, exhausted and lost. They got ropes around his horns and held him up against the side of the boat. Then, slowly, they took him to the mainland, a little over a mile away. The antelope was quiet against the hull, as if he knew he was being reprieved. Then, as the boat approached the shore and his feet touched bottom, he fought violently against the ropes. They tried unsuccessfully to restrain him for a few more yards but he struggled free, and sank like a stone beneath the boat. There was a similar instance with a large male warthog. Along with a boatload of other animals he was released on the mainland, the men leaping for cover because experience had proved that, likely as not, a warthog would instantly turn on its captors, seeking vengeance. In this instance the big, grunting hog whirled and ran straight back into the water. It was deep and he drowned before the men could get to him. Two years later a rhino did exactly the same thing. A sable cow was luckier. Her tag number was 488. Upon release in the shallows, she turned and swam out into open water, dotted with the upper branches of *mopane* trees. The rangers turned her and guided her back to the mainland. As she was about to emerge on to dry ground she lay down, her nose in four inches of water. Len Harvey got to her first and raised her head and then he, Rupert and Tom Orford lifted her ashore. She lay still for a few minutes and then lifted her head. Very slowly she got to her feet, shook herself and trotted away.

There was the odd occasion when sudden, unexpected events, having no bearing on the rescue, cropped up. In Salisbury, Archie Fraser, correlating game duties around the rest of the country as well as the Kariba operation, had received news that Danie Bredenkamp and his tracker had been mauled by a lion at the Chirundu Sugar Estates. A radio message was despatched to Rupert to investigate the matter. Rupert temporarily abandoned the rescue operation and took a Land Rover up across the escarpment and down onto the other stretch of the valley floor. From the nursing sister at the Sugar Estates clinic he learned that neither man was seriously injured, but that they had been transported to Lusaka hospital. Bredenkamp had been chewed up on both arms, his back clawed, and his right ear lobe torn off. The tracker, James, had been badly clawed on his arms and on his left leg.

Rupert visited the area where the attack had occurred, accompanied by the young African boy who had been with the other ranger at the time. The lion had been seen on the edge of the cane lands, feeding off a buffalo calf it had killed. On receiving this information, Danie Bredenkamp and his tracker had gone to the area, guided by the boy who had seen the lion. They found the lion immediately. It was midday and the animal was resting in some shade about 20 paces distant. The ranger had a 0,375 loaded with five solid rounds. One shot hit the lion through the shoulders and it reared up, snarling. Two more shots went straight through the animal's shoulders. It disappeared behind some bushes. The game ranger switched rifles with his tracker, taking the 0,470 double. Seconds later the lion charged. His first shot with the double missed, and as he fired the second barrel the lion was on him, sweeping the weapon from his hands. Lion and man were enmeshed on the ground, the ranger trying to ward off the creature that was concentrating on ripping away his stomach. To his credit the tracker did not run. He moved up to the struggle for survival, slipping off the safety catch of the 0,375 and firing at the lion. Nothing happened. Unwittingly he had put *on* the safety catch. For a split second everything was frozen; man, lion and man. Then the lion leaped at the tracker. The ranger crawled across to the dropped 0,375 and, finally, killed the lion. Both weapons were now empty. Seven shots. Two men. And one lion.

Rupert inspected the signs of the scuffle and then searched for droppings of the lion. He had already seen the skinned cat. An old animal, its teeth worn down to stumps. Amongst the droppings he found porcupine quills. Old age and pain had made the lion a still powerful adversary. Rupert cleaned Danie Bredenkamp's weapons, packed up his camp, visited him in hospital and was back in Kariba within three days.

Six months later, news of a man-eating lion in the wild, tribal areas of Karoi took Boyd Reese and a newcomer to the rescue team, Mike Van Rooyen, away from the lake. The lion had killed and eaten one man and had attacked another, but dropped him when it had bumped into a tree stump whilst dragging him off. The two rescue team members, accompanied by two game scouts, arrived in the area late in the afternoon. At sundown they heard the lion calling in the distance. Boyd and Mike decided to take turns sitting up and waiting for it. It was a reasonable supposition that the man-eater would visit them. They were camped at the collection of mud and thatch huts from where the first victim had been taken. The fire they kindled into a blaze was not only against the cold night air. Mike took the first shift. The night was silent. His companions dozed fitfully. All senses screamingly alert, he sat and listened. Nothing happened. Around 11.00pm he woke the American. For another two hours the night was quiet and peaceful. Feeling the tiredness taking the edge off his watchfulness, Boyd decided against re-awakening his companion. Instead he awoke the two game scouts. Giving them the shotgun and noting their precautions against an attack he returned to his bedroll a half dozen paces away. The game scouts were sitting back to back, with their flanks protected by a bicycle and by several empty paraffin tins. The night air was chilly, stars bright in a moonless, clear sky. Boyd drifted off to sleep.

One of the scouts lit a cigarette, blowing out the match. In that last instant of glare, he saw the lion springing at him, jaws open. The man screamed and dived over his companion with the shotgun. The lion bit at the bicycle as the two game scouts scrambled into a nearby hut. As the first commotion erupted, Boyd Reese leaped up and fired off some shots with his revolver, unable to see anything in the light of the softly glowing embers of the fire. The lion melted into the darkness. Dubious that there had been a lion at all, the two men stoked up the fire, chiding the game scouts still in the hut for their imagination. There had been no sound from the lion. As the blaze grew, illuminating the area, both men lapsed into silence. There in the dust and imprinted on one of the scouts' blankets, were the pugmarks of the lion.

Several further attempts were made to contact the man-eater. They set baits, spoored it, and even obtained traps from Salisbury. To no avail. Len Harvey joined the hunt. Still no success. Days and then weeks passed. The locals were impassively certain that the lion was acting on orders from the spirits. A headman's son, they informed the hunters, had slept with his own sister. And, when warned that the ancestral spirits would be angered at this violation, he laughed. Now, said the villagers, the keeper of the spirits in this area had sent the lion to them. At first it would kill innocent people in order to frighten the scornful youth who defied the spirits. And if the killings did not serve as a warning, and he failed to pay the required fine, he too would be devoured. They were wasting their time, the hunters were assured. And indeed, they were not having much luck in finding the lion. Spoor was fresh and baits were stolen from under their noses. Two weeks passed. And there was no more sign of the lion. It had gone. As they too left the area the game department men paid a final courtesy call on the headman. From him they learned that, finally, the errant youth had paid the fine ...

On the lake the rescue continued. More islands formed. More game was stranded. The level of the lake was not rising so rapidly now. The rangers noted this fact with relief. However, the pressure was still on them because now a new threat developed. The shrinking islands, even the large ones, could only support the feeding habits of so many animals for so long. Gradually the greenery of the islands was devoured, the process aggravated by the encroaching water. Some animals were affected more than others, while some quickly adapted to their watery exiles. The rangers kept a running dossier on specific observations of interest. With increasing frequency it was noted that baboons readily ate meat, in some cases taking determined steps to do so. On one island some of these primates were seen feeding off a freshly killed bushbuck. On another occasion Rupert and Tom Orford rescued a grysbok from the troop of baboons that were attacking it. In desperation, the tiny antelope had taken to the lake, but the baboons pursued it, and when the two rangers discovered the scene, the grysbok, already savaged, was 20 yards from shore. Surrounded. Another rescue team just managed to rescue a baby duiker, no more than three days old judging by the trailing umbilical cord. Two baboons were attacking the animal and had already inflicted wounds on its head. The rangers dressed the wounds and took their orphan back to base where it thrived on powdered milk. Even larger antelope were not immune to baboon attacks. On yet another island, four impala were found dead, their stomachs ripped out. The only other occupants were baboons and porcupines.

Nature shared more secrets with them. Four bush pigs were seen feeding on a fresh impala ram carcass. A leguaan was seen to attack a vervet monkey swimming between trees. A large barbel grabbed a grey heron chick which had toppled out of its nest, and pulled it underwater. On other occasions this same species of fish was observed nudging at half submerged maize stalks in a deserted, inundated village, then feeding greedily on the bounty of insects that was dislodged. And, while there was this seldom-before witnessed evidence of predation, so too did the flood produce some unlikely relationships. Virtually every island had its share of antbear burrows, down which there was usually a resident antbear. However, the rangers never ceased to be amazed at what other lodgers were discovered in the holes. It made a man's task that much more interesting as one grovelled down into one of these tunnels, eyes staring into the blackness while the brain hoped fervently that whoever was hanging onto your leg had good strong reflexes! The combinations were mind boggling. In one day, in four different antbear holes, the rescue team unearthed -

one warthog and a baboon:
one warthog and a porcupine:
three porcupines:
a baboon and a porcupine:
and in every case the antbear too was at home, the last to be dragged out, his claws caked with fresh soil as he burrowed for more room.

These cramped living arrangements did occasionally introduce a lighter side to the day's work. On one particular game drive, when a camera team and several journalists were present, a porcupine was seen to scurry down an antbear hole. One of the game rangers matter-of-factly kept an eye on the hole, earmarking it for a later rescue. A few minutes later the owner of the hole, a large, ponderous antbear, also disappeared down out of sight. Not too long later, another porcupine took cover in the hole. The game ranger raised an eyebrow. One of the cameramen had also noticed the antbear and wandered over, eventually standing above the hole. The cameraman peered into the slanted depths of the tunnel below him. As the game ranger silently commiserated with the antbear, sandwiched between two pin cushions, there was a sudden explosion of earth and antbear as it came bursting up through the top of the burrow. The cameraman shot up, high in the air, almost concealed by the shower of soil, as the disillusioned animal sought quieter parts.

In Tanganyika, Julius Nyerere, leader of the Tanganyika African National Union, was carried shoulder high through the streets of Dar es Salaam in wild celebration of the imminent African majority parliament. In Teheran preparations were in the final stages for the wedding of the twice married 40-year-old Shah of Persia to Miss Farrah Diba, who was 21. As Christmas approached, millions prayed for world peace and President Eisenhower and Mr Khrushchev dominated world headlines as unrest in Algeria continued. Iran and Iraq moved up troops in a Yuletide border dispute and China, no convert to Khrushchev's call for renunciation of force to settle world problems, posed a continuing threat with its claims to Indian frontier lands.

On Kariba the rescue teams worked into the new rainy season. In subsequent wet seasons the rescue operation would taper off, for the new rains would bring fresh succulence to the islands, a brief respite to the hungry antelope and rhinos. And the bush would be impossibly thick to work. But for now, at the end of this first climactic year, Rupert and his men worked on, seldom able to read the headlines about the 'other' world. In the blossoming civilisation of Kariba there would be parties and much frivolity. The club and the hotel and the nurses' home would see much revelry, and occasionally the game rangers would find an excuse to be there. Even Rupert, who drank little and smoked a lot, would get away from the lake a couple of times and briefly rejoin society.

CHAPTER 10

RHINO ISLANDS

During that first year of trial and error, the data and records which were so religiously kept, more often than not being written up late at night by the light of a hurricane lamp while the body was craving sleep, showed that some 1 700 animals, birds and reptiles had been saved. On the deficit side, 529 animals were lost. Some of these were found drowned, some died from a mixture of shock and hunger while being rescued, and some in the final analysis had to be destroyed, as there was no way to save them. Gradually this trial and error method evolved into a tried and tested system as the rescue teams became more familiar with the different reactions of species to this man-induced flood.

There were always the exceptions, and they cropped up every day. One warthog wasn't necessarily going to react like another once he was released on the mainland. One terrified dog baboon wasn't predictably going to head for the nearest cover once he was shaken unceremoniously from the confines of his sack. And one proud, furious sable bull could not be taken for granted once his hooves touched the bottom beside the boat and he started to use his horns in the classic, characteristic way of that species of antelope.

Yet progress was made. From the beginning Rupert made it a rule that any animal which died during capture would not be considered for their often barren larder. In doing this he ensured that the slowly increasing, often changing, gang of helpers could not take advantage of a rescue casualty. The habits of the many wild animals became a key role in the future planning of rescue operations. It was soon realised that impala were very loath to take to water and as this species of antelope was the most ubiquitous, a specific strategy had to be worked out. Netting became the most successful method of rescue. But this had its inherent problems. Islands, slowly being devoured from all sides by the rising waters, had to be of a manageable size before the men could rig the nets. And, the very nature of the Zambezi Valley bush, dense and inhospitable, made it an enemy. There were also the other marooned inhabitants to contend with. Lions and leopards, rhinos and elephants, zebras and sable, and others of the larger antelope species soon made short thrift of the web of nets painstakingly erected.

Warthogs, especially the larger boars, were best tackled in the shallows, where it was just that much easier to evade the slashing tusks. But, just as often, they were encountered on dry land enmeshed in the capture nets, or perhaps reversed defensively rear-end down in an antbear hole, ready to take on all-comers. Even the younger specimens, with mere stumps for tusks, would not hesitate to attack their rescuers. Several of the types of game were more easily handled in water. Monkeys and baboons, civets, genets, the small grysbok, porcupines and steenbok were easier to manage. Wild pigs would be unsnared from the nets or tackled in the shallows, this cousin of the warthog equally ready for a fight. On land or in the water the totally fearless hissing, growling honey badger was a handful for anyone, and always proved a wily, elusive ingrate. Along with the tusks and sharp hooves of his wild companions, this little animal left his mark on the would-be human saviours. The larger antelope, the waterbuck, sable and kudu were all capable swimmers, sometimes found miles out in the lake. But the males, with their heavy sweeps and twists of horns would tire easily, the weight remorselessly edging their muzzles closer to the water and death. These, and the calves, were helped along by the human sheepdogs, ropes and plaited stockings holding the heads up. Bushbuck fought desperately but tired quickly in their rescuers' hands. Duiker bleated continuously once they were confined within the bulwarks of a rescue craft and their plaintive childlike cries always heralded a boat's approach. Grysbok, quite capable of folding up and miraculously shooting through the six-inch squares of the hemp nets, quietened down quickly after capture and often seemed to take a wide-eyed interest in their surroundings. The strange, angular antbear, often the last species of animal to be taken off a drowning island because of its solitary, shy habits, was purported to be mute, no one in the past having had much close association with the species. However, the rescue teams were to hear loud, indignant domestic calf-like bellows emit from these nocturnal wanderers when they were handled. Zebras were poor swimmers and were especially hampered by the spreading menace of the *Salvinia molesta*. This thickening, seemingly uncontrollable, cabbage-like weed crept inexorably across the surface of this new Central African lake, often blanketing scores of square miles of surface. Animals and the rescue team boats found it very heavy going negotiating this plague and, coupled with the ever changing vista of submerging trees and shrubbery, new islands and drowned islands, men and animals often lost precious time in the daily battle for life.

Nevertheless, the start of 1960 was less chaotic than the previous year. Techniques were improved, a little more equipment was available, and the teams enlarged. For, with the publicity of that first year valued at £100 000 to the Southern Rhodesian Government, Salisbury could not afford to be seen allowing the rescue operation to lag. And wild horses would not have dragged Rupert and his band of scarred, water-logged rescuers from the drowning valley. Official mail to the leader of 'Noah' was now addressed slightly differently. In the New Year's Honours list he had been awarded the M.B.E. for his efforts. It was a subject that embarrassed him. There were other men in the team and most of them had sweated their guts out as much as him. And so he looked on the decoration as a team award, interpreting the inscription of his name as that of 'Operation Noah'. That his name, even then, was synonymous with the rescue effort, was as yet unrealised by him.

In the context of the rescue operations in that first year there were two events that caused Rupert extra concern. In both instances, despite a series of determined attempts, the rescue teams failed in their efforts to remove animals from rapidly diminishing patches of ground. And as yet neither Rupert nor the relevant authorities in Salisbury were clear as to how they were going to rectify the situation. On one occasion the rescuers had failed to remove a lone bull elephant from his island domain. Time and again they had returned to the slowly-vanishing patch of land, goading the animal with shots fired into the air, thunderflashes, low-flying aircraft and using themselves as bait to try and draw the stubborn elephant into deep water where they could guide him to the mainland. But the bull thwarted every attempt, never going more than flank high into the lake. The rescue team had many close shaves with the frightened, angry, stubborn animal. Apart from the encroaching waters there was the other enemy. Food. Or rather, the lack of it. The elephant was steadily eating himself out of sustenance. Eventually, on yet another visit to try to move the elephant, they found him dead. Loss of condition from the lack of food, and possibly pneumonia, appeared to be the cause. It was a sombre bunch of men who left the island, still not believing the elephant's stubbornness. The elephant problem would raise its head on several more occasions over the flood years. In the main, the elephant population had moved away with the gradual forming of the lake. They had been observed swimming over five miles, often from island to island, in search of succulent foliage. So the rising waters did not present these largest of all land mammals with the menace it held for lesser creatures. However, the rangers were to be forced to destroy elephants on several occasions, when reluctance to leave 'an urgent island' turned to truculence and total aggressiveness, seriously hampering the safety of hundreds of other animals. It was a painful weighing-up of the odds. How many impala and warthogs, or sable and kudu, was one elephant worth? In the four and a half years of Operation Noah ten elephants were destroyed for this reason. Twenty three were manoeuvred off islands, or found swimming in the middle of nowhere, confused by the never-ending expanse of water, and were shepherded to the mainland and safety.

A black rhino discovered on a diminishing island, some 200 yards by 75 yards, west of Bumi, was the game rangers' second major rescue failure. And until almost a year later, with the irascible creatures being discovered on new islands (these being named Rhino Island One, Two, Three ... and so on), Rupert and Archie Fraser would be searching desperately for a reliable method of removing two tons of rhino from an island, across varying distances of water in a variety of weather conditions, and releasing the animal on safe terrain. All this had to be accomplished with minimum injury to man or beast! It was a totally different logistical problem to that of the elephants, the criteria being that rhinos cannot swim. They would rather starve than get their knees wet. Unless they could be rescued, they were doomed to their patch of disappearing land, when they too would drown slowly beneath the rising lake. When one considers that, in the end, 43 black rhinos were rescued, then surely even the critics must concede that, on these merits alone, the effort was far from an emotionally-motivated waste of time.

They first discovered the rhino in mid May of 1959 and, shortly afterwards, Rupert made his first attempt at driving the animal off the island. At this stage it was still possible for the rhino to wade across to another island closer to the mainland and then similarly leapfrog several more until the actual mainland was reached. Len Harvey dropped off

Rupert and a game scout on the island shortly after 9.00am. Then he edged the boat back and began to ease it through the maze of drowning undergrowth that surrounded every island, trying to keep in reasonable parallel range with the rescue leader on land. The rhino was soon located. Strategically keeping climbable trees to hand, Rupert fired several shots in the air. His intention was to harass the animal into leaving. Torment it. Badger it. Make life on this small patch of earth intolerable. Man and rhino: 170 lbs versus 2 000 lbs. As he was to point out dryly later - he couldn't very well tuck the rhino under one arm, St. Francis style, and carry him off.

Apart from angry snorts and half-hearted charges, the rhino ignored Rupert. He tried another tack. Through the thick mass of hilltop bush he stalked the rhino, getting in close enough to pelt it with stones. For two hours this went on, with Rupert and the scout evading charge after charge. Up and down the island the game of hide and seek continued, the stone-throwing and the charges. Still the rhino showed no sign of even considering leaving the island. It had reached the stage when it completely ignored the stones thrown at it, even when direct hits were made. There in the small patch of drowning land, in the midday heat of the Zambezi Valley, Rupert shook his head and swore aloud. Plan C was needed. Again he stalked the grey mass of bad-tempered rhino. This time he fired shots into the tree beside the animal's head and into the ground beside it. Ricocheting stones and earth and bark at the beast. Reaction this time. Another charge. Another frantic scramble up trees.

This latest round had brought them close to the water where Len Harvey nudged the boat between trees, watching the events anxiously. Rupert caught a glimpse of the four-gallon jerrycans that were always carried in the boats. Some would be empty, he surmised. Good, noisy drums. A different sound to give the rhino. Warily, hastily he shinned down the tree, beckoning Len Harvey closer. Briefly he explained his next attempt. Then another stalk began, different this time, with the tinny, echoing beat of the drums pounding the bush stillness. From the boat and Rupert the sound bounced ahead of them. Rupert glimpsed movement ahead and then the crashing of the bush. It was tree time again. Losing sight of Rupert and the game scout, the rhino noticed the boat. Len Harvey had drifted in closer. With scarcely a pause the rhino continued its charge into the water, the spray from its churning feet soaking the other game ranger. He spun the boat away scant seconds before impact. Rupert persevered a while longer. Once, the rhino took to the water, floundering about ten yards before returning to land. After four hours Rupert called it a day. When the island was a little smaller they'd try again.

It was the first of many attempts to persuade Greta Garbo to leave her island. Later it transpired that, despite the nickname, the rhino was in fact a male. He was dubbed this eyebrow-raising title by a visiting cameraman who was filming a 30 minute programme for N.B.C. Television. One of many newshounds who would monitor the saga of the first rhino encountered, Hank Telouzzi was particularly liked by the normally media-sceptical rescue team. The withdrawn, rugged, often intimidating team leader and the ebullient, undaunted cameraman got on well from the start, despite the difference in characters. There was considerable leg-pulling and friendly one-upmanship between the two men. Frank Junor recalls the American daring Rupert to try and ride the rhino. With a characteristic slow consideration of the challenge, Rupert finally nodded. But there was a qualification. He could not afford a good quality camera and even the film he was using was murdering his salary ... if he succeeded, and the man got the unique footage of the event, he said, gazing at the film man's collection of equipment, ... how about donating this latest, most modern camera to himself? It was Hank Telouzzi's turn to ponder. Looking at Rupert and going over the past few days' happenings he declined the wager. Then there was the instance of his brand new Magnum revolver. Just on the market in America, it had been brought out to darkest Southern Rhodesia by the cameraman on a 'just in case' basis. It was the envy of the weapon-conscious rangers and the visitor needed little encouragement to demonstrate his rather mediocre ability with it. One day, before the assembled rescue men, he was shooting at empty beer bottles. A few were being hit. He motioned at Rupert, standing silently amongst the men, tapped the revolver and pointed at the line of bottles. The raised eyebrows and ironic grin said more than the spoken challenge. Grimacing wryly, Rupert took the weapon and hefted it experimentally. Someone replaced the bottles. There was an anticipatory silence. Familiar only with heavy calibre rifles, Rupert brought it up a couple of times in a practice aim. Then, with six smooth, evenly-spaced shots he shattered five bottles. The visitor never offered another challenge. Sadly, later, moving on to new headlines, he would be shot dead covering the Congo bloodshed in the early sixties.

Despite the repeated attempts to drive the rhino off, it doggedly resisted all persuasion. Everything that had been tried with the elephant was duplicated now with the rhino. To no avail. Rupert lost count of the times he was charged. Everyone received their share of 'her' stubborn frustrating anger. Even the boats were charged. The small fixed-wing plane they used once, was out of its range, but the huffing, snorting hatred it directed up at the annoying bird - thing left no doubt as to what it would like to do. Its hatred and frustration at the constant disturbance of its otherwise peaceful existence reached a peak one day when, before the wide-eyed rangers, it knelt down on its front knees and banged its head on the ground. In a seemingly uncontrolled, frustrated frenzy it then lay down and hammered its head a few more times. The men stared. Then it lay completely still. Unmoving. As if dead. Cautiously Rupert moved up to it and tossed a stone. The impact galvanised the rhino into action. For an animal of its size it was on its feet amazingly fast. Once again Rupert retreated before its angry charge.

On 2 July Frank Junor, Len Harvey and several other rangers revisited the island. Rupert was working on another part of the lake. The recalcitrant rhino had been dead for about two days. The island's foliage had been almost completely devoured up to the height of where the animal could stretch. Again it looked as if pneumonia induced by malnutrition was the cause of death. That, and its stubbornness.

In Salisbury, Archie Fraser had been conferring with members of the Veterinary Research Department. Drugs, so far, had been used to but a limited degree on some of the smaller game, mainly with regard to sedation and anti shock treatment. Everything pointed to drug application playing a bigger role in the coming months and years. The experiences with the elephant and rhino were evidence enough. Consequently, at the end of the year, Dr John Condy visited the lake. Liaising with Rupert, he wanted to study the effect of nicotine sulphate and other drugs on rhinos. Parallel with these observations it was hoped that a method could be devised to develop a technique for rescuing rhinos. Today, with the degree of sophistication reached in the evolution of drugs and wild animal capture, 35 years on, some readers may not fully grasp the enormity of the task about to be started. Names like Apple and Bill Gates were years ahead. The brave new world was still metamorphosing. Fax machines and the Internet were not even dreamed of. The space race was just above tree height. The silicone chip was only a year old. Laptop computers and video cameras were innovations still to come. Then, in 1960, with usage and knowledge of drugs in its infancy, the task ahead must have been more than a little daunting.

This period of experimentation was not made easier by the fact that the only two islands known to contain rhinos were as yet too large and unmanageable to work on. However, a start had to be made somewhere. Rupert, John Condy and some of the team carried out a series of recces on the islands. Step one was to trap a rhino ... the location of the animal was comparatively easy. Step two was to dart it and study the effects. Question. How did they achieve step one without harming the animal? Rupert started the ball rolling by setting foot snares along their trails and around their middens. The men waited patiently nearby. At sundown the snares would be disarmed, and reset the next day. The daylight hours brought no luck. At night rhinos were visiting their scatters, in one case even walking on the disarmed snare. Rupert advocated building tree platforms and sitting up at night. His suggested strategy that they could aim the dart gun by torchlight, once the animal was caught, and then truss it up while under the effect of the nicotine sulphate, earned him a wry sideways glance from the veterinary research man.

And so they reverted to plain straight-forward hunting, with the projectile being a dart and not a bullet. It was nerve-jumping, mopping-the-brow, dangerous work. The rhino were edgy, aware of the man presence, and behaved in typically characteristic rhino fashion. These early attempts were only successful in that they involved more and more observations of rhinos, often at close quarters, and consequently fed the minds of these few men with more information that they needed to discover. Their first subject was a big bull rhino on what they called Rhino One Island. They had stalked him well and got up to within 30 yards of the animal. The trigger mechanism of the dart gun was cocked. It made a loud, metallic click. The rhino bolted immediately. They could not get close to it again. During the afternoon of the same day they hunted Rhino Two Island where Rupert had ascertained there were two rhinos. Painstakingly they stalked one of them, eventually getting to within 25 yards of the rhinos. This time Rupert had risked cocking the gun in advance, weighing up carrying the loaded weapon through the thick bush against the earlier attempt. He fired. The dart touched a piece of branch, deflecting it so that it hit the rhino on the flank, harmlessly broadside on. The rhino snorted and spun, bolting in the opposite direction. Rupert muttered and retrieved the dart. It was not an auspicious beginning.

The rudimentary dart gun, coupled with the extra wariness of the rhinos, did not help the situation much more. More thought was needed. John Condy suggested putting a salt lick down at their favourite haunts. The rock salt would condition the animals and hopefully make them easier to locate in the future. He would return to Kariba again once a few problems had been ironed out. Rupert nodded his agreement, staring out across the lake at the distant rhino islands. Anything was worth a try, if they were going to rescue the stubborn animals ...

In the last week of April 1960 Doctor A. M. Harthoorn arrived in the colony. He was a leading veterinarian from Makerere College in Uganda and, together with Doctor J. A. Lock who joined him at Kariba, had considerable experience in the drug immobilising techniques of capturing the large mammals. Their invitation to visit the site of the largest-ever wild animal rescue effort had been initiated by Lt. Col. R. A. Critchley who, as President of the Northern Rhodesian Game Preservation and Hunting Association, was the instigator of the rescue operation on the north bank of the dramatically widening river. The Game Preservation and Hunting Association rescue team, headed by Tad Edelman, was smaller than that of their southern bank counterparts but with equal dedication spearheaded the Northern Rhodesian rescue operation. This aspect of the rescue efforts would cease in June 1961, two years before the end of the Southern Rhodesian Operation Noah. This was due to the scarcity of wildlife on the northern bank and the geography of the area, causing slower more shallow inundation of the land, trapping less game.

With the arrival of Doctors Harthoorn and Lock the preliminary steps were under way to solve the rhino rescue problem. It had now been established that four rhinos were stranded on different pockets of land in the lake. But there were still some logistical problems to be overcome. If the drugs the visitors had brought were successful and it became possible to immobilize and truss up two tons of rhino, what would be the best method of transporting the animal to safety? Rupert designed a raft, taking into consideration that virtually all of the components would have to be begged or borrowed from the nearby dam construction site. Consequently, forays up along to the various engineering sites of the hitherto unparalleled dam construction project were conducted, and in remarkable time a collection of planks, beams, rolls of wire, and most importantly, 18 empty 44-gallon oil drums found their way to the Game Department base in Kariba. With these items the rescue team constructed a raft that would, if all worked well, be sufficiently buoyant to carry a rhino, several humans, and a minimum of superstructure. For the manoeuvring of an unconscious rhino onto the raft, a sleigh of smooth tree trunks was built, constructed in a 'V' shape, which would aid the physical dragging of the sleigh through the bush. It was guessed that about 30 men would be able to drag the rhino-bearing sleigh from where it had finally dropped, to the raft at the water's edge. Then the rescue 'mother boat', *The Ark* would tow the lot to the mainland.

The island was reflected clearly in the still waters of early morning. It was a hilltop stretch of land, about half a mile long, and covered with a kaleidoscope of jumbled thickets, tangled thornbush and trees. Patches of rocky outcrops added their ragged obstacles to the arena. Rupert had reconnoitred the island several times, the last occasion being only three days before, accompanied by Dr Harthoorn. The leading inhabitant was a large bull, with a more irate temper than average, and he was only too ready to take on all-comers. The small party of rangers, the doctor and a photographer making a film for Caltex, headed for the island in a dinghy. Perhaps the following events are best described by Toni Harthoorn ...

"We landed on Rhino Island as quickly as possible, Rupert grumbling good-humouredly about the disadvantages of taking photographers along, while the younger rangers presented the bright side - that rhinoceros invariably charge the camera lens to the convenience and safety of the rest of the party! Only a few of us went ashore at first, while Ray, in the boat, quietly whistled the opening bars of Chopin's funeral march to cheer us on our way.

Our quarry was soon located, since we heard him just in front of us; but to see him, and above all to get into firing range, was quite another matter. We would see a small patch of grey hide, anatomically unidentifiable, or sometimes an eye or an ear. Occasionally we heard an ominous crackling as he charged, rhino-like, obliquely away or towards us. Eventually, at midday, we held a council of war and decided on other tactics. Since the rhinoceros clearly knew he was being hunted, stealth could be abandoned, and methods used of a more direct and forceful nature.

As marksman I was to be hidden in a tree on the waist of the island. The rest of the party, reinforced by several scouts, were to drive the quarry past the ambush. In this way the chances of at least seeing the target should be increased.

The syringe was reloaded, the gun checked and the tree position occupied. In twenty minutes the sound of the beaters approached. It was a tense time, as the target would be in view for a few seconds at the most, possibly too far in the bushes at the edge, or too near and below the tree. This was the last chance today. Suddenly he emerged, dark with sweat from the excitement and effort of running from the beaters. He came fast, but to my relief he momentarily slowed to a trot to negotiate some boulders at a comfortable range of thirty yards. Swinging the gun amongst the foliage as well as I could in best army tradition, I fired. To my instant relief I saw that the dart curved after him as if guided by the hand of providence, inserting itself in a favourable spot on the lower haunch where the skin is thinner and the blood supply good.

Seconds later the rangers were there. Looking up with questioning faces, too tactful to ask directly `hit or miss?' they displayed delighted grins at my thumbs up sign. I had very mixed feelings, for something could yet go wrong, since the drug used was at that time wholly untried on rhinoceros.

They paused only for seconds; then everyone fanned out to look for the animal. I had explained that I wanted to know immediately it stopped. Rupert, it later transpired, almost ran into it and had to rush up the nearest tree while the rhino followed rather unsteadily to take up its position glaring fiercely upwards. At last it sank to the ground. Rupert's whistle blast soon brought everyone to the spot. I looked apprehensively at the animal, struck as I have so often been by the shrinkage that a large and powerful animal apparently undergoes when it has fallen, but I was reassured by the movement of the heaving flank. A little antidote injected into an ear vein soon brought more life, and necessitated tying the legs for safety. A tranquilliser now brought sleepy indifference, and quite regular breathing; the embarkation could begin."

Once the 300 yards tug-of-war to the water's edge was completed and the rhino and sleigh hauled onto the raft, the last leg of the journey lay ahead. It was late afternoon and the surface of the lake had turned choppy. The mainland was 12 miles distant. Rupert eyed the raft anxiously. So far everything had gone well. Now the main consideration was the raft, with its precious cargo. Would 18 oil drums carry 2 000 pounds of rhino after all?

The journey took 90 minutes, and apart from the disturbance caused by several motor boats carrying journalists, was uneventful. The raft worked perfectly. The sleigh was hauled about 30 yards inland and the rhino's bonds untied. The tranquillised mound of prehistoric, armoured bad temper remained motionless. Rupert filled a can with water and splashed it over the sleeping animal. Instant arousal. The rhino scrambled up and the men scattered.

"Only Rupert remained standing, imperturbable as always, with various scouts hanging from the trees like overripe fruit."

Then the rhino charged the boat, splashing into the water and tossing one of the four gallon jerrycans high into the air. Satisfied that it had wreaked enough havoc, the rhino then lumbered off. That night, logging up the daily diary, Rupert wrote in the first entry dealing with a successful rhino rescue. It was 10 May 1960. Forty two more would be rescued.

By mid-July three more had been taken off the drowning islands. Each rhino provided different problems. Each rescue had to be approached as a separate exercise. Apart from the rhino they saved during the next three years, they 'lost' 14. The early experimentation with drugs resulted in the deaths of some of them, while at least two, on being released on dry land, wheeled and charged back into the water, sinking before the rangers could react. Rhino number three very nearly met his end this way. Apparently

not with the standard operating procedure of rhino behaviour, the animal had already swum 25 yards to attack the boat of the approaching rescue party. He had been almost invisible, standing neck deep in the lake in ambush, watching their approach. Then came his attack. Later, when the same animal was released, he swam at them again, attacking the outboard motors. This time he nearly drowned. He barely made it to the water's edge where he rested for over an hour, rear legs still in the water. The rangers were reasonably convinced that, had the effects of the tranquillising drug been completely worn off, the attack would have been even more determined.
On 20 August the daily newspaper carried a photograph of the release of the fifth rhino rescued. Christened 'Chippy', the cow rhino also attacked her boatload of rescuers, hammering her long front horn through the hull of the boat three times. Then she focused her anger on Rupert, who was standing on the raft, ploughing through the shallows, snorting and jabbing with that terrible front horn. As the rhino tried to get at him Rupert took off his shapeless, much ventilated bush hat and smacked the furious rhino half a dozen times across her face. Finally the rhino departed into the bush on the water's edge. The incident was witnessed by Archie Fraser, a cabinet minister and a visiting photographer. In the future Rupert was reluctant to discuss the incident. A shy grin would accompany his short explanation that he had merely waved farewell to the rhino.

By the end of that year eight rhinos had been rescued. One small calf had died after capture; it received the dart aimed at its mother, moving into the line of fire at the last instant and so getting an overdose. In May 1961 the tenth rhino was taken to safety. In September of that year, on a beautifully clear Monday, Rupert had his closest escape of the operation. On one of the islands of the Bumi complex the team had darted a half grown bull. The drug was not affecting the animal as well as it should, and the rhino was thoroughly annoyed. Time and again he would charge the men in the rescue team as they hovered close by, waiting anxiously for the drug to work. Rupert had the Cap Chur gun and was deciding whether or not to give the young bull a second dose. He didn't want to give it an overdose.

On the other hand, possibly the dart had malfunctioned and the full dose had not been injected. Always keeping a tree close by as an escape route, he eased closer to the restless animal. It wheeled and charged him and Rupert dived behind the protective bulk of a fallen baobab trunk. What he did not realize was that the tree trunk had been eaten out by termites, leaving only a fragile husk. The rhino charged straight through as if it were a pile of balsa wood. Rupert was pinned underneath the body of the rhino as it jostled to get him in a position where it could use its horn. Rupert's world was a pall of dust, snorting, grunting rhino and a close-up of the animal's underbelly. Now the rest of the team were shouting and waving at the rhino, trying to attract its attention away from the man beneath it. It stared angrily around, momentary confusion fogging its brain. Rupert wriggled out from behind its back legs and was helped to safety. A week later he decided to visit the hospital up on the heights. The bruises and lacerations were healing well, but his chest pains were not improving. The x-rays showed six broken ribs.

Frank Junor's buffalo incident and Rupert's close shave with the rhino were probably the most serious of the entire rescue operation. Certainly there were many other close shaves experienced by everyone concerned. There were almost daily occurrences. Slashes from warthog tusks, jagged, deep cuts from the hooves of several of the species of antelope - especially bushbuck and grysbok - bites from zebras, baboons, monkeys and honey badgers were an expected part of the day's work. Lofty Stokes came close to serious injury or worse when a leopard, running from a line of beaters, bowled him over. It didn't maul him, but it could have done. That more people were not injured or killed by some of the bigger animals was a combination of luck, cool reflexes and discipline on the part of the rescue members. Ex-director, Dr Graham Child, is adamant that Rupert's attention to detail and planning played an important part in keeping the casualties down.

The ubiquitous presence of all the dangerous snakes makes it almost unbelievable that no-one was ever bitten while floundering around the drowning islands. Equally difficult to believe is that no-one was ever taken by a crocodile. There were several instances when a member of a rescue team was splashing along after some animal, only to see a violent flurry of water close by and then the animal was gone.

As the world of drugs offered more efficient and tested products, so the task of darting rhinos became less complicated. Problems still occurred with the delivery weapons, and would continue to do so for years to come. Once Toni Harthoorn had returned to Uganda, a series of doctors added their experience to the science of immobilising wild animals. Dr Graham Child, then a long-standing director of the Department of National Parks and Wildlife Management of Zimbabwe, wrote his doctoral thesis on *Behaviour Of Large Mammals - Kariba.* In time, several other valuable papers would appear about the rescue effort. Archie Fraser perhaps summed this up best, when he noted that "every possible advantage was taken of the unique opportunity offered by Kariba to study animal behaviour and attributes."

CHAPTER 11

HOMELIFE, CRACKERS, AND ORPHANS

The bar up on the heights was full of the usual cross-section of people who had gravitated to this part of the colony with the emergence of Kariba Dam. Italian construction workers, visiting engineering hierarchy, hospital staff, a variety of persons who now called Kariba 'home', were all up in the pub which was built to catch the smallest reviving breeze drifting hesitantly among the hilltops. The crowd was thinning now. A hand hammered on the bar top, splitting through the cacophony of conversation, and the hubbub dropped expectantly. All eyes turned to one of the local residents as he stood, hand poised over the bar. Beside him, on the bar top, a small, nondescript, brown mongrel dog stood quietly. Before he lost the audience, the man informed the crowd that he was leaving Kariba shortly and that he was looking for a home for the dog. Glances switched to the dog and back again, without enthusiasm. He added ... "If anyone wants the dog they can take it now, otherwise I'll have to shoot it ..."

In a corner, a small knot of rangers back at Kariba base for the night, surveyed the scene. The crowd looked at the mongrel, which in turn scratched vigorously at a marauding flea. Finally, Tinkey Haslam stood up from the table and motioned to the dog. And so Crackers joined the rescue team of Operation Noah. At first glance, the only notable characteristic of the small, brown mongrel, with the streamlining of a dachshund and certain fox terrier-type tendencies was his questionable parentage. But, as time passed, he became the mascot of Operation Noah, working his way into the hearts of even the most hardened of the team members.

Almost as soon as Tinkey returned to camp with this new addition, Crackers transferred his loyalty and affection to Rupert, from whom, in the years ahead, he hated to be parted. For his part, it was seldom that the senior game ranger would embark on rescue tasks unaccompanied by the bright-eyed, ever-alert mongrel. Crackers, perched up on the bow of a boat avidly searching the water and undergrowth ahead for new sport, became a familiar figurehead. His shrill barks during rescue operations, either directed at wild animals, or any person he thought was a little slow off the mark, formed a familiar background chorus to the day's events.

Crackers, like his new master, was fearless. Impala or rhinos, buffalos or warthogs, baboons or zebras - all were so much sport to him in this new water and wilderness environment. To some degree the undaunted little mongrel became a valued member of the rescue team. Antbear holes were his *forté*! Prior to his arrival on the scene, recovering animals from these burrows was a time-consuming, sometimes hit and miss affair. However, he soon revelled in the exploration of the many subterranean hideouts. His rapid withdrawal from a hole, in a flurry of dust, accompanied by his barks of discovery, meant that, for sure, some form of animal or another was down there. His inspections of these holes saved a lot of digging on the mere suspicion that an animal may have sought refuge down there. During the searching of islands and the apprehending of animals dashing through the shallows, his short legs kept him at a certain disadvantage. Even two feet of water, for Crackers, was the deep end. However, this was not an insurmountable obstacle. He learned to take full advantage of any floating logs, running along them, balanced precariously like a lumberjack as they rotated in the water, and wherever possible he avoided unnecessary swimming - leaping as far as possible from a boat or the end of a log. His powers of agility, whether it concerned climbing a rough-hewn ladder or manoeuvring his way along the tops of a row of petrol cans, caused more than one person to wonder if perhaps there was a little monkey blood in his ancestry.

The longer Crackers stayed on Kariba, the more entrenched he became as a team member. The strength of his personality was boundless, his audacity unquenchable. His only periods of melancholy were on the infrequent occasions when Rupert had to leave him at base camp. Then, adopting a 'deserted again' look in his usually lively brown gaze, he would temporarily adopt another team member, and it became something of a status symbol to have Crackers' attentions redirected at one. If he accepted a morsel of bacon rind from a person at breakfast, even if he did bury it afterwards, one knew he was among the upper echelons of the Crackers' hierarchy. But whenever a boat arrived, or a vehicle, depending on where the latest base was established, the little dog would be gone. And if it wasn't Rupert returning, back he would come, tail adroop and a dejected look in his expressive brown eyes again.

In camp too there were always other newcomers. Mostly they were young animals and birds which could not fend for themselves once they were released on the mainland. And so, once a day's rescue tasks had been halted by the downing of the sun and the boats and men were back at their camp, work was by no means over. Upkeep of reports, repairs to engines, first-aid administered to the casualties of that day, the next day's strategy - all vied with the little time set aside for the main meal of the day. And there were the orphans to look after. The young impala, the kudu calf, the warthog with the sprained leg, the little genet which was released but which kept on returning, the pair of fish eagle chicks, and the half dozen baboons. Those were just current inmates. It didn't include the rhino in the makeshift pens at the back of the camp, released the previous day after being kept under observation for two weeks. Because Rupert hadn't liked the look of the swelling in its abdomen and had decided the animal should be nurse-maided for a while. Rupert had discovered this particular rhino had stomach ache and had sat up with it at night, on the fence poles of the pen, worriedly studying the animal. In the early hours of the morning the rhino had started rolling on its back, squealing endlessly. Rupert had telephoned a vet friend in Salisbury the next day, giving him the symptoms. Slightly nonplussed, the vet suggested that the rhino needed an enema. Rupert weighed up just how one gave a rhino an enema ... and eventually did just that. Drugging the animal, he carried out the operation with a stirrup pump, four gallons of warm water and two bars of blue soap. The rhino improved considerably but relapsed a week later. Another enema, plus two pounds of Epsom salts properly cured the ailing animal. Nor does it include the young sable bull, or the bushbuck ewe still suffering from shock; or the eight-foot-long Egyptian cobra that Frank was looking after, awaiting collection by the country's snake park.

Back at the permanent Kariba base camp, the wife of one of the rescue team members was spending a few days' leave, although her husband was away up-lake. The current 'orphan' inhabitants caused her some anxiety as she gradually discovered their presence around the scattered tents and huts. The warthog that had made the grass-fenced 'bathroom' its permanent home, resenting any intruders, was bad enough. The 12-foot python she encountered in the kitchen, put there by Rupert to discourage the stealing of provisions by the casually employed labourers, was even more unsettling. The same lady, it was, who on another occasion, awoke in the dead of night to answer a call of nature. Padding outside she startled Rupert who, totally unclad in the hot valley night, was watering the paw paw trees he had painstakingly planted and reared. It was habit, when he was in camp, to water them at night when it was cooler and there was respite from the fierce sun's rays.

A hot summer night in Salisbury, with the clock on the mantlepiece ticking its way to 2.00am. The house, at the western end of Rhodes Avenue, nestled comfortably among the tall, leafy trees which, in daytime, helped keep the house cool and gave some privacy from the neighbours. Salisbury and its suburbs slept. Suddenly, floating echoingly on the still night air, came the long drawn-out eerie call of a hyena. In the house Christine Fothergill nudged her husband awake. As he sat up, the last echoes of the hyena died away. Rupert quickly made his way outside. In his haste, he forgot about any clothing, sleeping nude as he did in the hot months. His main concern was quieting the hyena. It was just a pup, only four months old, and he'd had it for several weeks now. He'd found it in the bush, abandoned, and hyena or not, grisly reputation or not, he couldn't leave it there. So far it had behaved perfectly and was growing into a splendid animal. But not the howling. The neighbours were pretty long-suffering, with the menagerie of strays that found their way into the Fothergill home - and its surroundings. But this would be too much! He cursed as he tripped over a coffee table. Eventually he got outside. Already there were lights on and voices pitched querulously in the night. Torches flashed. With his own torch he padded naked around the garden, calling softly to the hyena. On the balcony of the double-storey house next door he could see an elderly lady in a voluminous nightgown peering anxiously down into the darkness. From that direction he caught a small sound and called softly again. The hyena pup bumbled out of the shadows with its shuffling, head-down, pleased-to-see-you, gait. Throwing a glance up at the balcony, Rupert manhandled the animal back to his house.

It was undoubtedly coincidental that their elderly neighbour succumbed to a cerebral thrombosis two days later. However, Christine, in quieter moments during the years ahead, sometimes wondered if it were possible that the hyena chorus, or possibly the sight of her naked husband wandering around the garden, did not help precipitate the attack. The hyena incident actually occurred several years after Noah, but the animal was one of a series of pets that found sanctuary in the Fothergill house throughout Rupert's game ranger years. Often he would be away, sometimes as in the rescue years, for long periods, and it fell to his wife to play nursemaid to the strays he brought home. Some were easily managed, others less so.

Like Zambezi and Sanyati, a young baboon and a young vervet monkey, the latter thinking the former was its mother, clinging upside down to its companion's underbelly as they scoured the garden for mischief. Hanging from the telephone lines, and raiding the neighbours' washing lines was just one part of their fun. And there were the dassies, those tiny rock hyraxes which are anatomically related to the elephant. They were no trouble really, not in the boisterous way of the baboon; and things were fine if you ignored the 'scalloping' of the curtains, eaten through most neatly, and managed to placate the lady next door whose flowers on the dining room table had been nibbled away. In a way they were even useful, the way they cleaned out the ashtrays. They loved tobacco and would eat cigarette stubs, or cigarettes, right down to the filters which they would then fastidiously spit out.

The clutch of fish eagles, a dozen of them of varying size and age, sharing Rupert's aviary at the bottom of the garden, presented even fewer problems. The birds, some just bundles of fluffy down whilst others were already growing their sub-adult plumage, were brought from the base in Kariba. There, where time was a premium, and with an ever-widening array of orphans being carried back to camp for nursing, it was proving impossible to care properly for the birds. So, back to Salisbury they came, until they were of the age to look after themselves. The daily task of slicing up raw fish and then manhandling the food down the young birds' gullets was certainly, thought Rupert's wife, one of the easier duties of being foster mother. It was just as well, being a nurse, that cutting up raw fish did not worry her overmuch.

The mopane squirrels, sent up from Kariba by Rupert, for what he anticipated would be a short spell of home care, were very sweet and appealing - and totally unaware of the family drama they caused. They came to the house in a section of hollowed-out tree trunk. Concerned for their welfare, and knowing little of their natural habitat, Christine felt it was most cruel to house the little creatures in that barren, draughty piece of tree. After some consideration, she transferred them from the log to the ever-handy aviary. It was only when Rupert made one of his sporadic visits home that she became aware that the squirrels had feasted handsomely off all the cockateel eggs in the aviary, much to his chagrin. Squirrels and tree trunk were transferred in haste to the bottom of the garden, into a large *msasa* tree. Their subsequent forays up neighbours' drainpipes and intensive exploration of the eaves was a minor trauma after the loss of the eggs.

The crocodile episode was one of the more publicised events of the 'animal house'. Young Martin Fothergill was already showing that he had inherited some of his father's passion for animals. A corner of his bedroom boasted a vivarium, holding numerous small reptiles and a few non-poisonous snakes, most of which were prone to escape with reliable frequency. To join this collection, from the flood waters of Kariba, came two young crocodiles and a water monitor (or leguaan to use its local title). His mother put her foot down at these additions becoming residents of his already crowded bedroom. Thus he was forced to construct, at the furthest point of the garden, a reasonably deep, well-drained hole, which was in turn cemented. The 'croc pit' was then securely fenced, including a chicken wire cover. Both parents inspected this new home and were well pleased at their son's attention to detail. It would indeed be a safe lair for the newcomers.

It was only a few Sundays later when the morning paper was retrieved from the front verandah, with members of the Fothergill family looking forward to a leisurely read over the first cup of tea of the day, that the leading photograph and article dispelled such thoughts. In the nearby St. Joseph's Home for Boys a crocodile had been caught in the chicken run, and had been killed by the night guard. Aghast, the family dashed out to their new orphans' enclosure. One leguaan and one crocodile impassively returned their anxious stares. Deciding to let sleeping dogs lie, Rupert refrained from making any announcements about a missing crocodile. The leguaan added a postscript to the incident a few days later. Once again it was an ever patient neighbour who was honoured with a visit from one of the Fothergill menagerie. Mumbling apologies, Rupert retrieved the reptile from its newly discovered lair in the stove.

Perhaps the affair of the genet was the most embarrassing and potentially expensive interlude of all. And, as with almost all the other escapades, Rupert was far away at the time, and it fell to Christine to pour oil on troubled waters. A local friend of the family had passed on to them a genet, the second one to join the clan and hopefully become a mate for the one already ensconced in the Fothergill home. However, the newcomer was totally unimpressed with its new surroundings and was unceasingly evil-tempered and bad-mannered. It was a complete contrast to the little spotted animal that already had the run of the house. Consequently, until it mended its ways, the new genet was relegated to the garage. Across the road from the Fothergill residence, the lady of the household was well known for her gleaming, polished floors and sparkling glassware. That she managed to keep the house in such fine array, despite two ubiquitous grandsons and a husband, was the envy of some of the neighbourhood. One fine sunny morning one of the grandsons appeared on Christine's doorstep, a somewhat hesitant emissary. The message he had was that his grandmother thought that it must be one of their animals which at that moment crouched in their cupboard. Animal! What kind of animal? The first stirring of unease trickled through Christine's mind. The lad shrugged. A funny animal.

Short minutes later Christine entered the house. Surrounding a large built-in cupboard, the whole family glanced silently at her before returning their gaze up into the cupboard's depths. Even at this tense moment, as she hastened forward to see what animal exactly, what 'funny animal' was in the cupboard, she marvelled at the shine on the wood block floor. Then she reached the small cluster of people and peered up. And her heart sank. There, right at the back, surrounded by gleaming, sparkling Stewart Crystal glassware, was the genet. The new, wild, bad-tempered, unmanageable genet. There was a pregnant silence. Christine's mind reeled. She'd brought a pair of her son's falcon gloves with her on impulse. Silently someone presented her with a small stepladder. Combined stares alternated between her and the genet as she gingerly mounted the steps. Now the silence was broken by her most genet-soothing repertoire of noises. The crystal glasses shone brightly. As the gloved hand approached, a low, ominous growl hissed from deep in the genet's throat ...

To this day Christine cannot believe that none of the crystal was broken. She remembers the silence, even after she had secured the animal and removed it from the confines of the cupboard. Not a word was uttered, even as she ruefully retraced her steps through the semi-circle of people - back along the beautiful, polished floor of the corridor and out into the sunshine.

There were many other orphans of the wild, in the Fothergill household. Bush pigs, hawks, an aardwolf, the bateleur eagle with the bullet through its left wing, the new arrivals kept coming. Apart from the years of Operation Noah, the man-induced flood years, when the camps and bases of the rescue teams resembled a wildlife orphanage, the house in the quiet, secluded avenues came to be a haven for hosts of other wild creatures. Back on the ever-expanding waters of the new Lake Kariba, the rescue operations went on. Seldom chronicled now, after that first hysterical year, the men were still going out. Week after week, month after month, well into the fourth year of rescue. There were fewer new islands being created now. The main rise of the lake level had happened already. Nevertheless, the islands that were left, the larger tracts of isolated land, were still being slowly devoured. And the islands, because of their very size and the nature of the rugged, entangled Zambezi Valley hilltop bush, were that much harder to work. The new threat became ever more critical. Starvation. First the grasses, then the low shrubs, then the low browse on the trees, and then the leaves higher up, at the utmost neck-stretching level. And it became a new race against time.

CHAPTER 12

PORTRAIT OF AN ISLAND

Today, few of the tourists who visit the luxurious Bumi Hills Safari Lodge and gaze out over the vista of the many moods of the lake and nearby Starvation Island have any inkling as to the origin of that rather sombre name. Now the island is a misleadingly large tract of land that remains invitingly green all year round. One can hire a boat from the lodge and within half an hour be cruising around its serrated shoreline viewing hippos, crocodiles, elephants, waterbuck, kudu and impala - the latter antelope being rather in-bred descendants of the flood generation. Inland, away from the green, cropped shoreline, the bush is dense. The Department of National Parks and Wildlife Management used to use Starvation Island as a breeding and experimental station, isolated as it is from the mainland. Only elephants make a habit of traversing the stretch of water, the beasts steadfastly swimming across, tips of their trunks breaking the surface like so many periscopes.

It was not always the idyllic oasis of greenery that today catches the tourists' gaze over the sundowners in the bar area way up on the contours above the lake. In the summer months of 1962, those barren, dust-swirling months that precede the first rains, the island reeked of death. From the early days of planning and charting the anticipated islands which would form, with some eventually disappearing forever whilst others would become new mini ecosystems standing as monuments to the flood, it was anticipated that the many hills and high contours in the area of the Bumi River would, in time, present unique problems of their own. Most of the slowly-forming islands of the 'Bumi complex' were large and unworkable. Throughout the months and years there were continuing reconnaissance patrols amidst this maze of islands, and when some of the smaller islands were deemed manageable, they received the systematic attentions of the rescue teams. Their tasks were not made any easier by the constant movement of elephants and lions crossing from island to island, either seeking new succulent grazing or exploring the 'antelope larder' situation on new ground. As early as August 1960, the men were experiencing elephant problems on one of the islands of the Bumi complex. Then, a cow elephant with calf at heel persistently hampered the netting and general rescue operations and things reached the stage where the animal started following and actually stalking the team. With time for once on their side and the island not yet considered urgent, the men postponed any further rescue work until the recalcitrant mother and child had departed. In the not-too-distant future, Rupert and his team would be finding themselves reluctantly destroying certain elephants who disrupted rescue work. Time had caught up with them again and they were just not able to wait extra days for the elephants to move, having ignored all attempts to drive them off. Other animals were dying of starvation and something had to be done.

Sunset, with a boat heading back to its temporary base on a large island off the east bank of the Bumi River. In the deepening twilight the wake reflected a slow kaleidoscope of different colours, from bright scarlet through pink to deep rich mauve, the colours changing with the movement of the wash, undulating lazily away. The sun had gone now, a red orb slipping silently between two midnight blue hills. Across the sky wisps of tattered cloud glowed pink, a surrealistic stain over the haunting blue of the Matusadona mountains, captured and reflected in the water of the lake. As the sun had dropped below the hilly horizon it splashed the sky with a myriad shades of scarlet, which was mirrored in this new expanse of water below. To Rupert, by the engine in the stern, it was as if they were afloat in deep red wine. By the time the team reached camp, twilight had been devoured by tropical darkness, with the trees starkly etched against the rich red waters.

The island on which they were now based was one of the Bumi complex. For the last two days Rupert had been inspecting the tangle of islands, determining priorities. It was not an easy decision. Their own island base was packed with game. In two hours he had seen over 50 warthogs, at least 200 impala, 30 zebras, 10 kudu, several of the smaller species of antelope, and three rhinos. But as yet the island was too large to work. Watching the vague, pale blur of Tinkey Haslam's arm at the bow guiding him through the trees, Rupert went over the day's events. They had been on the move since before first light, clearing one small, thinly-populated island by midday. Altogether they had moved a small herd of impala, four bushbuck, two antbears and six warthogs. In the darkness Rupert grinned to himself. With the warthogs it had been a little hectic. One casualty incurred by the team was back in Kariba hospital. The African had been lucky to get away with bruises and a badly gashed hand. The man had been putting up a stretch of net when the six warthogs had charged into him out of nowhere. Rupert, being the closest, had waded in among the irate hogs, literally pulling off two or three of the animals and hurling them aside. The remainder, encumbered by the net but still pressing in to attack, he fended off with his two bare hands and one foot until more assistance arrived. Now, as he smiled ruefully, he reflected that his usual method of slapping aggressive wild pigs and warthogs with his old bush hat would not have deterred this group. By late afternoon the animals had been released on safe ground and the team commenced a slow, meandering patrol homewards. Well away from any islands, they came across two adult hyenas swimming amongst the maze of half-submerged trees. The animals veered away from the boat, snapping savagely at any outstretched hand. Rupert imperturbably manoeuvred the boat closer, his attention fixed on the hyenas. With jaws recognised as being the most powerful in the animal kingdom at a kill, taking on left-over bones which a lion cannot break, he did not want to make a mistake. Eventually he saw his chance and gripped the first one by the ears from behind and, amidst a flurry of spray and growls, managed to hold it hard against the hull. The second animal joined it minutes later, a captive alongside the boat. On the way to the mainland their ears were tagged. Once released they trotted off into the undergrowth, pausing once for a long appraisal of their rescuers. It was another 'first' for the rescue unit, the hyenas being the first two of the species to be physically rescued.

Prompted by an unhappy incident that had occurred earlier in the week, the conversation around the campfire that night dwelt on leopards. They had often been encountered during the rescue operations, with Lofty Stokes' incident being the closest to ending in tragedy. In May 1960 a leopard had been discovered in the topmost branches of one of the myriad of half-submerged trees which presented such an obstacle course around every island. The attempt to capture it had failed when a dart fired by Stuart Klaasen had missed its mark and the leopard had leaped into the water and disappeared among the jumble of foliage towards the mainland. Like lions, the solitary spotted cats would often remain on the newly-formed islands, using the stock of trapped antelope and warthogs as their pantry, voluntarily leaving an island and swimming considerable distances to another larder once their island had been depleted of game. The leopard they had most recently encountered had swum at least 800 yards, and they kept bumping into another specimen that moved from one island to another as the game was rescued from them.

A few days earlier a magnificent male leopard had been discovered, perched precariously among the branches of what had once been a tall *mopane.* Now most of it was under water. Graham Child, Tinkey Haslam and a clutch of others in two boats circled the lone tree and its occupant, loading the Cap Chur gun. First the boat edged in to 10 yards from the tree, and then in again to within eight yards, as Tinkey darted the leopard. The cat leaped into the water, a few feet from the boat. The people circled the animal warily, and it in turn glared balefully at the human intruders, ears flat back against the skull. After five minutes the leopard's swimming motions were slower and they could see that the drug was beginning to take effect. Graham Child sidled the boat in closer and someone tossed an empty jerrycan close by it for it to use as support. One unsheathed claw struck at the can and the animal attacked towards the boat, trying to bound through the water in its determination. Graham Child opened the throttle wide, swinging the boat away, avoiding the attack by seconds. With the boat out of reach the leopard turned its attention to the jerrycan, savaging the metal container and ripping at it with all four clawed feet. The exertions made the drug course even faster through the leopard's system and it began to weaken visibly. The team swung the boat back, anxious to get close and somehow get hold of the tiring animal. It still evaded and tried to attack, slow and sluggish now, labouring. And then, in seconds, it sank. The magnificent, rosetted bundle of fury disappeared slowly below the boat. Perhaps the rescue attempt was doomed from the start, when one stops to wonder exactly how a leopard, even when drugged, could have been manhandled into an open boat, transported to safe ground and released without some damage being done to somebody.

By 1962 the rescue teams were spending weeks away from the Kariba home base. Rescue operations were being mounted two-thirds of the way down the 200-mile long lake. By now the new lake was approaching its eventual coverage of 2 109 square miles. Past Bumi Island (later to be dubbed Starvation Island) through the shrinking Sibilobilo narrows, past the basin of the Sengwa River and even further. As far as Chete Island, close to where Greg Gregory was pioneering the Chizarira Game Reserve, with the civilisation of Binga at the western extremity of the lake a day's boat travel away. The distance presented a new set of logistical challenges. The boats were the rescue team's lifeline. If some mishap befell *The Ark* or *The Tuna*, then food, petrol, medical supplies, capture equipment and the countless other necessities would be lost until another arrangement was made. The skippers, a succession of them, Boyd Reese, Rex Bean, Peter Moore, and the men of the teams, came to know the lake better than any. Breakdowns in transport there were, frequently, resulting in some varied and bizarre adaptations being initiated. At this time of writing there are a couple of Noah stalwarts who never again want to see a tin of fig jam. Not after eating virtually nothing but that confection when the sugar supply had mysteriously vanished, two weeks from base!

It was early on in the days of Operation Noah that a term evolved which is still used today in the phraseology of this country's game men. "Sadza and point" was first introduced by Rupert, at a time when there was a critical lack of available food. Sadza, the staple diet of most rural Africans (a white gruel made from finely ground maize pips) was always on hand. Very often, however, the men found themselves without any form of accompanying relish to go with the thick, doughy substance. And so, on a particularly hectic day of rescue operations, when his companions were hungry and a little temperamental and they still had no relish for their sadza, Rupert advised that on that day they would have "point" to relieve the monotony of the stodgy maize on its own. Eyebrows were raised inquiringly at this new dish. Grinning, he pointed in the direction of Kariba and its trappings of civilisation and suggested that his companions use their imagination. If they really tried, he said, they could be eating anything they wanted with the sadza. And so "sadza and point" became synonymous with a lack of sufficient food supplies.

A succession of new arrivals still drifted into the lives of Rupert and the longer serving rescue members, leaving the Noah men occasionally richer for these chance encounters but, more often than not, a trifle bemused at the type of person who descended upon them in their solitary, wild, inundated wilderness. There was the platoon of the Second King's African Rifles under the control of a young lieutenant, loaned to Rupert by the Northern Rhodesian government. It was early July 1962, during one of the milder seasons of the valley. For a week the soldiers felt their way through the rescue operations and then unanimously called it a day. Unless they were paid danger allowances, came the stipulation, they were not prepared to continue with this foolhardy pastime. Then there was a Lady somebody who accompanied the Governor's party on one of their 'get away from it all' sojourns on the new lake. An elegant, attractive, rather pale lady, she was not in the habit of wearing a *brassière* under her flimsy bush shirt. In 1962, amongst a band of rugged bush-worn game men who had become unaccustomed to such obvious femininity, her presence was felt, endured, with mixed feelings. Campfire philosophy reached new heights on those evenings of her sojourn. Then, the lady schoolteacher from one of the small towns in the east of the country surely never realised just how many names she was called in muttered epithets by team members. She had come to see *Operation Noah.* To *see* it. And *photograph* it. And of course, meet the famous Mr Fothergill! Rupert never found out how she had obtained permission in Salisbury to join the team. How she leopard-crawled into their lives. That she was a charming lady there was no doubt. And she was pretty, too. But the camera sessions just became impossible. She was everywhere. It seemed to Rupert that scarcely ten minutes would pass and there she was again ... *Please, Mr Fothergill, just a quick shot of me helping to put up this net ... please, Mr Fothergill, just a quick shot of me holding the tortoise ...* It was never-ending. However, she was a guest. Rupert persevered. John Condy and the other team members studied Rupert for signs of stress. The final straw was not long in coming.

They had rigged up nets across an island. Rupert and the team of 'catchers' were concealing themselves near the barrier at one end of the island. The beaters were waiting for the signal at the other end. The schoolteacher was with the beaters, safely ensconced in a tree. Rupert found it strangely peaceful. Suddenly one of the beater contingent came loping through the bush. He halted before Rupert. The woman, he said, wanted to see the boss, further up the island. For a few seconds Rupert's normally iron-willed control slipped. Then he strode away through the bush. At the tree where his guest perched daintily, he peered up ... *please, Mr Fothergill, would you take a picture of me up this tree ...* Rupert took a deep breath and looked around for the camera. Forestalling his question, she dangled the camera smilingly at him when he looked back up ... *oh, Mr Fothergill, you'll have to climb up and get the camera first ...* The boat that took her back to Kariba the next morning left before sunrise.

The months of June and July were hectic. Slowly the manageable islands were being relieved of their prisoners. The netting operations continued without pause. There were different net traps for specific environments. The shape of an island, what species of other game shared the land with the impalas, the depth of water around it and the degree of vegetation encountered on an island - all determined whether the team would use a box trap or a zig zag trap or a corner trap ... or maybe today's task needed 'Junor's Special'. Lions were common, hunting the islands. On Monday 28 May one lioness of a pride of five was trapped in a rough pole type 'cage' designed by Rupert, using a live sheep as bait. Two weeks later a second lioness was caught. When Rupert and the team inspected their catch, the sheep and lamb enclosed in the protected part of the trap were quite unconcerned at the proximity of the big cat next door. The rest of the pride swam off the island.

The silhouette of Bumi Island loomed larger than ever on the horizon. Right at the beginning of the 1962 season it was obvious to everyone involved in Operation Noah that it was going to be the most difficult island yet tackled. Two principal factors pointed to this. The first was its size, nearly 5 000 acres. The other was the amount of dangerous game on the island. Reconnaissance patrols had established that over 200 buffalos, 11 rhinos, four elephants and 11 lions inhabited the area. Before the other smaller game could be rescued the big game would, somehow, have to be removed. Adjacent to Bumi Island was another fairly large island where the base of operations would be set up to handle Bumi. Even on this island there were five elephants and approximately 400 head of various antelope, and it would have to be cleared before Rupert concentrated on Bumi. In due course all the 'lesser' islands of the Bumi complex were cleared, including the new 'Camp' island. Here the elephants turned aggressive and repeatedly charged the men, knocking down painstakingly built paddocks and plucking out the observation poles. It was a nerve-racking business. Time and again the rangers would attempt to drive the elephants off the island. The mainland was visible a mile away. In their turn the elephants seemed determined to drive the human intruders away. In the meantime the vegetation dwindled daily. And they hadn't touched Bumi Island yet. The stalemate could not be allowed to continue. Reluctantly, on 9 July, the team shot two of the elephants, hoping the shock would drive the rest off. To no avail. The skirmishes between men and elephants continued unabated. One of the team barely escaped a trampling. Three days later a third animal was destroyed; with no results. Eventually, all five were shot.

John Condy recalls vividly the feeling of tenseness that was always present on that island, almost tangible in its intensity.

"Tension Island', we dubbed it. The bush was very thick and we'd hacked squares out of the undergrowth. Here we dug holes and put up long poles which enabled us to get a view of the area and ascertain where the elephant and other animals were. No sooner would we erect the poles, the elephant would come and pull them out."

Eventually this island was cleared. The final step before Bumi was tackled - a task that would last through until the end of Operation Noah - was a recce trip along the southern coastline from Kariba to Binga, checking for any islands needing urgent attention. A few were inspected and cleared of their inhabitants. Preparations for work on Bumi Island then started.

Rupert's list of a dozen task headings is a typical understatement.

(a)Establish a camp.
(b)Build pens.
(c)Drive elephants off.
(d)Drive lions off.
(e)Transport rhino crates ex Natal White Rhino Operation to this scene of operations.
(f)Remove 9 black rhinos in the interest of safety.
(g)Transport rhinos from pens to Kariba en route to Wankie National Park.
(h)Capture of buffalos - adults and calves.
(i)Capture of antelope - kudu, waterbuck, impala, warthogs, duiker etc.
(j)Transport of buffalos and antelope to Kariba pens for sale to farmers, zoos and parks.
(k)Loading of these animals onto trucks.
(l)Transport food for animals to island.

Paradoxically, in January of that year, Rupert received instructions to cut spending. The spectre of lack of funds seems to have been ever-present, in the context of wildlife conservation at least. Largely because of extra finance spent on the ever-ailing outboard motors, (this aspect probably more than any other affecting the rescue operations), the rescue leader was committed to the most financially difficult year of all. No more aerial surveys were to be carried out, and the budget for capture equipment, medical supplies, fuel and clothing, suffered cutbacks.

In the last week of July, as Rupert prepared himself for the work ahead on this most challenging of the operation's tasks, a new set of instructions was relayed to him. He was to link up with Ted Davison, the doyen of Wankie National Park, John Condy and John Hatton and, finally, to pick

"Then an elephant appeared out of the bush, already in full charge..." — Page 72

PHOTO: WILDLIFE EXPLORATIONS

LEFT: Rupert on the waters of the new lake, 1960: the hat already showing signs of wear.
PHOTO: E. REYNOLDS

RIGHT: Captured impala, waiting for the boats.
PHOTO: M VAN ROOYEN

"Peter's Point...a far cry from the motley collection of scrounged tents and Nissen huts that sweltered on the baking rocky ridge..."
— Page 104

PHOTOS: F. JUNOR

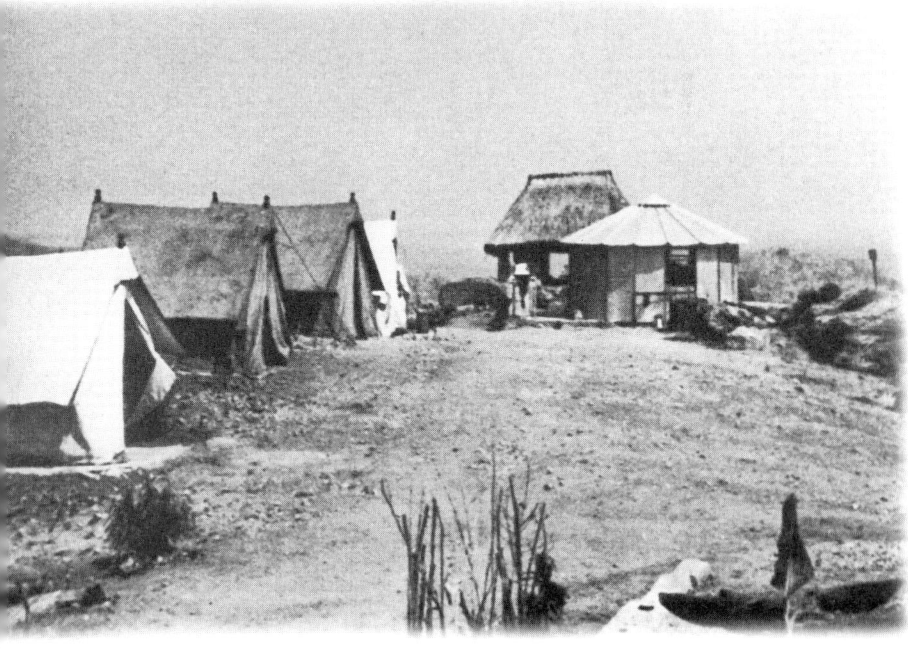

RIGHT: "Crackers, perched up on the bow… became a familiar figurehead." — Page 142

PHOTO: T. ORFORD

BELOW: "Antbear holes were Crackers' forte." — Page 142

PHOTO: J. CONDY

Catching a porcupine was only half the problem. Getting them out of the sack !ater, without having to cut the sack apart, was just as complicated.

PHOTO: MINISTRY OF INFORMATION

An antbear, thoroughly alarmed at the amount of activity at its burrow, bursts into daylight. Usually a net would be stretched over the entrance of the burrow.

PHOTO: MINISTRY OF INFORMATION

Rupert Fothergill, Kariba Lake, Southern Rhodesia, 1959, with young female bushbuck. One of the most widely used phtographs of him.

PHOTO: MINISTRY OF INFORMATION

Elephants on a drowning island. Note the spiderwebs in the trees, the spiders spinning their webs ever higher as the waters rose.

PHOTO: J. CONDY

A young bull is shepherded to safer haunts. Mike van Rooyen on the prow.

PHOTO: MINISTRY OF INFORMATION

A baboon's canines can rip a man open.
PHOTO: T. SPENCER

One of the 43 rescued rhino on its way to the mainland.

PHOTO: R. VAN HEERDEN

"On Friday 21 September 1962 the first ever adult buffalo was darted and transported to the mainland." — Page 164. John Condy and Rupert accompanied it.

PHOTO: R. VAN HEERDEN

RHINO DAYS: Time to leave…

PHOTO: MINISTRY OF INFORMATION

"...the cow rhino also attacked her boatlaod of rescuers..." — *Page 138*

PHOTO: MINISTRY OF INFORMATION

"Then she focused her anger on Rupert..." — Page 138

PHOTO: MINISTRY OF INFORMATION

The rescuers seldom had it all their own way.

PHOTO: J. CONDY

CHIEF OF THE DEFENCE STAFF

at Government House, Zomba.

10th October 1960

Dear Fothergill,

I am writing to thank you on behalf of my daughter, my staff and myself for having taken us out fishing on Lake Kariba and for showing us such very good sport in the short time available and in the heat of the day.

We were very lucky that Major Leng got those two fine tiger fish and the ten pounder put up a magnificent fight.

I was much interested by the description you gave us of removing the animals to safety, which of course all the world has heard about.

Please thank your assistant game wardens who came with the party too.

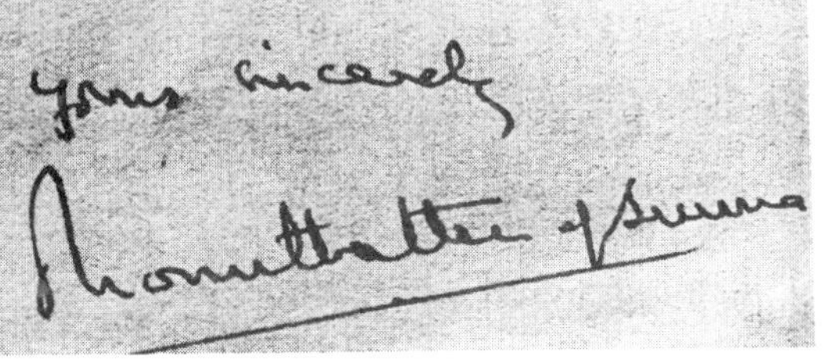

Yours sincerely

Mountbatten of Burma

Although the first hectic flood of visitors to Operation Noah had abated somewhat after the first frenetic year of 1959, Rupert and his team still hosted a variety of guests.

PHOTO COURTESY MRS C. FOTHERGILL

Rupert with white rhinos in Zululand, August 1962. Operation White Rhino saw the reintroduction of this animal to Rhodesia, crossing the border on 2 September 1962.

PHOTO: J. CONDY

up Tommy Orford from his post in charge of the new Kyle Game Reserve and travel south to the Natal province of South Africa. There they would liaise with the Natal Parks Board in the capture of eight white rhinos in the Umfolozi and Hluhluwe game reserves and transport them back to Southern Rhodesia.

The team was to end up spending several weeks away on Operation White Rhino. The first two weeks down in the coastal region of Natal were totally unproductive. The Natal wildlife men were unprepared for the capture exercise and used the initial period to show their guests around their wild areas. For Rupert it was a far cry from the spartan environment he was used to on the lake. The uniforms of the Southern Rhodesian game contingent were a little behind in sartorial elegance compared with the knife-edged creases of their hosts. Rupert's apparel in particular, after almost four years on the rescue operations, was a little worse for wear and his faithful battered bush hat caused a few raised eyebrows. There is a story, whose authentication the writer does not doubt, that when Ted Davison and Rupert first arrived at the headquarters in the Umfolozi Game Reserve, to meet their counterparts, they were kept waiting by the receptionist in the smart air-conditioned foyer. The vigil continued, the men fidgeted restlessly, and the secretary eyed them dubiously. To her the strangers were undoubtedly poachers. What was their business here? It took her a while before she nervously announced the rugged looking individuals, advance warning of the Southern Rhodesians' visit not having been passed on to her.

During August eight white rhinos were captured in the green-cloaked pastoral areas of remote Natal. Though normally placid creatures, considerably bigger than the other species of African rhinoceros that were being caught on the islands of Kariba, they tended to take longer to adjust to their capture. In due course the animals were crated and the convoy and its prehistoric cargo departed for home. On 2 September 1962 the convoy crossed Beit Bridge and for the first time in 50 years white rhinos were again residents of the colony. It is a sad fact that at the time of writing (mid 1995), the white rhino is extinct again in Hwange National Park. In a little over 30 years. And, outside privately-monitored conservancies and the four Intensive Protection Zones, the black rhino is sparsely represented. Kyle Game Reserve received four of the animals while four were transported westwards to the Matopos Game Reserve. For Rupert the six week busman's holiday was over and he returned to the lake in early September.

The rhino that had been nicknamed Hookhorn by the rangers wheeled in a flurry of dust under the baking October sky. It had reached the stage when, evil-tempered and unusually aggressive even by black rhino standards, it would charge the moment it was aware of the humans on the island. The men scattered, dashing helter-skelter for cover. It was difficult, as most of the cover had been eaten by the starving game and the trees on this part of the island made slender, fragile perches. Rupert had been stalking another rhino with the dart gun when Hookhorn exploded from nowhere. In his scrambling dash he glanced back. The rhino had veered away and was chasing one of the scouts. The man made for a tall, thin tree, only yards ahead of the strangely quirked tip of the horn which had earned the animal its name. Already up the tree were several beaters, the topmost man shinning higher as the man below edged upwards to give the approaching victim room to climb. He made it seconds ahead of the horn, adrenalin adding momentum to his efforts. Now the rhino snorted and swung away, searching for a new target.

It was imperceptible at first, the slow bending of the tree. Then with nine men hanging like paw paws to its branches, the top gained momentum and, in slow motion, unable to hold the weight of its refugees, it toppled slowly over. The movements of the panicking humans drew the rhino's attention back to the tree. It was a tableau that stayed forever in a visiting writer's mind. Tree slowly lowering its human fruit to the ground with the rhino trotting to meet them. There was pandemonium as they met and the swirl of dust that surged up, momentarily obscured the scene.

Miraculously no one was hurt. Bemused by the acceleration of nine yelling men all erupting away in different directions, seeking new sanctuary, the rhino failed to horn any of them.

Priority number one was the removal of the 11 rhinos. With them continually harassing the rescue operations, trapping the smaller game would be an impossible task . Rupert, facing this familiar adversary which appeared even more menacing after the docile white rhino capture, approached the task with his usual doggedness. The writing was on the wall. While, in that first week of September, the condition of the antelope and warthogs was good, it was only too clear that the rescue teams would have to move fast. The rains were a long way off and the food would plainly not last. Within three weeks seven of the rhinos had been captured, transported to the mainland, and released. Two more had died during the rescue. The remaining two, Hookhorn and another, would be captured only months later, as the operation finally, eventually, came to a halt. The lions and elephants were also harried and pursued until they vacated the island for quieter haunts. Which now left the two rhinos, over 200 buffalos and the many smaller animals. And October was with them again. Suicide month in the Zambezi Valley, on an island that was fast becoming a dustbowl; a death-trap, with too few helpers and no time left. For the first time during Noah, the teams had the use of a vehicle on an island. But one Land Rover was not going to help much.

It was gruelling work. The rescue teams never stopped. The men, all tough, fit individuals, honed down by the endless months of sweating the game off the never ending islands, lost more weight. Tempers became short and nerves strung dangerously taut. There were some new faces on the rescue operation now, names that would in the years ahead become synonymous with wildlife. But still they all lived on their nerves, and in each others' pockets, and watched with mounting frustration the plight of the animals on what was now called Starvation Island. As the leader, Rupert found he had more to contend with than the welfare of the game. When news from Salisbury filtered back on the grapevine that the wife of one of the team was dallying with a smooth-talking sewing machine salesman, he had his work cut out restraining the incensed husband. That the tough, irate young ranger did not invade Salisbury with his favourite rifle was due only to Rupert's perseverance in making sure that the man was kept away from any of the boats; until his temper had dropped below boiling point.

While the rescue team battled against the odds on Starvation Island, the world continued to turn. High above them John Glenn had become the first American to orbit the earth. Marilyn Monroe had died, and Tom Cruise was born. Amnesty International came into being. People in the big cities lined up to see the new film blockbuster, 'Lawrence of Arabia'. And, as the Cuban missile crisis put the world on the edge of nuclear war, the world population topped the three billion mark.

On Friday 21 September the first ever adult buffalo bull was darted and transported to the mainland. At first it was Rupert's plan to dart the adult animals and take them across on the faster, smaller boats, saving a lot of the time taken up by the raft-towing larger boats. After a couple of such trips, however, he decided against the method. A fully-grown buffalo and two men aboard the *Buffalo* or the *Christine* gave but a few inches of freeboard. A slight breeze ruffling the water, or a sudden, violent struggle by the doped, trussed animal would result in disaster. It was a tragic fact of life that had this transportation method been feasible, it would not have been necessary to destroy so many buffalos in the later stages of rescue.

Warthogs were the first species of wildlife to show signs of stress. They could not compete with buffalos and impala for the fast disappearing graze, and their plight was increased by the buffalo-created erosion, caused by the ceaseless patrolling of the big beasts, and so depriving the warthog of its main source of nourishment, the roots and tubers of grasses and shrubs. By mid-October the game rangers were encountering the first warthog corpses. Many others were not found as the weakened, emaciated animals made their final retreat into antbear burrows and died there. The smell of putrefaction wafted over the island. In late October a lone sable bull died of starvation and this was followed by casualties amongst the impala rams, weakened by an abnormal rutting season. Impala ewes started dying in early November and now the game was getting so weak that normal capture methods were impossible. They just would not be able to withstand the rigours of the chase. By mid-November the adult buffalos were dying, six carcasses being discovered. An inspection of the island, along the previously hacked-out bush tracks for the Land Rover, revealed 30 dead animals. It was Rupert's guess that a closer study of the dense dry bush would produce scores more. A final estimate of 200 deaths due to starvation was entered into the Game Department's report.

The nucleus of Rupert's team was Tinkey Haslam, Ron Van Heerden and the Coetsee brothers, supported by 50 African assistants. It wasn't enough. All budgets had been cut. Back in the shady tree-lined avenues of Salisbury, where the decisions were made about expenditure and policy, government civil servants evaporated from their offices at 4.00pm. On Starvation Island Rupert went to the manager of the tree-clearing operation based at Bumi and tried to bolster his meagre team. The man lent him 60 of his employees for a few days, for a game drive of the larger antelope. Rupert's team of 50, less hospital cases, those on camp duties or boat duties and penned animal attendants, was whittled down to 30. With the weakened condition of the animals precluding any further capture on a large scale, the next objective was to provide food. The buffalos were failing rapidly now. Consignments of lucerne were scattered in heaps over the island, being brought up lake by boat, purchased or donated by private sources. A pall of dust hung permanently over the island, kicked up by the hooves of the shuffling, ever-searching buffalos. White patches of mange flecked their loose, grey hides. Most of the warthogs were dead now. Drifting high up in a white-blue sky that was mockingly devoid of any cloud, vultures spiralled down from the heat thermals, to squabble noisily over the booty.

The bigger antelope, like kudu, fared better than the smaller game. There were fewer of them, and competition for the higher browse was less.

Waterbuck too seemed to be coping. A few buffalos had been removed before the starvation crisis reached its peak. Rupert's team, with the assistance of the ever helpful John Condy, removed five adults. Then they ran out of drugs for the darting equipment and there was no response from Salisbury as to when new supplies would be arriving. So Rupert went after the buffalos with the Land Rover. In the gloom of the dust pall, amidst the snorting, lumbering, desperate animals, they looked for targets. As the younger animals slowed and dropped behind, the men would race from the vehicle and, bare handed, through force of numbers and in desperation at the plight of the game, wrestle the buffalo to the ground. Then the creature would be trussed up and carried to the raft. More often than not the bellows of the calves would bring angry mothers charging back and a free-for-all would ensue. Again Rupert got more cracked ribs, in this running down of calves, there under the high, bright sun of October, amidst the dust and the starving game, with the menace of Hookhorn ever present.

He had recently turned 50, the event celebrated by warm Cokes from Bumi. Only very occasionally using a therapeutic drop of liquor, he didn't miss the raising of a glass at his fiftieth. Now and again he did crave ice-cream though, down here in the valley heat. He had heard there were all sorts of new flavours out, back in civilisation. And he loved ice cream. It was one of the plus factors of town life ...

By the end of November the first smudge of rain clouds had drifted reluctantly over the lake. The heat became more oppressive than ever. The carcasses increased, despite the lucerne. If there were to be any survivors, the rain had to fall soon to regenerate the browse and the grasses. It came one night, the first rain of the season. The heavens opened amidst barrages of thunder and white, jagged lightning. It poured on wild animals and on the men in their makeshift bush camp. Four inches in one night!

Eventually, nearly 200 animals were rescued off Starvation Island, apart from the elephants and lion that were chased off by the team when they first started operations there. Sixty four buffalos were either physically removed or driven off and shepherded to the mainland. In the final months of Operation Noah many buffalos had to be shot on the few remaining large islands when all efforts to move them off failed. The rhino Hookhorn and the other remaining rhino, a female, continued to thwart all attempts at capture. It was as though fate was against the game rangers. They took more and more chances. The equipment would fail at a critical point of the proceedings. On three separate occasions the dart fired at Hookhorn pierced his tail, close to its junction with the body, with the needle appearing through the other side, uselessly squirting the drug into thin air. A marksman on his best day would find it impossible to hit that part of the animal intentionally, three times in a row! The more attention focused on Hookhorn the more vindictive he became. Rupert began to wonder if the animal was jinxed. If perhaps he himself was jinxed.

The saga ended during June 1963, the last month of Operation Noah. On the third day of that month, at twenty minutes past one in the heat of midday, Rupert darted the rhino in his front left shoulder. In character, right to the end, Hookhorn created complications. He took to the water and, with the drug pulsating through his system, had to be roped to the side of the boat, the men struggling to keep his head above water. Then they towed him back to shore and loaded the subdued giant on to the raft. The last part of the task was to tow the rhino across to the Matusadona Game Reserve and release him. The diary entry was typically brief.

Monday 3/6/1963
Rhino Male Adult (Hookhorn) rescued today.
Tag Numbers L. Ear 3691
R. Ear 3692 (Yellow Plastic Tags)

The next day the female rhino was rescued. Like Hookhorn, she too plunged into the lake after the dart containing 1cc hyoscine, 10cc's largactil and 1gm of morphine entered her left shoulder. Once again the men retrieved the animal and brought it back to the island, from where it would join the irascible rhino with the strangely quirked horn tip, on safe ground.

On 30 June 1963 Operation Noah stopped. It was judged that the final level of the lake's rising waters had been reached. New islands were unlikely to be created and the existing islands were unlikely to become smaller. In the last six months 761 animals were rescued: 42 either had to be destroyed or died during capture. This figure excludes 94 buffalos that had to be destroyed on the 'Bumi complex' and Sengwa Island. Nearly five years had passed since Rupert had witnessed the first effects of the strangled river flowing back against itself and overflowing its banks. And a task that many had said was impossible, and which some called a waste of time, was now completed. It was a task without precedent in the problems it posed for the senior game ranger, and his succession of helpers. With his return to Salisbury imminent, his children now five years older and his wife adapting in advance to having a husband at home permanently, a chore almost as daunting as the rescue operation would have to be tackled. This would be the correlation and compilation of five years of diaries, technical data and other paperwork.

The confrontations with Hookhorn, Rupert reflected, were a far pleasanter proposition than the mountain of paperwork that awaited him.

November 1963 was to bring another milestone in the history of the Game Department. After existing for more than a decade as separate government bodies, the Federal Department of National Parks and the Southern Rhodesian Department of Wildlife Conservation were merged, the move coming about by the impending dissolution of the Federation of Rhodesia and Nyasaland on 31 December 1963. It is difficult to deny that the years of Operation Noah, so recently completed, helped to lay the most enduring cornerstone for the country's new Department of National Parks and Wildlife Management. Sadly, today, there are generations in the country now called Zimbabwe who, despite inheriting a wildlife heritage that is second to none in Africa, have never heard of Operation Noah.

PART THREE

NEW DIMENSIONS

CHAPTER 13

HYENAS ... AND OTHER 'VERMIN'

Under a full moon three hyenas detached themselves from the shadows of the trees surrounding the cattle paddock. They paused at the barbed wire fence, heads lifted as they scented the air. In the moon-silvered darkness they seemed larger, these big, blotched, hunch-shouldered dog predators. They shuffled forward, into the grazed greenery of the paddock, and their body language showed they were ready to start. A hundred yards away, the group of cows, a nursery herd, all with calves at foot, and still feeding their young from low hanging, full udders, milled nervously as they watched the shadowy intruders.

The hyenas broke into a deceptively fast, loose-gaited trot, tails high, and then into full speed. And then they were among the cattle. The big female hyena ran easily alongside a terrified cow and with one lunging snap ripped its udder off. Crimson gushed black over the grass and the hyena's muzzle, and she snapped again, opening a jagged wound in the guts. The cow bellowed in agony, slowing and standing splay legged, its calf on the far side, away from their attacker. Though mortally hurt, the mother bobbed and jabbed her horns at the hyena. The animal circled, dodging the horns with ease, and then darted in again, huge-jawed, savaging the gaping wound a third time. The cow tottered, screaming. In another part of the paddock the other hyenas were exacting a similar toll. Two calves were dead, ripped apart, whilst another cow, lurching from wounds, bleeding badly, tried vainly to hold off the snapping, relentless killers. The blood on the grass shone silver in the moonlight.

There are those who consider the hyena cowardly and stupid. The reject of the animal kingdom that lives on other animals' leftovers, or the killer of defenceless, newborn calves. The spotted hyena (*Crocuta crocuta*) does both, but he is not a coward, and neither is he stupid. Cunning, yes. Survival-conscious, yes. Today it is well chronicled that these animals, in various parts of Africa, are very capable of attacking and killing of their own accord such worthy adversaries as sable antelope and buffalo. It is no great feat for them to drive lions from a kill.

At first glance, usually a glimpse at night or during the first early hours of daylight, it is not an impressive animal. The rounded bears' ears and dull, yellowish coat patched with dark irregular spots register on one's senses only after one notes the shuffling, almost sheepish, slope-shouldered gait. Yet this creature, with its massive shoulders sloping down to what looks like a crippled rear, can manage an easy thirty miles an hour and can carry a goat slung across his back, leaving no sign of its burden on the ground, for two miles. And the jaws of this scruffy-looking, shuffling, unimpressive bush opportunist are recognized as being the most powerful in the animal kingdom. It will crack the biggest of bones, left unmarked by lion, with ease. Indeed, its white dung is proof of its ability to crush and devour the strongest bones. And, like the lion and the vulture and the ant, the hyena has a part to play in nature.

In African superstition and folklore the hyena is a leading character, albeit not a popular one. In wild, unfettered Africa too many of the old and infirm have been a part of the hyena's diet. And, even today, amidst progress and civilisation, on more than one occasion an African is to be seen with part of his face missing, or a foot, or a part of his nether regions. In the wilder areas, sleeping in the open beside a campfire, lions or leopards are not necessarily the main hazards. The hyena, or *bere*, as he is known in the main language of Zimbabwe, is not fussy about what he eats. Many are the bush camps that have been the target of the hyena's wide-ranging eating habits. Nothing is safe. Whether it be drying meat, safari trophies, camp chairs, cooking pots, shoes, your favourite bush knife, the well-loved, much used binoculars ... it is all food. Nor are you, gently snoring behind your mosquito net, immune from the hyena's attentions. Rupert, who would become involved in many hyena control tasks, never ceased to wonder at their powers of digestion. In the stomach of one male hyena he discovered two pieces of half-inch rope, one handle of a plastic bucket, a lizard skin, feet and hair of a rock hyrax, tree bark, cattle droppings, two pieces of red cloth and a baby bushpig. And to add to this already dubious reputation is a rumour which some people still believe: that the hyena is a hermaphrodite. This is not, however, the case. This unfounded belief has come about because the female clitoris is unusually developed, resembling the penis of the male. Coupled with this anatomical curiosity, a pair of swellings of fibrous tissue resembling a scrotum have helped spread the fallacy.

And so, together with his appearance, his reputation, the fables, and man's readiness to label anything that is not easily understood, we have the hyena. Cowardly, brave, cunning, scared, stealthy, he is all of these. He is also the characteristic sound of Africa, sadly, now not heard as often as it was only a few years ago. To the uninitiated, the hyena's symphony is chilling, but there are few bush camp habitués who dislike his voice. The term 'maniacal laughter' has often been used to describe his voice, and certainly the wildly insane chorus of screams, shrieks, giggles, whoops, howls and sniggering chuckles that can be heard at a successful kill, or during mating, or during their eternal warfare with lions, could come from the witches' scene in Macbeth. But his most often-heard call, his roving, questing night call, has a haunting eerie beauty. And a campfire that does not have that long drawn-out 'wooooOO-UPPP' floating on the night air, making its distance almost impossible to gauge, lacks some of the magic.

Today, in Zimbabwe, it is unlikely that a person will hear a hyena outside a national park. With progress and civilisation evolving at its roller coaster rate, hyenas outside protected areas are labelled as vermin. And, along with baboons, jackals, and the lion or leopard that takes a liking to domestic stock, they have been destroyed relentlessly. Where game became scarce and stock plentiful, hyenas became a menace to livestock, and because of their cunning and rapid appreciation of man's normal hunting methods, poisoning became the most effective control measure.

In the months after the end of Operation Noah Rupert returned to normal duties. The situation now was considerably different. With the amalgamation of the two game bodies into the Department of National Parks and Wildlife Management and the new dimensions which this event heralded, the way of life, as Rupert knew it, began to steadily change. He was now a warden and in his fifties and in the 'new order' were many younger men, some with degrees, to take on the field work. In some circles he was considered an anachronism, a dinosaur - like the rhino, a relic of a bygone age. As is common with amalgamations in most spheres of business, and certainly no less so in the civil service, there was the predictable jostling for positions in this new government department. Rupert, by virtue of his management of the long rescue operation and the accompanying experience, and his age, was a candidate for a less rigorous life and promotion. To him promotion was synonymous with never-ending desk work and office politics, and it was slow death. And consequently, in this new dramatic turn of events, he anxiously sweated out reshuffles and transfers, and threw in an occasional idea of his own. His new title of Roving Warden was the result, and he was not unhappy.

To a large degree it meant a return to the duties he carried out before Lake Kariba formed, only now there were more declared game sanctuaries, more men in the field, and not quite as much control work. Things were changing rapidly since the time when he was one of only two game rangers in the Game Section. On his visits to head office in the shady backwaters of the capital there were always new faces. He made his visits as brief as possible. After five years on Kariba, there was a certain mundane air to some of the work he now had to do. He had long since had his fill of killing, and the rescue operation had cemented that feeling. But it was a part of the job, this control work, and unavoidable in the face of development. The crop-raiding elephants were still a fact of life, as were the lions and leopards killing the stock, but more and more time was being devoted to the eradication of smaller vermin. The hyenas that were reported to be scavenging around settlements, eating anything from old skins to rotting maize husks, became a continual problem. The jackals, allegedly the main carriers of rabies, and certainly being encountered more frequently now suffering from this disease, developed into a similarly never-ending problem. There were also the depredations of the baboons on the ever-expanding maize lands. At least, reflected Rupert on occasion, they let me carry out the control work like I did in the early days. Just me and the trackers and off we go; elephants, lions or hyenas. He was never to become involved in the new elephant culling system which evolved in the Wankie Game Reserve in 1966. When the restricted compressed herds of elephants, breeding at their normal rate and increasing their numbers within the small sanctuaries, trapped pockets of nature in the mass of progress, became too many for the land to feed. Destroying their own habitat, and that of their fellow creatures, so that, in the end, the Game Department people had to do *something*. And the strategy evolved into the systematic culling of entire family units. In minutes, spotter planes and automatic weapons reduced a herd of two dozen animals to motionless grey hulks on the veld. And it *had* to be done. Quick, merciful death from an efficient marksman now meant no slow, lingering, starving death later. *It was progress!*

Rupert was back on the road. Darwin, Zhombe, Melsetter, Tjolotjo and everywhere in between. He covered the four points of the compass in his tasks across the country. In the northern Mangula area, lions were making cattle-killing a habit. An art form, almost. The local farmers tried everything; poison, tracking, tree platforms and night lamps. The lions became very educated, and no less bold. The summer nights of late September 1965 saw Rupert and his trackers, Langton and Kosiah, sleeping amongst the cattle, waiting patiently. In the early months of 1964 several areas experienced problems with elephants raiding gardens, breaking fences, and generally 'bucking the system'. Rupert was tasked with hunting them. One here, two there, three up in the north-east border area. On the Mazoe River in the Pfungwe Tribal Trust Land close to the border with Mozambique, in a late evening in April 1964, he finally caught up with a herd which had been destroying Africans' maize lands. Carefully, methodically stalking the herd, he selected a target, a tuskless adult cow. With her gone, he hoped, the herd would get clear of the district. At the sound of the shot, as the elephant dropped, the rest of the herd attacked. In the fading twilight Rupert wheeled, facing charge after charge. At the end of it, nine elephants lay dead. There was then a four-hour hike through the dark back to camp. Crossing the Mazoe, one of the tribesfolk, acting as guide, was taken by a crocodile. In midstream, amidst the panic of the rest of the team, Rupert fired through the darkness into the water, hoping to scare the big reptile into releasing its victim. But it was in vain. The man was never seen again.

Further north, weeks later. On the Hunyani River, not many miles from where it enters Mozambique on its way to joining the wide, reedy expanses of the Zambezi. The bush was still green and thick from the rains, but the season was almost over now, sliding into a short autumn and then the dry, parched days and cold, clear nights of winter. Elephants, again, were the cause of Rupert's visit to this part of the Zambezi Valley. A different valley, this, to the wild areas almost untouched by man, two hundred miles to the west. This was Tribal Trust Land and its accompanying scars. Villages, of mud and thatch, scattered amongst the harsh Zambezi Valley bush, for miles and miles. A rare mission station, whitewashed walls gleaming bright, incongruous in the maze of horizon-to-horizon bush. A German-run mission, this one here on the Hunyani, at a place called Chitsungu, where Rupert stopped briefly on his journey north. A small oasis of tended lawns and gardens. A cross. Civilisation. And then bush again, and the patches of maize, more frequently planted now. The trouble spot. Elephants, ripe green maize plants, and people struggling to exist. Irreconcilable. And something had to give.

The journey had already provided a surprise. Rupert had come across a party of four schoolboys camped on the upper Hunyani. The oldest lad was 18. They were, they informed the Roving Warden, hunting buffalos. Rupert surveyed their campsite dubiously and then inspected the boys again. How many have you shot so far? A shuffling of feet. None. Have you hunted them before? A long pause as each one waited for the other to answer. Finally, no. Rupert grimaced and asked what weapons they were using. Weapon. One rifle ... an old 9mm Mauser. Rupert shook his head and called their guide across. He was not, he ordered, to take the youngsters into any thick bush. Not at all. And, he hoped the guide was not allowing the boys to swim in the large pools. Not with the crocodile population as healthy as it was in this river.

Rupert hunted along the Hunyani for four days without finding fresh sign of elephants. He moved camp to the smaller Mururudzi River and hunted downstream to the meandering, swift-flowing Angwa. After two days he found fresh spoor in the sand of the river bed. He and the trackers followed it into the green maze of *jesse* bush. When they eventually found the herd, the *jesse* was so thick that an elephant five paces away was invisible. The wind changed. The herd broke and ran, smashing its way through the scrub. Rupert followed. Two hours later at noon he found them again. He worked his way in on them under a hard, bright sun and managed a quick, fatal shot at one animal that was lagging. When he inspected it he found a big, festering wound high up on its left back leg. A bullet wound. He traced the bullet, from its entry point to where it had lodged in the spine. The elephant's right tusk was cracked and the nerve badly decayed. He left his trackers to supervise the removal of the ivory and to inform the local people of the fresh meat booty. He'd done his work, another elephant was dead. Another problem was solved. There was more meat for the humans to feed off.

Rupert came out of a light, rejuvenating sleep. He lay still on his camp bed, wondering what had disturbed him. What alien sound had penetrated through the usual night noises to bring him awake. Tree frogs, crickets, in the distance a nightjar. Then the sound came again. Something at the foot of his bed, sniffing. He could hear the soft whufflings clearly now. A local dog, he surmised. Perhaps from that last village they passed. He lifted his head slightly and shouted softly at the animal. He could do without their scavenging around camp. Minutes slipped by and he drifted back into bush sleep. A log in the fire on the far side of camp collapsed lower into the embers, sending up a small shower of sparks into the darkness. Close by, a Scops owl chirruped. Close also was the same sound again, some scuffling. Rupert sat up, as his tracker switched on a torch. In its beam, frozen by the sudden light, a full grown male leopard looked at them. The intruder was no more than five paces away. He was busy trying to get at a line of elephant meat that had been hung up to dry. Soundlessly, he melted into the night.

Rupert lay back and looked up at the stars. A mosquito whined past his ear. From far off he caught the sound of drums, a repetitive tremor in the night. A village party, he mused. Then, more soft noise. Within their ranks again. The metallic scream of the ratchet, from the reel on his light rod, startled him. He scrambled upright, fumbling. His rod was propped next to his bed. The line continued to scream off into the night. As he grabbed the rod, Langton switched on the torch. Gasped aloud. On the far edge of camp the leopard tugged at the meat on the line, bait from fishing Rupert had done the previous evening. That moment in time stayed with Rupert forever. He'd caught a leopard. It was a bizarre tableau. The leopard, eyes reflecting in the torchlight, and the game warden hauling on the fishing rod, the two joined by a thin, taut line of nylon. Then the line snapped and the cat was gone.

They scattered a bundle of dry maize stalks beneath the ribbon of hanging meat strips, as a different warning system. The leopard would have to make some noise if it returned in its determined bid to get at the meat. The men went back to bed. As the minutes became an hour, the breathing of the trackers and game warden lapsed into a slow, steady rhythm. Then, noise. Different this time. The lapping of water. This time Rupert had the torch. He flicked it on. In the morning he measured the distance exactly. It was less than nine feet. Three paces away from his bed, the leopard was crouched on its belly drinking from a dish of soapy water in which the plates had been washed that evening. For long seconds man and leopard stared into each others' eyes. Then, silently, the leopard stood, higher than the human now, large and menacing in the thin wash of light, and walked away. Twice again the leopard returned. Finally, exasperated, Rupert cursed and threw a shoe at it. A low growl was their last evidence of it. And the mosaic of pugmarks in their camp when daylight filtered over the bush.

There are two types of jackal in this country, the side-striped jackal and the black, or saddle-backed jackal. Both of these small predators are fairly ubiquitous although the side-striped jackal is more secretive and nocturnal in its habits. Both types eat rats, mice, birds, insects, wild fruits and carrion and the more striking looking black-backed jackal is prone to raiding poultry and small livestock in populated areas. Because of these habits, which also serve to bring it into contact with domestic animals, the jackal is a much persecuted animal. Coupled with this situation is the fact that today, erroneously or not, the name jackal is often synonymous with rabies. Thus, outside the game sanctuaries, it is often harried and destroyed.

In the years following Operation Noah, in between the control duties and translocation work of the larger game species, Rupert found that more and more time was being spent tracking down these small, alert predator/scavengers. The frequently-occurring rabies outbreaks made their survival more precarious than ever, as from all corners of the country reports told of staggering, foam-mouthed jackals attacking people, animals, and even cars. Today it is a fact of life that the large majority of reported rabies cases stem from the unchecked masses of scrawny mongrel dogs in ruralareas. However, during the middle and late 60s it fell to Rupert to sort out the problems of jackals/rabies, and at times there were as many as four vermin control units out on call. On one jackal foray, close to the home base of Salisbury, Rupert encountered jackals running in packs, in some cases the packs constituting as many as seventeen animals. Because jackals have close knit family relationships, with well defined and defended territories, these roving packs were something out of the ordinary. What made Rupert wonder even more was that these biggest of conglomerations were hanging around the city's crematorium.

The animal which exacted the greatest toll of domestic livestock was the hyena, and the local subsistence farmer fared worst of all. One example was a lone hyena in the Mtoko region which, in the months of September and October 1964, killed 22 head of cattle. That was quite apart from many other cows mutilated. Ironically, many was the occasion in a 'hyena problem' zone that the local people showed no interest in offering any kind of help to the roving warden when he appeared on the scene to sort things out. Faces went blank, doors closed, headmen were away. *Hapana*. Not today, thank you. When the shutters went down, that was it. Rupert was on his own. Sometimes he wondered if there was some dimension that he just was not seeing. Fear, maybe. Witchcraft? But it didn't really play out like that, he judged. It was just plain and simple recalcitrance. And it frustrated him.

Baiting was the most successful method of dealing with hyenas, and even this was not foolproof. The first step was to procure a goat or a donkey as bait. Constant refusals thrown in his face would tempt Rupert to call it a day, leave them to it. Let them sort out their own problems, catch their own hyenas. The tribal areas of Msana, Masembura and Chikwakwa, in the Bindura district, were the worst hit by hyenas. And, paradoxically, it was the tribespeople of these areas who were the most unhelpful. However, one way or another, Rupert would finally acquire some form of bait. An important criterion was the type of bait. Small pieces of meat, or birds, could be eaten by other animals, and a hyena would wander miles away before the poison capsules hidden in the meat would dissolve. A goat or donkey, well secured to a tree, was the ideal bait. Then several capsules could be secreted in the meat and the area around the dead animal could be scattered with concealed gin traps. Over the years Rupert achieved a considerable degree of success in the control of hyenas but, nevertheless, there were times when they stayed a step ahead of the crowd, and proved more than a match for their would-be destroyer.

November. The first month of the rains. Scattered, noisy, cloudbursts at first interspersed with hot, oppressive, leaden days. Operating from his base on the Nyagui River, Rupert had located several hyenas' lairs and established their nightly patrol pattern. On a previous visit to the area he had destroyed six hyenas. More had invaded the area and had so far killed a dozen goats, seven donkeys and mauled a young boy. Despite this predation, and the subsequent cry for help from the tribesfolk, he still experienced difficulty in obtaining bait. Finally a sacrificial donkey was reluctantly offered. He had baited for three nights now. Two hyenas had taken the poison on the first night. One had been found 50 paces away from the carcass. The other's spoor had been followed for three miles before it had succumbed to the poison capsules. The carcasses were buried deep and stones placed over the area to stop their fellow clan members digging them up. The last two nights had been fruitless and it was clear that the remaining hyenas were not stupid.

The donkey carcass, treated with over 40 strychnine capsules, was surrounded by gin traps. The ground around this trap area was swept to make the reading of spoor easier. In addition a nearby shallow stretch of river where the hyenas were in the habit of crossing was 'treated' with another two steel-toothed gin traps, underwater, imbedded in the sand. Rupert inspected the area on the second morning. Three of the gin traps had been painstakingly and deliberately exposed, the soil over them scraped delicately away. Clearly evidenced by the tracks was the attempt two hyenas had made to drag the donkey carcass out of the danger area. Only the thick wire around the donkey's neck, attached to a tree, had prevented them doing so. Rupert raised an eyebrow and shook his head. During that night a hyena laughed continuously from the direction of the river crossing. Rupert lay awake, listening to the array of vocal sounds, amazed as ever at the repertoire. At first light he checked the river. A mongoose had been caught in one of the underwater traps. Along the river bank was heavy hyena spoor and places where one hyena had sat and studied the plight of the unfortunate mongoose. More surprises were to come. The body of the hyena buried near the donkey bait had been dug up and carried away. There was no sign of a drag mark for over a mile. Rupert scratched his jaw thoughtfully. A different plan of action certainly looked essential.

It took a month to account for seven hyenas - six males and a female. A cub which was heard deep in a small cave was caught and brought back to camp where Rupert washed it, treated the sores on its hide and patiently persuaded it to eat. Although weak, it was still savage and would not hesitate to bite and it was a while before Rupert gentled it and tamed the creature. Christened 'Buster', the young hyena has already been mentioned in an earlier chapter.

From the high, green slopes of the Chimanimani mountains where the wind keened through the acres of pine trees, and the mantle of bracken conjured up visions of other distant lands, Rupert was recalled to Salisbury. He had been investigating the reasons for the decrease in the eland population in that part of the Eastern Highlands. In a little over a year the resident population of these largest of all African antelope had been reduced from 250 to about 60 animals. With the meat of eland often considered the tastiest of the wild grass-eaters and the weight of a bull reaching 2 000 lbs, these docile, good-natured creatures are prime targets for poachers. Rupert discovered that this was in fact the reason for the alarming decrease in numbers in the remote highlands of the eastern border. Back in Salisbury, similar news awaited him, and the vermin control was not restricted to animals.

Isolated, fragmented reports had been reaching the Game Department headquarters of poaching in the north-east of Rhodesia. The tribal areas of Chesa and Pfungwe straddle the Mazoe river on its journey eastward to the mighty Zambezi, and wedged between these areas of rural African civilisation, bordered by the Mazoe and Gwatera rivers, is the Umfurudzi wilderness area. Stories of African poaching parties, armed with Second World War issue 0,303s, stolen 0,22s, shotguns issued by the district commissioners for crop protection, and packs of dogs, had been causing alarm amongst the Game Department staff for some time. However, despite their increasing personnel, it was still difficult to monitor the whole country, and priorities had to be established. Reports of increased poaching throughout the territory were on the increase and the killing was being done by both white man and black man. Now, in these tribal areas on the Mazoe, stories of a white man shooting crocodiles and rhinos, elephants and hippos were becoming more frequent.

And so Rupert transferred his attentions from the cool, green, high country on the eastern border northwards to the wild, jumbled terrain of the low-lying northern frontier area. His love of prospecting gave him the perfect cover he needed, and so it was that the local people of the area met him, a newcomer in ragged clothes who searched for the different coloured metals of the earth. In the timeless African bushveld, where living and staying alive are as fundamental as sunset and sunrise, any slight deviation from normal day-to-day events causes a ripple; a slight disturbance in the pond of the people who exist in this simple, uncluttered part of the fast developing country, with the ripples eventually reaching even the furthest of the inhabitants. It took very little time for Rupert to hear of the other white man who had been visiting the area, not to find the things of the soil as he was doing, but to hunt the many different kinds of meat that lived there. The tribespeople called this man *Motomoto* (Fire, fire - because his guns became hot from much shooting) and within days the game warden found the carcasses of two rhinos, three elephants, a kudu, and six hippos. Together with those discoveries he learned that this *Motomoto* supplied the tribesmen with ammunition for their weapons in exchange for their help skinning crocodiles; had shot another 16 hippos for use as crocodile bait; used a Land Rover with false number plates; had a false bottom in a 44-gallon petrol drum where he hid skins; and that he had maps of the entire country showing tsetse fly rangers' camps, rangers' camps in all the non-hunting reserves, police stations and all known pools and rivers containing crocodiles. It did not take Rupert much longer to establish the man's proper name, plus those of his companions, which were forwarded to headquarters. The name was well-known to the Game Department. He had already been in court for crocodile poaching and was known to have shot 35 leopards, doing his own tanning so that no records were found in the books of reputable tanning companies. Rupert hunted the area harder now. Stories and hearsay were not good enough for court. Nor were the bleached bones and tuskless, rotting carcasses. The man had to be caught red-handed, gun smoking and animal still newly dead. The game spoor was plentiful. Eland, zebra, waterbuck, kudu, lion and, most exciting of all, black rhino. He found more carcasses. Another rhino and, further north on the Ruya River, many crocodile skeletons. He and Langton and Kosiah crossgrained, walking against the natural contours of the rugged terrain, and found extensive meat racks where animals had been cut up and their meat salted and sundried.

Gradually Rupert built up a dossier. He knew the man now. By sight and by reputation. He had seen the rotting carcasses. He had spoken to the bush Africans who had accompanied the man on his hunts, who had skinned the crocodiles, had hacked off the rhino horns and chopped out the tusks. He had had long conversations with the men who owned a small gold mine in the area, where *Motomoto* had camped and broken the seal of a bottle of brandy over the campfire, boasting that, when the Game Department eventually got too close, he would leave, and publish a book and show 16 mm cine films that would humiliate the game rangers. Rupert continued to file this information back to Salisbury where, in turn, they began to systematically delve into the operations of the tannery businesses, the butchers who specialised in venison and the expensive furrier houses who advertised up to 50 leopard-skin coats a month. By now Rupert had enlisted the aid of the police and together they set about relocating the Africans who would be suitable witnesses in a court case. It was not enough. The poacher, this man *Motomoto* who was slaughtering the game, had to be caught out there in the bush. Committing murder. Otherwise, with a lawyer who knew his business, he would laugh his way out of court.

And even without this commercial murderer, poaching by the local inhabitants had reached endemic proportions. The guns and the dogs and the snares were wreaking havoc on the wildlife population. In that December of 1964 Rupert wrote an impassioned four-page report to the Department of National Parks and Wildlife Management recommending that the rugged area of Crown land in the vicinity of the junction of the Gwatera and Mazoe rivers be declared a rhino sanctuary. The so far healthy presence of these ancient-looking beasts, together with the remaining resident elephants, buffalos, lions, eland, roan antelope, sable antelope, zebras, leopards, hyenas, bushbuck, reedbuck, warthogs, wild dogs, hippos and crocodiles would make an ideal nucleus for a new game sanctuary. He stressed that it was ... *vitally important that a game ranger and game scouts be stationed there immediately, otherwise it will be too late! Poaching is rife.*

Sadly, two years later in September 1966, a disillusioned Rupert Fothergill was despatched to the area again, to undertake further anti-poaching patrols. He found the area badly denuded of game and most of the countryside burnt out. Still the guns and the dogs and the snares were taking their toll. Waterholes were poisoned. Game was scarce. Poachers' tree platforms were found overlooking almost every source of water. The hyenas and vultures looked healthy. In a last attempt at the end of his patrol report, he entered a page long summary of his observations.

1. *The Area is being heavily hammered by African poachers from the surrounding Native Reserves.*
2. *Do we intend giving these rhinos any protection, by declaring a small area as a sanctuary for them? Two years ago there were 22 rhinos, since then five have been destroyed by poachers etc.*
3. *If so, game scouts and a game ranger must be posted to the area immediately, otherwise within six months there won't be a living thing to be seen.*
4. *The D.C. Darwin, should be informed for the second time that the African farmers in Chesa N.P.A. are not using their shotguns for protection of crops, but for hunting purposes only.*

In the early seventies the area was proclaimed a safari area, managed by the country's hunters' association, and then in 1975 new legislation proclaimed it the Umfurudzi Parks and Wildlife Land. Yet the sophisticated poachers, with their four-wheel drive vehicles and mesmerising shooting lamps, and the endless sorties of African hunting gangs from the bordering tribal areas took their toll. In September 1980 a massive air and ground operation managed by the Game Department and utilising army and air force personnel, scoured the area. The task was twofold. They had to discover the extent of poaching activities, evidence of which was great, and to undertake an evaluation of the game surviving in the area - which was minimal. Sable and kudu antelope, together with some of the smaller species of buck were reasonably well represented. Waterbuck, zebras, eland, impala, bushpigs, reedbuck, lions, roan antelope and black rhinos were tabulated as being either extinct or on the verge of extinction in that area.

Postscript Rupert finally succeeded in getting the man with the name of *Motomoto* into court without actually catching him bloody-handed in the bush. The result was as he guessed it would be, without irrevocable, damning evidence. The poacher smiled mockingly at the game warden when he was acquitted.

In 1970, four years after Rupert's last written plea concerning the formation of a rhino sanctuary, where the Gwatera and Mazoe rivers meet, the Department of National Parks and Wildlife Management undertook to capture and translocate the surviving black rhinos in that area. Of the 23 animals rescued, many had old bullet wounds or festering snare wires embedded in their bodies.

CHAPTER 14
OPERATION RHINO

James Bond smoked his fiftieth cigarette of the day, at three in the morning. It was a Balkan and Turkish mixture made especially for him by a tobacconist in London. A chilled, half-bottle of Clicquot nestled in the silver ice bucket beside him as he leaned against the bar and surveyed the patrons of the casino. Three hours at the baccarat table had left him jaded. When the girl walked in to the Casino Royale his rapier gaze took in the sleek black hair, the deep blue eyes and, of course, her plunging neck line.

A Saturday afternoon in September 1964, the fifth to be exact. In the hard, wild Sizemba area of the Sengwa River, in the Rhodesian Zambezi Valley. Rupert Fothergill let the latest exploits of the world's best-known secret agent drop beside the camp bed and dozed in the heat. Away behind the camp the uproar from the five rhino pens had abated, only temporarily he was sure, as the beasts rested before their next bout. The big troop of baboons which visited the camp regularly had also stopped their barking and carousing near the pens and Rupert's senses took advantage of this brief respite to catnap.

They had stopped hunting, for the moment, he and the younger ranger attached to this task from the Wankie Game Reserve. The stockades were full. Full of five big, indignant, bad-tempered black rhinos. For the last three nights they had been creating merry hell as they tried to get at each other through the thick, scarred *mopane* poles of the pens. Sleep had been minimal for Rupert and Ron Thomson and the rest of the capture team. The chief culprits were the two that Rupert had darted two days ago. The 10th and 11th rhinos caught in this first ever exercise of its kind - a cow, christened Sinanga, after the unyielding, inhospitable bush of that name; and a large bull with a 24-inch front horn, named Kadigidigi, after one of the scouts, were making a lot of noise. As the newest arrivals, they were ready to take on all-comers, as well as each other, and the cacophony of roars, grunts, snorts and squeals echoed across the hot, dry bushveld. In a day or so Ron Thomson would escort one of the rhinos on its 300-mile journey to Wankie, crated and belligerent atop the lorry, negotiating some of the roughest terrain in the country. Then one of the pens would become vacant and the hunt would be on again. There were still plenty of rhinos to keep the game men busy, here in the *mopane* scrub and the belts of almost impenetrable thorn thicket. In September, with the daily temperatures rocketing past 130°F, and with every day bringing the dart hunters within paces of a violent, bloody death, the coming dog days of October had little worse to offer.

Over two months they had been here now, the crusty, middle-aged game warden and the young, fresh faced ranger, together with their motley band of scouts and trackers. Operation Noah was history now for Rupert. Five years of rescue on the nearby lake. Thousands of animals. Over 40 black

rhinos saved. For Ron Thomson, with four years under his belt as a ranger in Wankie and several years before that hunting, the opportunity to work with the man who was already a legend in the wildlife conservation world was manna from heaven. In time, over the years, he would take over the mantle from Rupert, pupil from teacher, and his keen, academic approach and his flair for the unorthodox would make him the specialist of the rhino capture world. Paul Coetsee and others would, in their turn, become synonymous with rhino survival. But now, in the last week of July 1964, as they built their base camp and rhino pens, and completed their preparations for the hunts over the long weeks ahead, it was Rupert who planned their campaign and marshalled the recce patrols through the wild, rugged landscape of bush and rocky hills. Black rhinos are territorial creatures, especially so where their beloved *jesse* is thickest. Seldom will they move outside their couple of square miles of home range. And so, gradually, Rupert and young Thomson worked out an estimate of the rhino population in this small, forgotten part of southern Africa.
Ironically this largest of man-made lakes, which now covered 200 miles of Rhodesia's border with her northern neighbour, was still governing Rupert's life. Years before, as the dam wall was still creeping inexorably up the sides of the gorge known as Kariba, over 50 000 Tonga tribespeople had been moved from their ancestral tribal lands along the Zambezi River to new areas well above the final levels of the lake. In a scattering of areas in the valley, often in country which was a far cry from the rich, alluvial soils of the banks of the Zambezi, they had begun new lives and tried to adjust to their new homes. Then, once the dam wall was finally completed and the mighty Zambezi River ceased its hitherto unmolested, eastward journey, and slowly crept back on itself to form a vast inland sea, it had been the turn of the animals, whose plight had not been as seriously considered as that of the humans.

Altogether, as the months slipped into years and the animals rescued in Operation Noah were relocated on safe ground, along with the animals that preceded them of their own accord, *and* the animals that already inhabited the areas, *and* the tribespeople that already inhabited the areas, *plus* the recently relocated tribespeople to the areas, things moved gradually towards crisis point. Wild animals and humans, outside prescribed sanctuary areas, seldom go together. And by mid-1964, a year after the end of Operation Noah, the area was in turmoil. Elephants, buffalos, rhinos, the antelope and the baboons destroyed the meagre hard-won crops of the tribespeople. They in turn shot, trapped and snared the game. In the end, for the game, it was a no win affair.

For the tribespeople have at their fingertips progress and civilisation, in the form of a myriad of government departments, responding to their pleas for help. And the rhino, in this case the black rhino, is the worst affected of all. For, in a fast downhill slide, it is becoming extinct. Its limited territory and inability to adapt as readily as other species, together with its confused, irascible nature and myopic eyesight, have caused it to be killed, and killed, and killed. At the time of writing, the world population of *Diceros bicornis* has plummeted to less than 3 000 animals. In present-day Zimbabwe, privately-owned conservancies and four governmental Intensive Protection Zones (I.P.Z.s) are the last hope for the survival of the remaining 300 or so black rhinos.

Back in 1964, the rhino had not been declared Royal Game. That is to say that a person could still obtain a licence from the relevant government department and hunt and shoot black rhinos. Only in 1968 was the animal made Royal Game. In the area of the junction of the Sengwa River with the new Lake Kariba, the rhinos were being snared and killed. Beforc long there would be none left. The Department of Internal Affairs, keen to keep the people happy, was about to add to their demise with instructions to shoot out the black rhino population in the area. The odds against the animal were mounting.

In the newly evolved Department of National Parks and Wildlife Management there was consternation. In Wankie there was a small breeding nucleus of black rhinos, all rescued on Operation Noah. There were several bulls, but only two or three cows. A desperate first time hit or miss operation was planned. Rupert, with a small team, would base up in the trouble spot and they would locate, dart, capture, reorient and, finally, transport as many rhinos as possible out to the safety of Wankie. Again, funds were to be the problem. Sister government departments loaned a truck here, a Land Rover there. Rupert and his new assistant would have to sort out the rest of the logistics, not the least being the totally contrary, impractical, dart weapons and drugs. It is just short of miraculous that more casualties were not incurred because of this unreliable equipment. Today, during modern darting exercises, a comfortable range of 80 yards is possible with updated equipment. Helicopters are often used. Then, with drug dart capture in its infancy in Rhodesia, and the very thick bush involved, Rupert and Ron Thomson were stalking to within five paces of rhino, to ensure that their leaking dart guns would put the needle of the dart satisfactorily into their quarry. The closest range, as reminisced by Thomson, was achieved by Rupert. Two paces.

Their first rhino was successfully darted on 10 July. For 12 days Rupert had been in the area, establishing camp, building the pens, bringing in crates ... and weighing up the task at hand. It was not, the 52-year-old warden judged, going to be a picnic. Before dawn they were out in the *jesse* thickets. They had already established particular rhino territories, their paths through the tangle of bush, the waterholes and favourite drinking spots along the lake edge. Already they were very aware of the other species of big game that also inhabited the area. All of the rest of the 'big five' were well represented, and in the coming days elephants, buffalos, lions and leopards would bring complications to the rhino capture exercise.

In the cool, sharp air that comes with the dawn, sounds travel further. A rhino on its way to water, or chewing on the dry twigs of the *jesse* is that much easier to locate there in the claustrophobic, skin-scratching, shirt-ripping maze of scrub at that time of day. Every hunt was a contest. A contest between the dart teams locating and stalking a rhino silently enough to within darting distance, and the rhino or its attendant oxpeckers becoming aware of them and blundering away in fright. Or charging. In *jesse* scrub, climbable trees were few and far between. It was midday before Rupert could get close enough to the rhino that they had stalked for four hours. Because of the noise two people made, no matter who, in *jesse*, the final stage of the stalk would take place alone. Ron Thomson, the scouts and trackers waited behind as Rupert eased his way closer to the indistinct smudge of grey hidden in the haze of grey thorn scrub. It took another 45 minutes to manoeuvre closer, close enough to send the dart on its way without it being deflected by a twig. A dozen paces ... ten ... nine. Fifteen minutes. He could see the rhino reasonably well now, parts of it very well. From its regular deep breathing he realised it was asleep on its feet, dozing the midday heat away. No birds. No jolly oxpeckers around this one. Hurrah and hooray. Carefully he raised the Palmer Capchur Gun, selecting a target area on the grey, wrinkled hide. The flat report blended with the whooshing grunt of the rhino as it was galvanised into full safety-seeking stride. Straight away from them. But it was no go. Nothing. Frustration. Sweat pouring. Adrenalin already slowing its surge through the system. *Dammit*. The needle at the base of the flying syringe had broken at the base on impact with the rhino's hide.

It would happen again. Often. After many long, painstaking stalks. Bang. And the needle broken. Until they fixed it, properly. Using some common epoxy putty supplied by a hardware store. But that was still to come.

They went after it. Under the midday orb of the sun.

As long as Rupert had his two old Mazoe bottles full of sweet, cold tea he would go on forever. They found it again, two hours later. Another stalk. More difficult this time. The rhino was alert, wide awake. Not sleeping now. Listening for its pursuers, testing the wind. Rupert went in again. Slowly. Step by step. Also testing the wind, hoping fervently that it wouldn't shift. He fired the second dart at five minutes after three that afternoon. This time it stuck. This time the rhino bolted with the dart dangling from its rump.

After it again. Along its spoor. Senses screaming alert for the animal ahead. It was difficult spooring. Time-wasting. The clover leaf spoor mingled with other animal tracks, and for a while it had run with a herd of buffalo, its spoor obliterated completely. Rupert and Thomson and the trackers circled, backtracked. Cast further afield for new signs. And then they picked it up again and went after it.

They found the rhino. Eventually. Two and a half miles later they found it. All big, armoured, chaffing, tick-ridden, grey mass of him. Out for the count. On his back (now they could see he was a male) snoring, feet in the air. It was close to sundown. He was christened right then, out there in the *jesse* with the shadows lengthening, with his four great feet in the air. Chacadama, the trackers called him. Which referred, quite naturally, to his feet stuck aloft.

So now they had reached Phase Three.

They had found a rhino and darted it successfully. They had lost it for a while, and then relocated it, successfully. Which meant they were about half way. The next trick was to get a vehicle in; to get the transporting truck through the jumbled maze of scrub and bush to the comatose rhino. And then they had to load him, the recumbent ton-and-a-half of him, six feet up on to the back of the truck, and drive him back to camp. And then they had to unload him. And administer the antidote that would bring old Chacadama round. Then, very probably, there would be hell to pay, when this rhino, their first capture of the operation, found himself in a new environment. In a pen, even if it was a large area, with the man smell all around.

As Rupert inspected the drugged beast he smiled fondly, his usually sombre features lightening. He had been in the wars, had Chacadama, judging from his tattered ribbon of a left ear and the wound near his testicles. Which, to be sure, was not going to improve his humour.

It was a reasonably accurate prediction. They eventually got the rhino into his pen and the injection given. At a few minutes after ten that night Chacadama was on his feet again. Groggy and swaying slightly, he surveyed his new surroundings, shifting one way and then another, taking it all in. He was not impressed, nor was he happy. He snorted and charged the feeding crate, his front horn probing and smashing at the top planks. Turning them into driftwood. Then he circled the enclosure, searching for a new enemy. Anything. Anyone. Huffing, snorting, wild-eyed in the light of the lantern. All night he performed, nearly breaking his way out once. Extra *mopane* poles to prop up the mangled remains of part of the fence were put up just in time.

And he was the first. There was still three months ahead and God knows how many rhinos to be caught. There was no limit. They would catch as many as they could. Save as many as possible in this one effort, because they might not have another chance. Three months. Over 90 days of *jesse* bush and rhinos, and faulty dart guns, and stalks to within five paces of their horned quarry.

And slowly they did catch them, these unpredictable, great, horned heavyweights. First working as a team and then, once Thomson had grasped the intricacies of the dart hunt, hunting separately over the area around the Sengwa's meeting with the great lake. Every hunt was different. Each stalk was made under new circumstances.

There were failures, many of them. There had to be with this new game of hide and seek. It was not possible that every stalk, no matter how painstakingly made, no matter how perfect, could end in success. There were too many odds against them. It was a brand new ball game, this version of man versus rhinoceros. And the very nature of the terrain, the unreliability of the various dart delivery weapons and, that great equaliser of all, pure and simple luck, good or bad, made the whole exercise a bit of a stacked deck. During Noah, Rupert should have been caught, looking at the odds. And now, in their daily contacts with rhinos, surely Rupert or Ron Thomson must get gored.

The scientists and academics, the heavily degreed persons who are involved with animals, wild or otherwise, look askance at anyone who shows any sign of anthropomorphism. Animals should just not be judged against human standards. Their actions and responses should not be paralleled to those of the far-advanced human animal. Intelligence is a word avoided by the boffins, in the context of animal behaviour. Yet the tactics the rhinos employed, often, to avoid capture, left no doubt in both men's minds that there were still things to be learned. And that animal intelligence was not to be scoffed at. For instance, time and again they would stalk a rhino and, one way or another, the animal would become alarmed and aware of its would-be saviours. And it would bolt. More often than not, it would seek refuge amongst a herd of elephant, or buffalo. In this way it not only had the extra advantage of its wild neighbours' senses, it also managed, with exasperating monotony, to considerably delay any spooring, its own tracks being interspersed and lost amongst those of its temporary hosts. Many was the occasion when a rhino, fleeing from the man presence, would adopt one of two escape routines. Either it would bolt pell-mell along an established game trail that it habitually used, snout to the ground as it sniffed for scent of its human tormentor, or the beast would depart in a rushing tail-erect scramble, not along the game trail, but parallel to it, traversing the roughest ground it could find. Making subsequent spooring difficult and time consuming. And, during later capture attempts, with time running out, when Ron Thomson set up dart loaded trap guns on rhino paths, the animals very quickly learned the habit of first hooking their horn under the tripwire and walking backwards until the gun discharged harmlessly, before continuing their journey. And the wildlife men experienced this not once, but often. Intelligence? Or a keen sense of survival?

Throughout July they hunted on. One Cap Chur Gun was useless after firing two darts. The other two were leaking and could only be used well within 20 paces of a target. It was an achievement to get within ten paces of a rhino, beating the noise, wind, and oxpeckers. But the achievement turned sour when the dart bounced off the rhino's hide and you had to scramble frantically to get out of the way of the animal. They succeeded in capturing a second rhino, a young bull, that month. There were fresh claw marks on his back from an unsuccessful lion attack, but otherwise he was in good condition. Towards the end of the month a new version of Cap Chur Gun was sent to the rhino capture team. It was a revolver model, and leaked just as badly as the others. Two rhinos in a month. Not an auspicious start, and the two men went at it harder.

Ron Thomson darted his first rhino in mid August and, two days later, they captured a further two animals. Things were improving. A crossbow, made in Bulawayo, joined their armament. It was only slightly better than the guns and it proved to be a clumsy hindrance in the confines of the *jesse*. Every twig and thorn seemed to ensnare itself on the string and a variety of tuneless string sounds would echo through the bush.

The capture tally was not a true reflection of the efforts being made by the capture team. Every day they were out in the scrub before a new sun had risen to cast its glare over the valley. And every day they encountered rhinos, in varying circumstances, and elephants and buffalos. The days merged into weeks. Rupert lost all track of time. Only the daily chore of writing up the field diary kept him in touch with the passing days. And so he knew it was a Sunday, some Sunday, when he got himself too close to a family herd of elephant.

It was the usual story. He had been stalking two rhinos when they caught his scent and bolted. Patiently he followed up. Soon he found that they had taken refuge amongst an elephant herd. Rupert circled cautiously and stalked up behind the bulk of a termite mound, trying to close on the rhinos from another angle. The best laid plans can go awry. As he eased himself over the crest of the mound ... " I found myself almost within hand-shaking distance of two elephant cows and calves. I retreated backwards like a crab, nose to the ground in the hope that I would be mistaken for a baboon ..."

Rupert circled around the elephants and picked up the rhino spoor again. And promptly got amongst another elephant herd. The warden made a tactical withdrawal, only to land himself in amongst a third herd. As he extricated himself from the latest herd he reflected there must be more leisurely ways of spending a Sunday morning. He lit a pipe, taking his time. Hoping the rhino duo would give him another chance before the sun got too high in the sky.

They changed their tactics. By now the rhinos in the area sensed that they were being hunted. And they became more difficult than ever to catch. One pair, a mother and calf, were only coming down from the nearby hills in the dark to drink at their favourite water hole. It was pointless darting a rhino amidst the rugged terrain of the high ground because it would be impossible to get the carry vehicle in there. So Ron Thomson built a tree platform overlooking their drinking place. There was a full moon now, and the night-time African bush became a surrealistic frieze of moonscape silver slashed with liquid, black shadows.

At a few minutes before eleven that night he darted the mother as she ambled past beneath him. The smooth-rubbed fibres of her front horn reflected silver in the moonlight. At first light they were tracking her up towards the hills, and Rupert and Thomson were worried that she would make the bad ground. Then they found her with the calf close by her side, worrying, nuzzling at its sleeping mother. It turned and faced the humans and snorted loudly and prepared to defend its parent with its stubby five-inch horn. They darted the youngster as well, and that made their seventh capture. There were healed snare wounds around the mother's neck and leg, great welts of scabbed skin on the armoured grey hide. She had managed to break free. She was one of the lucky ones.

Then they had captured ten. A dozen. And by the end of September they had caught nineteen. There was a regular shuttle service now, from the rhino camp westwards to the haven of the great Wankie Game Reserve. Time was not measured in days, but by events. From their second capture, the young bull, which was remembered by the pride of lions they disturbed whilst following him up, to the eighth capture when Rupert had to edge quietly away from an old, smooth, worn-bossed buffalo bull which had approached unseen as he was filling a dart syringe with drug. Curiosity rather than aggression had kept the old buffalo coming, slowly, head up, staring until he was less than 15 paces away.

The rhinos themselves were remembered, and sometimes christened, according to the circumstances in which they were caught. There was Mankah (Young Woman) darted by Ron Thomson. He'd had to use three darts on her, persistently keeping after her when the needles kept breaking. There was old Ben, named after one of the trackers, blind in one eye with, again, almost healed, weeping snare wounds. He had kept going for two miles after he had been darted.

Maceh (Stones) had taken a long time to track down after the dart went in. Three hours and a mile-and-a-half later, over rocky, stony ground that left little sign, they found her. Drugged but on her feet still, with her great head stuck into a thick *jesse* bush. There was little four-month-old Mbira (like a rock hyrax with no tail) caught with its mother. Hyenas had chewed its tail off and the raw wound had to be treated back at camp.

The rhino Rupert remembered best, they never darted. In the game warden's words he was "... the oldest rhino bull I have ever seen." Christened, automatically, Madallah (Old One) by Rupert and his game scouts they reckoned he must be the father and grandfather of all the rhinos in the Sengwa. With a massive front horn he was easily identified on later occasions. Rupert had been tracking rhino spoor in the *mopane* woodlands and he had heard a rhino approaching. Climbing trees he and his men had waited for a target to move into view. Rupert eased the Cap Chur Gun into a ready position. Then Madallah appeared, walking like an old man, carefully selecting the spot to place each foot. He passed under Rupert's tree, and then stopped to ruminate under Langton's perch. The scout swung silently from his branch and hung suspended, feet gently resting on the old rhino's back. There was no reaction. The African nudged a foot on the wrinkled, grey hide. The old rhino plodded calmly away. Rupert watched the animal disappear, dart gun forgotten. At Langton's silent, raised eyebrows query, he shook his head. The old boy would die of old age in a year or so, he reflected. Why disturb his life now? He probably wouldn't be able to take the drugs anyway. Let him die peacefully on the Sengwa. (A year later the old rhino was darted mistakenly by Ron Thomson and died from the shock of the drugs. Perhaps it was a mercy, for on the old rhino's hide old and new scars evidenced the increasing interest of hyenas).

In mid-October the operation ceased. Nineteen rhinos had been captured and relocated in Wankie, in three-and-a-half months of first time ever back-breaking toil. Under his belt Rupert had 63 black rhino captures, including the Noah rescues. And he was still in one piece. That was it. For this year at least.

* * * * * * * * * *

There was a brief, hoarse scream of warning from the game scouts. It came too late. As he turned he caught a fleeting glimpse of the grey bulk of the rhino before it hit him. Hit him with the power of a locomotive, all 2 000 pounds of grey, snorting, prehistoric belligerence of it. Rupert never felt the horn go in. He was just conscious of the impact of the animal hitting him, and then he was in the air, suspended above the hooking, jabbing rhino. Impaled! Desperately, his hands scrabbled at the horn, trying in vain to stop himself going deeper on it. Then he was off. Spinning, reeling, falling, a small part of his mind noting the crimson on the rhino's front horn glistening in the first rays of the climbing sun. He cursed again the worsening deafness in his left ear. Then he was on the ground. On all fours. Battered, bleeding, but mind working lucidly. Cover! He must find some sort of cover, any cover. The scouts ... Langton ... where the hell were they? Why weren't they diverting the thing away from him? Fire a shot with his rifle. Do something, before ... The rhino hit him again, missing him with its horn on its first swipe, and he could see the blood plainly now, his blood, covering the entire horn, and it hooked at him again with its massive, armoured head. He was smashed sideways, sprawling, blood-spattered across the ground. And he felt his shoulder go with a distinct crack. The force of the swipe sent him yards away and he could feel the pain in his gut this time. Then he saw the *mopane* stump and he kept rolling and crawled ponderously behind it. He lay there, battling to keep his panting quiet, eyes glued to the rhino as it moved to and fro, scant feet away, hunting for him, snorting its anger in long, whooshing roars. Head down and swinging as it tried to find the human again and kill it properly. Snuffling, squealing, dust swirling thickly up. And Rupert knew that if it had another go at him, that would be it. End of story. No more rhino darting for him! He couldn't dodge it now. Without moving his head he flicked a glance downwards. Saw the spill of his intestines, bunched pinky grey on the ground beneath him. Seconds had elapsed. Years. There was more noise now, more dust. He flicked his glance back to the rhino, and his heart lurched anew. The two other rhinos, the ones he'd been after, concentrating on, waiting for a better chance to put the dart in, had joined his attacker. Now he had three rhinos within yards of him, shaking the very earth itself as they stomped around, looking to kill him. And he dare not move. He watched them.

Then they were off. Going! Heading off into the maze of *jesse*. The newcomers had distracted the one that got him, their noisy, excited appearance switching his attention away from his search. And now, unbelievably, they were gone. Rupert eased himself upright, cradling his spilled guts in one hand. When the game scouts got to him, eventually, he was carefully, gently, removing the dust and dirt from his intestines and

pushing them back. Back through the ripped, jagged holes of his jersey, shirt, trousers and underpants, and into the hole in his lower abdomen. Once he'd got the mess back he squirted almost the entire contents of his small yellow plastic bottle of wound powder (Animal Wound Powder from Millborrow & Co) into the wound. It was a laborious task, with only his left arm usable. But he got it done. Then he walked over a mile back to where they had left the Land Rover, skirting a herd of edgy elephants in the process. Langton helped him with the gears, getting back to camp. Where the first order of the day was a pot of hot, strong tea.

Despite a lot of crossed wires, Rupert was evacuated to the main hospital in Salisbury. An indistinct radio message, via the Game Department's radio network, was picked up at the Wankie Game Reserve and relayed to Bulawayo. In turn the Air Force base at New Sarum near Salisbury was alerted and an Alouette helicopter of the Royal Rhodesian Air Force was despatched, collecting *en route*, from the hospital grounds, the Medical Superintendent, Dr Laidler. In the meantime, the District Commissioner at Binga, on the lake shore, some 150 miles from Rupert's camp, received the information that Rupert had been gored by a rhino and was dying. A shocked D.C., Ian Findlay, broke into the locked area ranger's office to get at the radio and managed to make contact with Rupert. The calm, unflustered response from the injured man helped reassure the D.C. that things were not *that* critical, and he wondered if he had perhaps been too hasty in despatching an Air Force spotter plane that had, by chance, been stationed at Binga in conjunction with a survival exercise. Ian Findlay had made up a hasty medical pack to be dropped into Rupert's camp, the principal inclusion being morphine tablets. The least he could do, he had thought, was to ease the pain in the warden's last hours ...

Rupert was gored, eventually, maybe predictably, at about 6.40am on Sunday, 8 August 1965. It had to happen sometime. That it did happen, and that the end result was not more serious than a broken arm, a neatly severed appendix, and a chip out of the pelvic bone was, at the least, fortuitous.

The 1965 rhino capture operation had been in action for little over six weeks. The conditions were the same as those experienced the previous year. The bush was just as thick, and the capture guns were just as unreliable. Out of six guns only two were usable and, as usual, only if the hunter was very close to the rhino. The crossbow, with its inherent disadvantages, was also being used. And the remaining rhino population, either remembering its harassment of the previous year, or because of the pressures coming from the tribespeople, or perhaps reacting to the very obvious predation on its young by lions and hyenas, was more hostile and wary than ever.

The start to this year's capture had, once again, been inauspicious. In late June they had come back to the Sengwa rhino camp. It was overgrown now, and the elephants had destroyed the huts. The pens, however, were still in fair condition, and only needed some strengthening. Testing the crossbow, it was discovered that the cross-shaft had cracked and had to be bound. As assistants on this capture operation Rupert had Tom Orford and, temporarily, Viv Wilson. Due to arrive at the camp soon were Dr Harold Roth and a vet from Cambridge, Richard Jones. They would be bringing a new immobilising drug known as M99, which was allegedly superior to the morphine sulphate that was being used.

Their first darting attempts had been frustrating and unsuccessful. After the usual careful approach, one rhino had been darted in the shoulder but ran off and was not located. Two days later Rupert darted a large bull, but at the moment of impact the beast wheeled and broke off the needle of the syringe against a bush, before the drug could be injected. They followed him up, encountering three different herds of elephant and a herd of buffalo. But the rhino was wary now, and annoyed. And a troop of baboons followed the proceedings noisily, making it impossible to get close to the quarry. The next day there was another rhino. A replay of the previous day, with the needle breaking. More charges. More trees. Rupert switched from using the crossbow back to the Cap Chur Gun. Nothing. Not a dicky bird. No dart. Just a loud, echoing, metallic click and the rhino cow charging without hesitation. Barely beating the animal to a tree, Rupert tried a second shot from his perch. Again, nothing. The gas had leaked out.

That afternoon he tested one of the other weapons and, rather than do nothing, took it out on a new hunt. On a narrow peninsula jutting into the lake they found two rhinos. Rupert lay in wait whilst the trackers disturbed the rhinos and they charged past him. He almost cheered out loud when the dart stuck firmly in the buttock of the leading animal. They followed up on the sets of tracks. When these split up, they debated which set to follow. Rupert tossed a coin. Tails! They went off on one set. And, of course, it was the wrong ones! Retrace the route and follow up on the other spoor. And there it was, at unbelievable last, its head resting comfortably in the fork of a low tree.

Twilight. Darkness just around the corner. They got him, Chavuta, their first rhino for that operation, back to the pens well after dark. It was early July. Mid-winter in Rhodesia. Clear, star-studded skies. Cold. A probing, gusting, chill wind.

The fifth rhino to be captured had seen it all before. Rupert felt an extra tenderness for this particular animal as he inspected the much battered ear tags. The left ear tag was 3347, the right number read 3348. The rhino, a male, was christened, not surprisingly, Kariba, from whose waters he had been rescued over two years previously, in March 1963.

Eight rhinos were captured by Fothergill, before he was gored. Eight in six weeks, and all the near misses in between. All the stalks to within a cocktail-bar's length of an animal. All the pell-mell, heart-thudding, 'only just' scrambles for safety when the wind changed, or the oxpeckers gave warning. Or when the dart went in. The visitors, with their new drug, had tended to be a trifle superior. Initially. After all, their experience with drugs and reactions was certainly wider than that of the taciturn bush-worn game warden. And yet, in time, even they learned.

One of the darted rhinos was lying comatose whilst they measured heart beats, pulse rates and so worked through their check list of required data. Rupert, watching the rhino carefully, grunted. It did not feel right, did not look right. There was something wrong with the animal. The visitors regarded him dubiously. Wrong? Like what? They had their stethoscopes and other paraphernalia tuned in to the beast's reactions, did they not? And, as far as they were concerned, everything was fine. Rupert grimaced and shook his head glumly, silently. And quietly unpacked his antidote apparatus, and made it ready. Minutes later the whole demeanour of the drugged rhino changed. As is characteristic of the species, it was slipping away, rapidly. The visitors, startled, scrambled for the antidote. Rupert slipped it into one tattered thorn-torn ear.

Some men, only some, get a 'feel' for such developments. An intuition. Rupert had it. Some of the other men, like Thomson, Orford and the Coetsee brothers, also have it.

Ron Thomson came down from Binga and took over the rest of the operation, having in turn more than his share of close shaves. There was rhino number nine, Siamweri, named after the headman of a small village near the lake shore who reported its presence to the game ranger. Before eventually being captured, it led Ron a merry chase through herds of eland, impala and elephant, in turn stalked the ranger, took refuge in the lake three times and eventually charged right through the middle of the village, sending the locals shinning up every near tree.

For one week Ron tried trap guns on well-used rhino paths, setting them at night and disarming them at first light. The end of this experiment came when he discovered one of his trap guns set off and followed the spoor for almost a mile to find a young bull fast asleep. The ranger inspected the beast, searching for the dart. Nothing. Nonplussed he finally checked under the animal's tail. Still no sign of the dart. With the sun's rays fast becoming hotter, he removed his bush jacket and dumped it across the rhino's withers. Suddenly the rhino was on its feet, lunging at the man near him. Ron dodged the horn and scrambled out of range. The rhino quickly lost interest in him and started to browse peacefully off some thorn scrub, attended by a trio of chattering oxpeckers. The ranger watched the rhino for a long time. There were no drug effects whatsoever. He found it intriguing to think he'd been examining a healthy, snoozing black rhino.

Ron Thomson captured another 11 rhinos, including the rhino that almost killed Rupert. Like his mentor, the young ranger hunted ceaselessly, out in the *jesse* before first light until late at night. The deadline was the end of September, and there would be no extension of this time. There would not be an opportunity to try again on capture operations in the Sengwa area. In future any animals interfering with the tribespeople would be destroyed. This was the final solution.

Rupert returned to the rhino camp in the last days of September. All that was left now was to wrap up the rescue mission, nurse the most recently captured rhinos and get them adjusted to their travelling crates. And wonder how long the four remaining rhinos, the ones they hadn't managed to capture before the deadline, would last.

CHAPTER 15

TO CATCH A LION

The golden-red orb of the sun oozed hesitantly over the craggy thrust of the escarpment. The slate grey waters of the lake changed to mother of pearl. A goliath heron shifted from one long sentinel's leg to the other and a small wash of ripples trembled away from the reeds; dove grey, guinea fowl purple with finally the clean, metallic blue of a roller reflecting upwards in the suffusion of light. Rupert and the other members of the game rescue team picked their way through the sparkling, dew-laden grass towards the area from which the ghoulish goose-bump sounds had issued during the night. The carcass of the elephant, the young, irascible bull they had been forced to shoot the previous afternoon, in its eighth charge of the day at the rescue team, was gone. They blinked. Eight thousand pounds of dead elephant had disappeared overnight. Then Rupert saw the uneven, bloody swathe through the grass, leading towards the edge of the lake. Now the sun teetered on the rim of the escarpment and the water burned orange. They followed the trail, studying the maze of clawed reptile spoor, the grooved belly marks, and found where the crocodiles had eventually dragged the elephant into the shallows and on into deep water. For forty paces the crocodiles had dragged the mass of elephant! A game scout shivered and Rupert felt his hackles rise. And he wondered how many of the crocs there had been.

The only other animal on the African continent which equals the rhino as a living example of prehistoric survival, is the crocodile. For 170 million years the saurians have inhabited the land and the seas of this planet. And in Africa the crocodile (*Crocodylus niloticus*) has killed and eaten more humans than any other animal. As a highly successful, very competent killer, this reptile has only one peer. Man! In the country that is now Zimbabwe, very few river systems in the less developed parts of the country do not have a presence of crocodiles. And few villages have not had dogs or sheep, goats or cattle, or a relative, taken by this cunning, ultra survival-conscious killing machine. A little way above Victoria Falls, on a beautiful, late afternoon not long ago, the author's dog, Nelson - canine scholar and gentleman - was taken in seconds. Another croc statistic.

In the opening months of 1968 it was this reptile which was the subject of Rupert's attention in the featureless monotony of the patchwork of African communal lands covering the east of the country. Here the Macheke and Mare rivers meander across the flat lands to flow into the wide expanse of the Sabi which travels due southwards, parallel to the barrier of the Eastern Border Mountains, searching for a break before curving away eastward, through Portuguese East Africa to the warm waters of the Indian Ocean. For two months Rupert had been waiting in concealed blinds close to tethered goat or sheep baits, or silently stalking the ghostly red orbs which gleamed malevolently out of the darkness in the beam of his hunting lamp. His first intentions had been to trap the animals, but he had run out of time. Then he hunted them. The results had not been good. The crocodiles had been hunted before, and knew the rules of the game. And it was the wrong time of year to hunt crocs. The rivers were warm and the reptiles did not need to leave the shelter of the water and reeds to stabilise their body temperatures by basking in the sun on a sandbank. June/July was a more suitable time, for then it was winter, and even a tropical winter turned the waters cold, driving the animals out into the sunlight. And providing a target.

In his usual fashion, the roving warden persevered, trying one method and then another. It was not an area he enjoyed. There was very little sign of game in the district. There seldom is in the communal areas, for game is meat and therefore should be killed and eaten. The previous year, here in the same part of the country, the local people had complained of raiding baboons. A vermin extermination team had travelled from Salisbury and had successfully poisoned all the baboons in the area. Now the same people complained to Rupert that leopards were killing their stock. They were not interested when he explained the inevitability of this, now that the baboons, the leopards' main natural prey in this area, were gone. The leopards must go as well, they demanded, once the crocodiles have been killed. Rupert was not unhappy to receive a radio message to return to headquarters.

REPORT ON THE RHINO POPULATION IN THE RUYA RIVER P.E.A. BORDER AREA

On a recent patrol in this area, a small pocket of Black Rhinos were located approximately 10+. These Rhinos are normally resident between the Mudzi River and the Shamba River. The terrain is quite unsuitable for African settlement, as it is mountainous country. The District Commissioner Mount Darwin agreed with me on this point as he had flown over the area. It would be impossible to drug these Rhinos and remove them from the area because of the nature of the terrain. Black Rhinos in Rhodesia are becoming scarce, and in my opinion, from evidence gathered over the past three years, the Black rhino population of the country has been greatly overestimated! These animals occur in small pockets wherever there is a suitable habitat for them. Poaching, snaring and predators, such as lions and hyenas take their toll.

In the Binga Area alone, since 1964 - 63 poached Rhinos have been located. On the Sengwa River the carcasses of six baby Rhinos were located, death due to predators. At this rate, it is my opinion that in a few years' time, we shall have fewer Black than White Rhinos.

As the Ruya river Rhinos are in a Native Reserve, I should like to suggest that the higher authorities in the Native Department be approached, and the position be put to them, in the hopes that a small area of 6 x 6 x 6 miles of Mountainous country be set aside, in order to preserve these Rhinos. The area required has been plotted on a map, attached to this report. African settlement into this area would be fatal for these Rhinos.

Warden Roving Control
R Fothergill.

This report of Rupert's at the end of May 1968 was the culmination of two months' reconnaissance in the extreme north of the country. There, right on the border of Portuguese East Africa, in the rugged, inhospitable foothills through which the Ruya River carved its way to another country, he searched and tracked and scoured the remote wilderness for the animal he had come to love more than any other. Black rhinoceros. It was obvious to the game warden that unless definite steps were taken to protect this isolated pocket of rhinos from the surrounding communal areas and the meat-hungry populace, there was little chance of their surviving. And a few more of these animals which God had so far allowed to exist, would perish. Still fresh in his mind were the other rhinos in the Umfurudzi, only a few score miles away. And the carcasses. Rotting, bones bleached white, gone. More each year. Despite his repeated pleas to the hierarchy to do something. Thousands, millions of years of survival, of evolution, dead. Extinction waited just around the corner.

His reports and pleas eventually stirred reaction. After the Umfurudzi rhino rescue operation in the middle months of 1970, when 23 of the animals were darted and captured and relocated in the south-eastern sanctuary of Gona-re-Zhou, the Game Department turned its attention to the rhinos still surviving in the area of the Ruya River. In late 1969, largely due to Rupert's report, the Secretary for the Department of Internal Affairs, one of the most colourful personalities of the era, had declared that small, little-known portion of Rhodesia, a sanctuary. This was fine, in theory. But the area was too remote and too small to warrant a permanent post being initiated there.

And so it happened that in the late winter months of 1970, two years after Rupert's report, Ron Thomson and Paul Coetsee led an operation in the Ruya area, which located and rescued 24 black rhinos. By now the quietly-spoken, youthful looking Thomson was the Game Department's leading rhino capture expert and there in the dry, arid, baked earth country, amidst the dry river beds and ugly hills, he displayed the skills learned from the Sengwa rhino captures.

* * * * * * * * * *

Some 18 miles from the Kariba Dam wall, south-eastward across the lake, there is an island called Tsetse Island. It is a 20 minute journey in a modern speedboat, considerably longer if one is travelling on the *Sikwasi*, the Fisheries Research vessel. Behind Tsetse Island, between it and the reed-fringed estuary of the Gache Gache River, coming in from the escarpment, is a smaller, less conspicuous blob of an island which is known simply by a number; 174. Here, on this side of the lake, in this part of the Sanyati Basin, it is a different world from the bright lights and tourist babble of Kariba. Visited only by fishermen and game viewers by boat , the little island was used as a study area by staff of the Department of Tsetse and Trypanosomiasis Control, in their observations of relationships between the fly and wild animals. Game introduced onto the island years before had thrived and increased, with each year seeing new, wobbly-legged calves appear amongst the resident sable, kudu and impala. During a normal dry season, which lasts from around April until November, the level of the lake drops and Island 174 ceases to be an island. A thin tongue of land, once a ridge before the valley was drowned, gradually emerges above the shrinking waters to connect it with the mainland some 500 yards away. And the expanse of water separating it from the mainland becomes a stretch of shallows and sand bars, and the trees now exposed look like skeletons, to be covered again by the white droppings of the water birds.

It was here that Rupert came, back to the wide, horizon-squinting expanses of Kariba Lake that was now nine years old. He brought with him a trap cage which he had used often during Operation Noah, which seemed so long ago now. For headquarters had tasked him with another capture exercise. Lions, this time, were to be the subject of his attention. Since May, two lions had been systematically depleting the herds of antelope on the study island. Easily negotiating the shallow channel, they had killed 18 of the 26 sable and soon all those resident on the grassy, *mopane* tree-studded island would be killed off. Research came to a halt. It had initially been hoped that the lions would tire of the island then move on, but the handy private larder had proved too good to abandon. If Rupert did not succeed in trapping them they would have to be shot.

He found fresh spoor of one lion on his first inspection of the island and soon set about selecting a site for his trap. On a narrow neck of the island, he and some of the tsetse staff manhandled the trap into position. It was a simple enough plan. A small, but very stout pen was built, where a sheep would be installed with lucerne and water. The rectangular, steel barred trap cage would then be placed end-on against the pen, so that, looking through the open trap door, the lion would see the sheep. The whole arrangement would be covered by scrub, leaving just the door open. When the lion entered to get to the sheep it would trap itself, triggering a release mechanism hidden in the floor, which caused the heavy steel door to slam down behind it. The sheep would be safe in its pen, the intervening iron bars of the cage keeping the big cat at bay. For the first night Rupert left the pen empty, to see how the marauders reacted to this new part of the island's scenery. On his return from the Kariba base the following day, he was pleased to see that the lions had inspected the trap thoroughly, the ground around it scarred with their pug marks. You've been having it all your own way for too long, he reflected, as the game scouts ensconced a bleating sheep into the pen. You've become too sure of yourselves. Careless. Well, we'll see how things turn out tomorrow.

A brassy, burnished wilderness of water. The sun inching higher into a clear, blue sky, already hot at seven in the morning. The lilting, haunting cry of a fish eagle. And then the spitting, coughing grunt of an angry lion. Explosive rasping growls ripping through the early morning tranquillity. Rupert, Peter Moore, the Kariba Warden and an old Noah hand, and a handful of labourers warily approached the area of the trap. The snarling continued, louder now. Then they could see the trap, with a lioness inside, and a second lioness prowling around outside the cage and pen. At the sight of the humans, the trapped lioness attacked the steel bars in a spitting, clawing, yellow-blurred paroxysm of fury. But Rupert was more intent on her companion. She crouched beside the trap cage, haunches drawn up tight, tail flicking, all steel sinews and yellow glaring eyes. Clear off, old thing, the warden implored silently, easing off the safety catch on his rifle. Go on. Don't spoil things. I don't want to have to kill you. The lioness continued to stare balefully at the men, the growling becoming one continuous gurgling rumble. Rupert and his companion walked slowly on towards them. The trapped lioness was going berserk. The other one stood up, lips curled, front fangs gleaming, mesmerising white. Growling louder now. "Go on, push off!" Rupert spoke aloud now. "Begone! *Hamba*! Getaway!" He kept moving. The lioness backed up. Now only 30 paces separated men and lion. In full charge a lion can cover 100 metres in five seconds. One and a half seconds separated Rupert and

Peter Moore from a violent, bloody end. That, and Rupert's rifle, which he was hoping he would not have to use. Peter Moore bent down and picked up some stones and clods of earth. He stood up, eyeing Rupert. The game warden nodded, without taking his eyes off the lioness. She's lost her edge now, he thought. She'll retreat; back away. I think. I hope. But I thought she was going to come at us. At first. She was talking herself into a charge then. But we did the right thing, keeping on, walking in. Now Peter Moore was throwing the clods and stones at her, swearing, shouting, baffling her with noise. Almost 20 paces now. Reluctantly, begrudgingly, with much noise, the lioness was moving away from the trap cage. Then she turned and leaped away into the scrub. A tawny wraith, there one second and gone the next. But, thought Rupert, not far away. We shall have to watch that one.

It was impossible to get near the cage. Unsheathed, raking claws reached between the bars in determined, angry, savage efforts to get at her captors. Rupert had his next steps planned, but for the moment he was staring into the shadowy interior of the sheep's pen, puzzlement creasing his features. The sheep was no longer there. And he could not fathom how it had escaped. Then he peered closer, inspecting the area furthest from the trap cage. There, the story was plain. The second lioness had methodically removed the barrier of thorn scrub from around the pen. Then the big cat had dug out a hole beneath the thick circle of mopane poles, a gap no wider than six inches. And through that gap, by sheer strength, she had pulled the sheep. Rupert never did solve how she had been able to get at the sheep to kill it in the first place.

Now he focused his attention on subduing their new prisoner. Inserting 33 grains of phenobarbitone sodium into a chunk of meat, he then manoeuvred the treated meat into the cage. His watch said it was 10.30am. It would take a few hours for the lioness to calm down and eat, and for the drug to react. Which, he reflected in good humour, is a good enough excuse to do some fishing. One trap, one night, one lioness. Reasonable results. Then we have got number two lady lion to catch.

They left the captured lioness still growling and cursing and took the *Sikwasi* further around the island.

At five that evening the meat was gone and the lioness only mildly sedated. She attacked through the bars with renewed vigour. Rupert sat near the cage until last light but she showed no signs of succumbing to the drug. He treated another chunk of meat and left it outside the cage for the other lioness should she visit her trapped companion. The next day scuff marks showed where the free lioness had lain down beside the cage during the night. But she had not touched the meat. Their 'guest' was still a most irritated animal, vociferously making her feelings known. The drug seemed to have taken more effect for now she could not stand upright, but nevertheless she lurched and lunged at the men on the outside of her prison. Rupert went back across the lake to Kariba. The dosage was plainly not enough. Somehow he would have to obtain more and, he surmised, the hospital seemed his best bet. His drug mission successful, he returned in the late afternoon to Island 174. By now the lioness was fully recovered and had taken out her frustrations on the metal water container. Now it resembled a sieve. Rupert decided to leave her alone for another 12 hours, to ensure no repercussions from the continued drug intake. Again he left the meat out for her companion, this time with 54 grains of phenobarbitone.

The third day of the lioness's confinement dawned. Rupert checked the spoor. Again her companion had visited and had lain near the cage. And had ignored the meat. During the next two days the lioness continued to suffer no effects from the drugs and, eventually, took to scattering the doctored meat outside her cage. The second lioness had left the island during the third night. Rupert followed her tracks across the shallows to the mainland. Now that their prisoner would not eat any treated meat, Rupert switched his approach. He would have to inject the lioness with immobilizing drugs. But somehow he would have to first restrict her movements within the cage so that he could get near her without having his face ripped off. He studied the cage for a while, and the restless, pacing occupant.

It was simple, really. By inserting *mopane* poles through the bar spaces, her area was reduced and, pushing her further back to the end of the cage, where she was eventually unable to turn, Rupert safely injected 10cc's of largactil into her rear end. Then the poles were withdrawn. Five hours later she was drowsy, but exploded into action at the slightest sound. Rupert shook his head. This was becoming monotonous. Six days had gone by since he had first captured the lioness. He sent Peter Moore back to the hospital in Kariba to try and obtain 50 grains of phenobarbitone in liquid form. He returned the next day empty-handed. The hospital could not make it up in liquid form. He had telephoned Headquarters and an aircraft was flying up the following day with the required drugs. That night the second lioness returned from the mainland and prowled around the cage. It was a fleeting visit. At daylight she waded back to the mainland. Again, they penned the lioness up against the bars, on the last day of August.

It was a Saturday. In Salisbury people thronged the rails at Borrowdale Race Course, or dotted the cricket pitches and bowling greens, making their plans for the rest of the weekend. Perfect weather suggested a game of tennis at the club, or drinks around the swimming pool.

On Island 174, Rupert Fothergill gave his lioness an intramuscular injection of 6ccs of acetylpromazine and 43ccs of largactil. An hour and a half later the lioness was asleep, showing no reaction when she was gently prodded. Now time was of the essence. For no-one could accurately predict how long she would remain unconscious. Rupert instructed that the trapdoor be hauled up, and entered the cage. A litter of poles and grain bags had been improvised and was in place at the mouth of the cage. Rupert took care in roping her legs together, for if she came to while being carried, or while on the boat, the bonds would be their only safety factor. Giving everyone the seconds they needed to get away before she broke them.

Four men carried the litter down to the boats. She and Rupert would be towed by the *Sikwasi* in a smaller craft to the shore of the Matusadona Game Reserve. Two hours away. Rupert checked the ropes again. At midday, they carried the still sleeping lioness off the boat and deposited her gently in the shade of a leafy fig tree. Rupert covered her with branches so that she would stay cool when the sun changed direction later in the afternoon. At sundown she was still asleep. Rupert and Peter Moore shared the deck area with the labourers and slept the night near her. At dawn she showed no sign of coming out of her slumber. Rupert checked her pulse and took her temperature. Everything was normal. He grinned wryly, echoing Peter Moore's thoughts. She took long enough to get under, he mused, and when she went she really went deep. She's really keeping us waiting. Typical female!
At midday she opened her eyes. Two hours later she lifted her head and growled when Rupert pulled her tail. Rupert seriously regretted not having had an antidote to inject. It would have been all over by now and he could have had a final search for the other cat. At sundown she was still there. Rupert checked her again. As he got close to her she raised her head and snarled and swivelled upwards onto her brisket, her movements slow and unco-ordinated. But she was improving. Another night aboard the Fisheries Research boat. Tea and stale bread sandwiches with chunks of bully beef and raw onion. Overhead the canopy of blue ink sky was sprinkled with a giant's handful of glittering jewels, blending on the horizon with the hilltop lights of Kariba. A nightjar swooped. From away inland a hyena called. Mosquitoes attacked in formation. Hippos grunted, raucously jovial, nearby.

In the morning she was gone. Rupert traced her spoor down to the edge of the lake where she had drunk. Her claw marks were splayed deep in the mud. Then she had headed inland. The tracks were purposeful, no lurching or weaving. Rupert spoored her for half a mile and returned to the boat. For another four days he tramped the shoreline of Island 174 but found no sign of the other lioness. It appeared that the disturbance and the disappearance of her partner had driven her away for good. Rupert dismantled the trap, loaded the gear aboard the *Sikwasi* and headed back across the lake, as he had done a thousand times before. Island 174 dwindled in their wake, tranquil, timeless.

Kariba. Six weeks later. October now. A merciless sun, leaden heat. Shirts soaked with sweat. Rupert returned with the trap cage. Another capture task had been assigned to the roving warden. It was a different quarry this time. A different island, Sampakaruma, taking its name from a chief whose people had lived in this part of the valley before the flood. An island that was a hilltop. And on it was a leopard which had been there since the lake formed, driving it and baboons and grysbok to the safety of high ground. For a long time the leopard lived well. But, over the years his appetite surpassed the breeding rate of the baboons and small buck, and they became harder to catch as the leopard got older. Now people visiting this island close to the boundary with Zambia had reported seeing a leopard which looked in poor condition, and the word had passed through the Game Department network. Now Rupert had returned to Kariba. In the days ahead even he would find his years of bush experience taxed by the activities of this beautiful predator, who seemed to write its own rules of play.

He had carried out his routine reconnaissance of the island, noting the ubiquitous spoor of the leopard, learning as much from the pug marks as he could. The trap cage had been assembled and nudged up against the newly-constructed pen which, this time, would house a goat as bait. The leopard had not come anywhere near the trap during the first test night. The next afternoon Rupert installed the goat and returned to the Game Department base on Peter's Point. So far so good. He was reasonably certain that the following day would see the hungry leopard trapped in the heavy, steel-barred cage. The goat had been bleating continuously when he had left and the spotted cat was bound to investigate. The roving warden was entirely correct in his summing up of the situation. The leopard did just that. And then it escaped.

Rupert could not believe it. He studied the telltale spoor in and around the trap. The goat had stopped bleating and now dozed in a corner of the pen. The leopard had entered the cage, in the normal required fashion. And, in the normal required fashion, the release mechanism had been triggered and the heavy steel door had crashed down. And there was one trapped leopard, which had then got away. Rupert could see how the animal had done it, and marvelled at the leopard's strength. Something like 120 pounds of cat had forced open enough gap in the door to crawl out. To pull the door up needed a concerted effort by two full-grown men. Between the bottom of the door and the cage floor was a three-inch gap, especially constructed like that so that an animal's tail would not be crushed when the door came slam-banging down. The leopard, by all accounts no longer in its prime, and undernourished, had forced its paws into the gap and patiently, determinedly, inched the door upwards and somehow manoeuvred itself safely beneath it, to disappear amongst the scrub and rocks of the island. Doubting very much that the leopard would revisit the trap, Rupert reset the trap door, this time manhandling a large, heavy rock close to it. Then he and the game scouts lifted and wired the rock on to the steel mesh of the door. It was an arduous, time-consuming task, made more so in Rupert's mind as he had little hope that the cat would return. The capture team returned to Kariba.

Rupert seldom swore aloud, but the next morning he muttered several invectives as he surveyed the trap site. The leopard *had* returned. And had been trapped. And had escaped, *again*. And again it had forced its way out through the same gap. To add insult to injury, the leopard had then pulled all the brushwood away from one side of the pen and had managed to maul the goat through the four-inch-spaced *mopane* poles. Half the goat's face had been torn off. It was still alive and Rupert had to put it out of its misery. Then he entered the cage and had the scouts release the door. It crashed down. Rupert braced himself in the best position and began to lift the door. He could lift it no higher than 14 inches. Okay, he thought, that's twice. Third time lucky. And this time we'll really make it difficult.

Two hours later, a larger, heavier rock was secured to the trapdoor and the bottom of the door was heavily wired with mesh. The pen was painstakingly re-covered with the sharpest thornscrub, and rocks were piled on the roof. The goat carcass had been secured so that the mauled, bloody head protruded through the back bars of the cage. Finally, Rupert was satisfied that the preparations had been sufficiently thorough, and they departed.

It was a case of third time lucky. For the leopard. After it entered the cage, the door had slammed earthwards. And had jammed halfway. The leopard had consumed the head and neck of the goat at its leisure and had departed under the half-closed door. They reset the trap, adjusting it so the door would not jam again. The following day they were greeted by the sealed trap cage. It was mockingly empty. A gusty, bullying wind had sprung up during the night and the vibrations of the door had slipped the release catch. Outside the entrance was a large hole where the leopard had attempted to dig its way *into* the trap. A slow grin crossing Rupert's face gave way to a chuckle. This was quite ridiculous, he thought. Four times the trap has been set, and four times the damned cat has stood right where he was standing and worked out the ins and outs of the situation. And it was still out there. Playing games with him. Well, round five coming up. And it must be very hungry. It had only been able to have a snack off the goat so far, so by evening it would be keen. It remained to be seen if Houdini's luck would hold!

The leopard was there, caught, the next morning. But only just. It was very thin and in poor condition and had managed to squeeze itself through the six-inch spacing of the bars at the end of the cage and into the bait pen, where it had consumed the rest of the goat. When Rupert arrived, it was busy trying to dig itself out of the pen. There was no hissing, snarling paroxysm of fury when the humans appeared. Unlike the lioness, the leopard just ceased its digging and crouched silently, unblinking yellow gaze fixed unwaveringly on the men outside. Looking at its condition, Rupert found it even harder to accept that it had forced its way beneath the

The Sengwa rhino capture operations, 1964 and 1965: Rupert loading drug into darts.
PHOTO COURTESY MRS G. KNIGHT

"...with her great head stuck into a thick jesse bush." — *Page 202*

PHOTO COURTESY MRS G. KNIGHT

"...crated and belligerent atop the lorry negotiating some of the roughest terrain in the country..." — *Page 192*

PHOTO COURTESY MRS G. KNIGHT

Horn meets nose: taking measurements.
PHOTO COURTESY MRS G. KNIGHT

The string of the crossbow tended to snag on every bit of bush.
PHOTO COURTESY MRS G. KNIGHT

A drugged rhino about to be hauled on to a sledge.

PHOTO COURTESY MRS G. KNIGHT

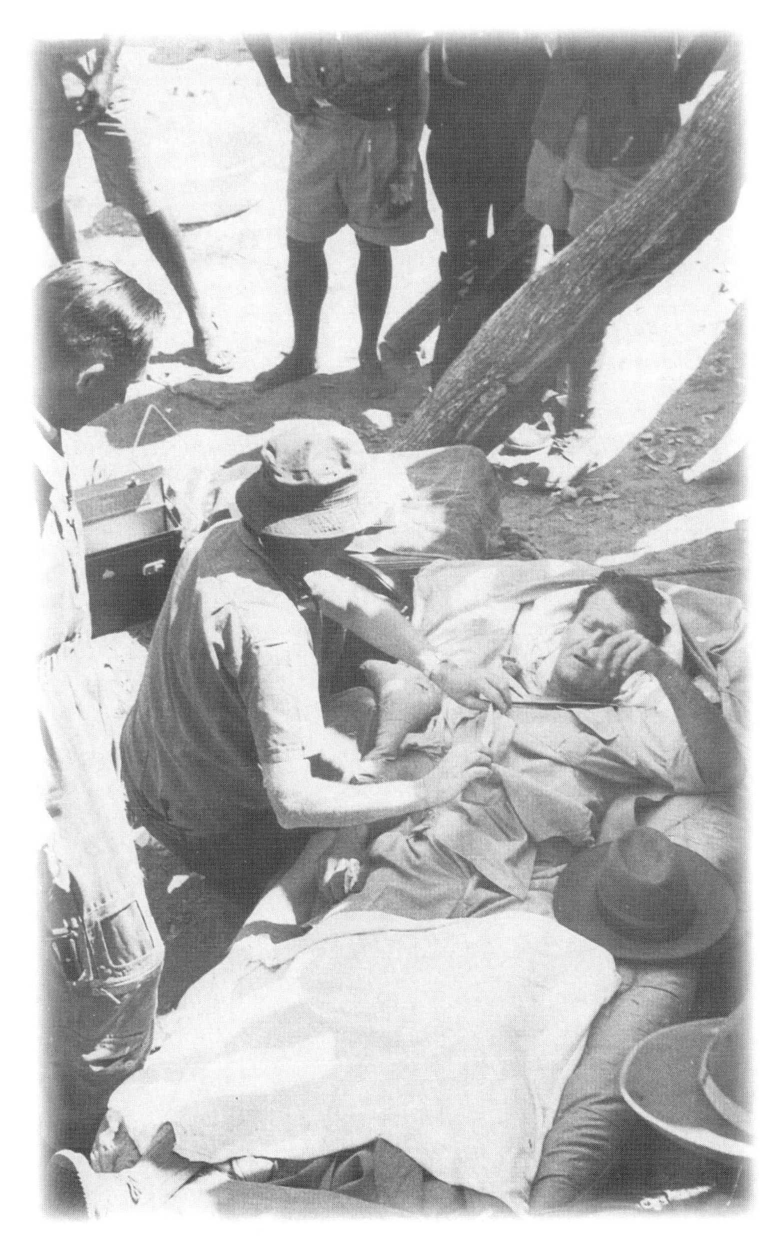

"…gored eventually, maybe predictably." — Page 206. Rupert in the shade of a rhino pen being tended by Dr Laidler.

PHOTO COURTESY MRS G. KNIGHT

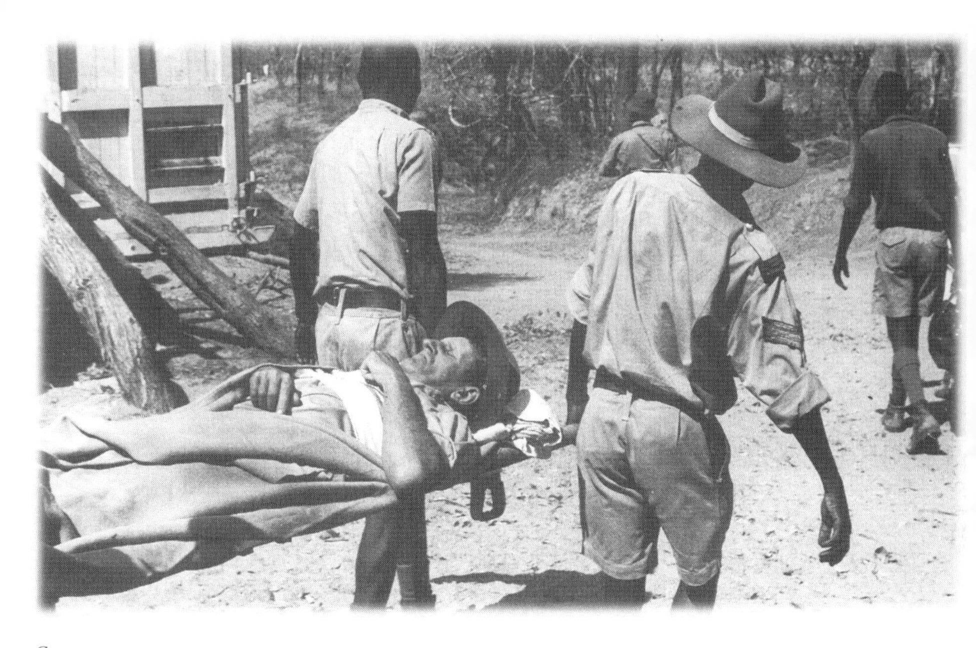

Casevac.

PHOTO COURTESY MRS G. KNIGHT

Bush hat and boots.

PHOTO COURTESY MRS G. KNIGHT

Rupert in Binga, October 1965, two months after his near-fatal goring.
PHOTO: I. FINDLAY

sheathed raking claws reached between the bars..." — Page 218

TO: P. MOORE

Rupert with trapped lioness.

PHOTO: P. MOORE

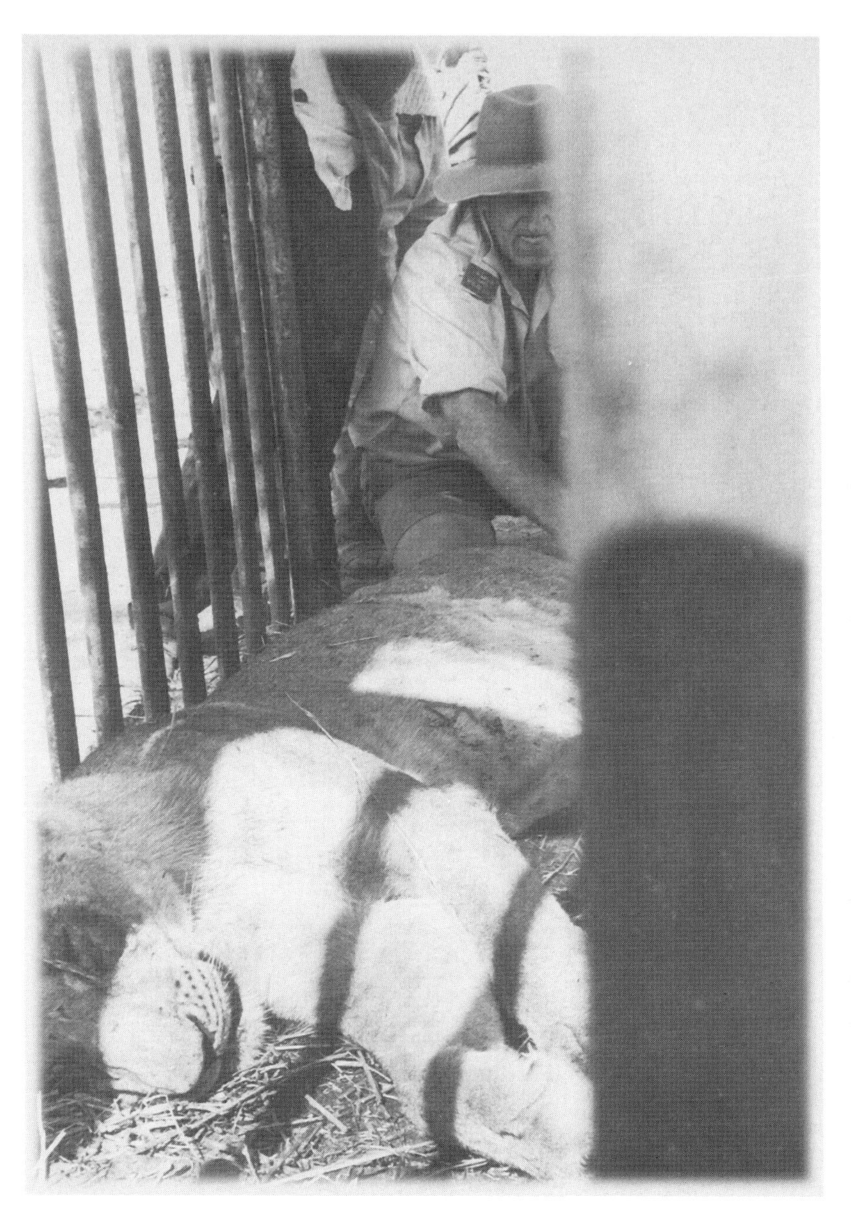

"Rupert took care in roping her legs together..." — Page 220

PHOTO: P. MOORE

Mana Pools revisted, 1969, Rupert and his team, which included Clem and Paul Coetsee, the late Robin Hughes and Tim Paulet, planning a capture exercise.

PHOTO: H KENYON

"Men and impala weaved and bobbed to and fro, a maelstrom of flickering, half-seen bodies." — Page 231

PHOTO: H. KENYON

A haggard Rupert with Paul Coetsee. He would find out only some time later, back in Salisbury, that he had suffered a heart attack.

PHOTO: H. KENYON

This simple steel plaque is cemented into a small rock overhang in the first folds of the escarpment overlook the Sengwa basin.

PHOTO: K. MEADOWS

trapdoor. He lost no time in blocking off the entrance to the pen with poles and having the cage turned around so that the trapdoor faced the blocked entrance. Then poles and trapdoor were unlimbered and the leopard was chivvied through into the cage. Only now did it growl. A low, ominous, grating sound.

Wary of the spotted cat's ability to negotiate narrow spaces, Rupert did not accompany it on its journey across to Matusadona. The smaller boat bobbed along behind the *Sampa*, another Fisheries Research vessel, with the leopard braced against the swell. Nudging the shore of the game reserve that had been born from the formation of the new lake, the crew and game rescue team watched as a rope attached to the trapdoor was hauled over a pulley. As the heavy steel barred door lifted, so the last phase of the exercise was completed. The leopard was free to go. It did not have to force its way out of the cage this time. The mainland, the wilderness of Matusadona, was a few yards away. The prison of the island was gone. The leopard slipped out of the cage and stood silhouetted against the water. Rupert waited for it to leap on to the bank. Instead, it disappeared beneath the prow of the boat. Rupert ordered the skipper of the Sampa to drift the launch closer to the dinghy. Sundown was an hour away. Pebbles and clods of earth tossed into the boat brought no reaction. Rupert sighed. It looked like another night sleeping on the lake ...

CHAPTER 16

RETURN TO MANA POOLS

The feeling of Mana is felt long before one actually reaches the place. The spell of this wilderness starts to tug long before one is down on the expanse of floodplain encountering the plethora of wild animals amongst the cooling patches of shade offered by hundreds of scattered evergreens. Before even the Rukomechi River, the western boundary, is crossed, clearly identified from the air during the first months of the year by the broad swathes of ghostly pale *Acacia albidas* which follow its meandering course. Before the traveller encounters the thick *mopane* scrub and woodland whilst traversing the Nyakasanga Controlled Hunting Area. Up on the escarpment at the neat stone and thatch administration centre of

Marongora, where there used to be the single magnificent mounted tusk, weighing 116 pounds, the first tickle of excitement and anticipation causes any wilderness lover, who has heard of Mana Pools, to instinctively try and hurry the sometimes brief bout of required paperwork that is encountered at all the country's sanctuaries. And then the layby, further down the escarpment, on the right of the main road, with its signboard

ZAMBEZI VALLEY ESCARPMENT
ALTITUDE: 764 METRES ABOVE SEA LEVEL

tells the traveller that he is just about there. In the Zambezi Valley. And the panorama which greets him, stretching further than the eye can see, a grey-green ocean of bush, never- ending, is testimony to that. Down there is Mana Pools, on the great Zambezi River, and now it is only a couple of hours' drive away.

On the first day of May, 1969, Rupert and the Coetsee brothers paused there briefly, as was Rupert's habit, on their way down to this valley paradise. Since his first visit to Mana Pools in 1936, Rupert had habitually stopped at this point of the twisting, snake-backed route down onto the valley floor and had taken time to reflect on the grandeur of the view. To give it a few moments of silent homage. On this trip he looked out over the wilderness with mixed feelings. Ahead lay many weeks of hard work. This was not a problem. Hard work was no stranger. In the coming weeks he was to head an exercise in conjunction with warden Paul Coetsee which would have to remove 3 000 impala. Remove by capturing and, when and if this process proved too slow, by culling. In addition he would be involved, for the first time since its innovation two years earlier, in the culling of complete herd units of elephants. This latter task was an experience he had so far managed to avoid. Now it had caught up with him. It was the opinion of the Government's research department that both species of animal had become overpopulated in the area and thus needed 'managing'. Rupert wondered about that now, as he took a last look across the valley. The game had managed itself quite well so far, without the heavy human hand of interference. Had conditions changed that much down there? He had not thought so, on his last visit. The Mana area was vastly different to Wankie National Park and its inherent concentration problems. The coming trip, despite being in an area he dearly loved, was not something he looked forward to. In fact, ruminated the ageing game warden, it was not even getting off to a good start. Not with the report they have to check on that day.

For, via the bush telegraph, that indefinable amalgam of rumour and whisper whose tendrils of information spread with the speed of a bushfire with the wind behind it, word had come of a killed rhino. The animal had been shot by a member of the security forces operating out of a base near the Sapi River. Rupert and his companions had a map reference where the incident was believed to have taken place. They were on their way there now, to search the area. To find and inspect the carcass, and study the spoor pattern which could tell them exactly what had happened, what had been the reason for someone to kill a rhino like that, apparently out of hand? It was not, Rupert thought again, a good way to start a new job.

They did not find anything in the area of the grid reference they had been given. On the way back to the Mana Pools base they stopped at the army camp and enquired about the story of the rhino killing. Contrary to what Rupert had anticipated, one of the officers readily agreed that a fellow officer had indeed shot a rhino. The poor animal, he said, was sick; dragging a back leg which was full of suppurating sores. Rupert nodded. Did the animal have any evidence of being snared? Did it charge? Was it vitally necessary to shoot it? Why weren't the Game Department people up on the escarpment notified? The officer concerned was out of camp at present, was the reply. Rupert nodded some more, and made arrangements for Clem Coetsee to meet the officer concerned the next morning. And see the remains of the rhino. It was just the first day, he reflected soberly. They had not started yet. With the impala and the elephants ...

* * * * * * * * * * *

The eyes reflected yellowy orange and then glinted green in the beam of the night lamps as the impala turned its head. From the back of the open Land Rover, the young cadet ranger operating the lamp swivelled the light, catching the reflections of the rest of the herd, and their pale, two-tone tan-coloured forms fidgeted and stared back at the mesmerising orb of glare. Clem Coetsee edged the Land Rover closer, keeping the engine sound down, approaching the herd of some 50 antelope in a deceptive, oblique, curving pattern. The lamp stayed on the animals, flicking over them, hypnotising, holding them there. Behind the first vehicle two other Land Rovers followed, each beaming out its pinning, hypnotic light. In each vehicle were two or three wardens or rangers and eight game scouts. They were close now, Clem Coetsee's vehicle no more than 15 paces from the impala. The capture teams braced themselves for the chase. Any closer and the animals might break out of their trance and panic and scatter. This was the fifth night in a row they had been out on capture and already there were signs that the impala were becoming wise to the meaning of those dazzling big eyes in the dark. It had taken much longer this time to work in close to the animals.

So far they had captured 60 impala, with four dying from shock and injuries sustained in the mad, hell-for-leather scrambles during the capture exercises, as they hurtled through the night with the beams of light stabbing through the blackness. The bizarre scene resembled some artist's latest surrealistic canvas, with men and impala appearing and disappearing amidst the rays of light. The pounding of hooves blended with the gasps and grunts of the men as they chased pell-mell through inky blackness, doubly blind after a brief interlude in one of the beams of light, and colliding with trees, each other, clumps of bush, falling, tripping over trees pushed over by elephants. And these were the least of their problems, these innate natural obstacles. There were other animals, many other animals, here on the Mana floodplain. There were other species of antelope, elephants, rhinos, and the predators. Each night had brought its share of adrenalin-pumping incidents. For, in attendance with most of the herds of impala were the lions, leopards and packs of hyenas. Darkness brought the time of the hunt and the men had come face to face with all of the predators on one night or another. A pride of 12 lions during one night, with cubs ... and protective mothers. A leopard during another night, disturbed in its stalk of the impala caught in the beams of their night lamps. And the previous night there had been four hyenas loping along amidst the frenzy of the capture, homing in on one impala ewe and bringing her down amidst a snarling, teeth-snapping, bleating death flurry of dancing shadows. Now, on this night, as the men keyed themselves up to leap from the Land Rovers, each wondered what extra excitement lay in store for him.

For long moments all was still. Land Rovers were quietly stopped. Men were ready, waiting for the night's lead man to go. Impala stood frozen by the lamps. Tonight Paul Coetsee led the chase, bursting from the back of the lead vehicle, the powerful beam momentarily catching the back of his head in mid leap. Then he was on the ground, and everyone was there as well, leaping, running, dodging fallen trees and stumps, their shadows running black ahead of them, grotesque, liquid silent. And the impala were starting to react, starting to scramble away, spell almost broken, the first tentative leaps of alarm, escaping. But the dazzling, mind-puzzling, mesmerising beams of light still played over them. The giant orbs still glared down at them from up on the vehicles, and their reactions were stilted, stumbling. Then the capture team was in amongst the herd and already some of the animals had been caught. Now the man smell was strong, drowning the metal petrol smell of the vehicles, and the panic surged. And the impala broke away, ran, leaped high, kicked and stabbed with their lyre-shaped horns, and their shadows leaped with them, black spirits drifting amongst the beams of dust-blurred light. Men and impala weaved and bobbed to and fro, a maelstrom of flickering, half seen bodies. Men who had caught animals in the initial charge and carried them kicking, struggling, eyes rolling, to the care teams waiting by the vehicles, now returned to the fray. One man was down, thrashing on the ground. Rupert, pounding after a young ram, stopped and knelt by the game scout. Blood gleamed wetly crimson in the darting light. The man moaned, clutching his knee. It was Langton. He had tripped over a *mopane* tree stump and the jagged end had ripped deep into his knee. Rupert carried his long-time companion back to the vehicles, laying him in the beam of the headlights.

Out in the darkness and kaleidoscope of search lights the men continued to chase after impala. There were several lying at the feet of their warders by the vehicles, soothing, clucking noises and gentle hands calming the fearful animals. The remaining men were further away from the Land Rovers now, chasing, running, heedless of anything but the now scattered impala herd. Then. *Lion*! And they were heading back for the vehicles, running very fast for the shelter of the Land Rovers and the covering rifles. Paul Coetsee came in last, staring back over his shoulder into the darkness. Someone aimed a lamp over him and there they were. Two lionesses. One standing, the other still crouched, tail thrashing. He reached the vehicles, only slightly breathless. It had been close. He had seen them, glimpsed them, at the last moment. Flattened out in the grass. Scant yards away. Angry. Frustrated. Disturbed in the middle of their stalk of the impala.

They moved on to a quieter area. To another herd. In all that night they caught 17 impala, returning to camp close to midnight. Seventeen impala, one badly injured game scout, and a near miss for Warden Coetsee with the lions. That now made a total of 73 animals captured. It was going to be slow work, this night capture. And, sooner or later, someone was going to get hurt, when they grabbed a lion or leopard by mistake.

Rupert was not happy. He could not see any successful way of capturing the impala being developed. Not with the number Salisbury was talking about. As yet, the bomas of plastic sheeting, light, relatively cheap and easy to handle, had not evolved. It would happen years later. Rupert still had 3 000 impala, minus 73, to capture. And to cull. That fact alone gnawed at him. Quite apart from the crazy night-time antics they were presently involved with. Netting would have to be attempted, he thought. Though with 140 yards of nets, compliments of Wankie, they were not going to achieve much. But they would try. Try netting at night, after a few practice runs in daylight. Hopefully it would be better than running around like bloody mad things and bumping into lions and whatever else was hidden in the grass.

Night-time netting was not, as he had expected, successful. Now the herds of impala were alert and wary of the lights which approached through the darkness. And there weren't enough nets. Over several more nights they tried various ways of outwitting the impala herds. To no avail. They would have to get more nets and then attempt to drive the animals into the enclosures in daylight, without the hindrance of darkness. In the meantime, Rupert acquired another 400 yard of nets - confiscated from the villagers living further inland, who used them for trapping. They were made of baobab bark, braided and entwined, and much of it was rotten. It was better than nothing. Rupert and his team set about a new plan of action. They built bush fences in carefully selected areas, guide fences of natural grass and poles, which would help channel the driven animals into the circles of netting. And they rebuilt the holding pens at their base camp, replacing the pigwire and thatched grass with rows of mopane poles. Too many of the penned impala were breaking horns and damaging themselves in the pigwire. Rupert wondered whose idea that had been. Some livewire from H.Q., he surmised sourly. Headquarters were not his favourite people at the moment. Not with their target of 3 000 impala, to be caught and culled. And the elephants ... Already many of the captured impala had been transported up out of the Valley by various farmers keen to establish these beautiful, graceful antelope on their farms and ranches. More bush fences were built and sites selected for new netting operations.

The first day scheduled for daylight netting dawned. The crimson ball of the sun climbed from beneath the wide, meandering blueness of the Zambezi, into a cloudless sky. The teams set out early, searching for suitably close herds to drive into the fenced channels and thence into the nets. It was a time of more frustration and disappointment, more failure. The game men were herding a large group of impala steadily towards the grass hedged 'funnel' when the wind changed. Blowing the feared man scent off the nets back into their nostrils. And that was it. No go! Pandemonium! The animals had that hated smell all around them now and they broke. Leaping, bounding, exploding away, high graceful arcs of impala escaping. And so it went. The daylight captures, petering out into failures. The night capture exercises, later and further afield every night, with fewer animals being caught. They needed, by Rupert's reckoning, a good 2 000 yards of netting, and at least another 80 men to act as beaters and to cover more ground during capture work. Three weeks now they had been down at Mana. They had caught 99 impala. Ninety nine impala, each one caught by hand, run down, chased, in the black night hours, with the wavering, stabbing beams of light. But it was too slow, far too slow, this process. In the daily radio schedules with Headquarters there came a strong hint of impatience. The culling would have to start. Soon. With the capture relegated to secondary importance, interspersed amongst the cropping. Culling and capture at the same time, mused Rupert. It did not make for a very successful combination.

Blackness. Night lamps. Eyes reflecting. Shooting. The sickly-sweet smell of freshly spilled blood. Forty-five impala the first night, the night of 21 May. Eighty the next night. The sound of the shotguns echoed through the night silence of the bush and rolled back from the sides of the distant escarpment. Carnage. SSG and AAA shotgun rounds did not always kill adult rams, outright, especially in the flickering, bobbing beams of the lamps. This left the axe work, the *coup de grâce*, to be carried out. Then there was more blood. Rupert hated it. He thought the whole exercise was a disaster, that Research and Headquarters were totally wrong in their approach to this task. How was he supposed to hand-capture a respectable number of impala? And how was he supposed to net them, netting being the only way, Noah had proved that, with a few hundred yards of nets, and all of 20 labourers? And using shotguns! Shotguns, to kill 3 000 impala!

Now they were also hunting elephants . And that was not turning out too well either. It was too early in the year. Too close to the rains. There was still plenty of water on the surface. Too many scattered waterholes and pans and small seasonal rivers. And the elephants were scattered as well. Only a few small bachelor gatherings down at the paradise of Mana Pools. Which was now, for a while, becoming a part of hell. In the dry months, October especially, there were hundreds of elephants. If culling had been deemed essential, that would have been the time for it. Particularly with the new method, the extermination of an entire herd. So the panic did not spread to the other elephants who lived down here in this stretch of valley. Now, in May and June, it was difficult to locate elephants in a suitable culling area, where they could be certain of destroying every beast. There were no spotter planes in use, apart from some assistance from a locally-based military aircraft. Every stalk ended up in a thick, impenetrable maze of *jesse* bush which dotted the area. And that would be it! . Without aerial spotting, there could be no certainty of getting every elephant. So, back to camp, to get ready for the impala culling, or capture, that night. They were very long days. And they were not very happy days.

In the last week of May they managed to cull 13 elephants, a group of four and a group of nine. By the end of July a total of 60 had been culled. It was a far cry from the forced elephant population reductions of today in the game sanctuaries where four figure numbers are taken off in one, several-week-long exercise, because the game reserves, or national parks, or sanctuaries, cannot cope with the increased animal populations, compressed into them by the outside pressures of human progress. Humans breed and breed, unchecked. Wild animals breed, and have to be 'managed'. Culled.

For another week, Rupert and his men concentrated on developing a successful capture technique. He, and the Coetsee brothers, Clem and Paul, Dave Scammel, Robin Hughes, Tim Paulet and the other younger rangers worked long, long hours. But they had too little resources to do too much. Not enough men, not enough nets, although now they had been sent an extra 1 000 yards of hessian, and not enough time. Their most successful netting operation cornered 20 impala. And two zebra stallions. Which made short work of the fragile baobab twine nets, smashing easily through, with most of the impala following. They captured eight impala that night. Five another night. Sixteen on their last capture attempt. One hundred and thirty impala, altogether, captured and transported to other areas.

Then the culling started. Every night. Out in the Land Rovers. The night lamps meant death now. Not capture. It seemed endless. One hundred and twenty four one night. 118. 191. 155. One hundred and seventy seven dead impala another night. On and on. The commercial company which had contracted to collect the carcasses, by refrigerated vehicle, for sale in Salisbury, was making daily runs down into the valley: the slaughter run. During the day there were the elephants. In one climactic 24-hour period, during the dark hours of a Sunday night, 22 June, 121 impala were culled, followed the next morning by 15 elephants. Rupert was sickened and he did not know if he could handle it for much longer. A visit to the area by the Director sparked him into drafting a ten-page report on the situation.

The Director
Nat. Parks and Wild Life
Mana Pools Game Reserve
Observations and comments
1.The figure of 3 000 impala to be culled is too drastic a knock to the impala population in this area.
2.Has the Research Dept. taken into consideration when settling for this figure of 3 000, the numbers which are accounted for over a period of a year, by the predators? i.e. Lions, leopards, hyenas, wild dogs, jackals etc During the course of the culling and capture work, the lions, leopards, hyenas have been seen alongside the impala herds. The hyenas hunted in

packs from three to four. A hyena was observed chasing a doe impala. Three freshly killed impala carcasses and a pack of wild dogs was seen near one of our netting sites ... If 3 000 are culled, does this not create a food problem for the predators? The danger is that the few impala which remain, are going to have a tough time rearing their calves; the predators will see to this. The increase in population may take years!

Vegetation

The valley has had a good rainy season; approximately 39". There is no starvation problem here, this year there is more than ample food for the various species of antelope.

Flood Plains

I have visited the Mana Pools area in 1936, 37, 38; 1953, 54 and 56, and I cannot see any marked or obvious change in the scenery ... Damage to Acacia trees by elephants, is not obvious or extensive, what damage can be seen, such as bark in patches ripped on the odd tree and which has not killed the tree I would say is normal and to be expected where elephants are resident ... One reason given to me here, for culling impala, is because pockets of shrub on the plains is desirable; the idea is fine, but the danger is a take over by the shrubs, eventually finishing up like a miniature jesse bush, a grass flood plain is a far better proposition than a tangled mass of undergrowth ...

Impala Capture

The hand catching method of capturing impala is out, it is not a success, if large numbers are required. Initially a few animals are caught, then they become wise to the spotlights. The hazards to the men doing the catching are numerous ...

Some of the casualties to members of the team

1.Game scout: mopane stump in knee and head injuries.
2.Game scout: deep split between thumb and finger.
3.Research officer: bad fall off Land Rover. Head injuries and jaw.
4.Ranger: fractured collar bone.
5.Warden: injured collar bone.
6.Warden: nearly grabbed a lioness instead of an impala.

<u>Netting</u>

This would be the most efficient method of capture ... Unfortunately this would require a lot of equipment; 2 000 yards of nets and 4 000 yds of hessian, which we do not possess ... Capture and culling just do not go together, it must be one or the other; the shooting disturbs and scatters the animals; they move out of the area. A lot of patience is required; which is lacking here ...

<u>Culling of Elephant</u>

This has been badly timed: October would be the best month. There is a scarcity of elephants at this time of the year in Mana Pools ... end up in the jesse Bush, where it is impossible to destroy the whole herd.

<u>Mana Pools Game Reserve</u>

The shooting of rations for the Mana Pools Game Reserve compound, should be done on the borders of the reserve, and not in the vicinity of the pools area. All the old tame buffalo bulls seem to have disappeared, and the numbers of animals shot for compound rations appears to be excessive!

* * * * * * * * * * *

Rupert sat on the trunk of a *mopane* tree which had been pushed over by elephants, and enjoyed the warmth of the sun. Soon he would take his jersey off but now, a little after eight in the morning, the chill of a winter night in the valley was still there. The Land Rover was parked beneath a fine, leafy evergreen *Trichelia emetica*, the immense patch of dark shade almost cathedral-like. Langton was collecting some twigs to start a small fire for tea. It was very quiet. A yellow-billed hornbill sailed over him in its characteristic front-heavy flight. Amongst the mahoganies and sausage trees a troop of baboons foraged, also enjoying the warmth. Further away, impala and waterbuck were grazing, the sunlight catching the moisture on their coats from the dew-laden grass in minute, flashing crystals. The escarpment was clear in the washed atmosphere of a new day. He had left camp early, at sunup. He craved some peace and quiet. Away from the responsibilities and hubbub of the base. Away from the killing. Away from the routine visitations of the refrigerated trucks and their cargo. And so he had left it behind and headed inland, towards the escarpment, to Ketepa Springs. He had been here before, in the past, often. And always he had seen rhinos here. It was especially good rhino country. This morning he had checked the spoor around the waterhole and their tracks were plentiful. And so he thought he would spend the rest of the day here and unwind. Drink lots of tea. Smoke too many cigarettes. He felt very old on this day. A low hiss from Langton made him cast his glance across the springs. There, a way off still, a large bull rhino was ambling through the mosaic of shade-splashed sunlight. Heading towards the water. Rupert watched the animal fondly.

For the last three days of June, Rupert stayed in camp. He felt under the weather. The teams went out at night without him; and during the day, after the elephants, without him. The craggy features of the game warden turned to haggardness and his usual easy nature changed to tight-lipped grimness. The rest of the team eyed him anxiously, dubiously. He had never been known to be out of the running for very long. Three days was a record. Then his demeanour improved and he returned to be almost the man they knew. Two days later he was amongst them fighting a bushfire which was threatening to sweep the length of the plains. On 8 July 1969, the culling quota was reached and the killing stopped. The winding down process began. Another operation finished. An operation he hated.

It was only two weeks later that he discovered, visiting his doctor under protest, that he had suffered a serious heart attack. Brought on, undoubtedly, said his doctor, by the long days and rigours of the Mana exercise. Rupert was non-committal. It was a good enough reason, he reflected to himself. That, and the killing.

CHAPTER 17

BACKWATERS

Operation Warthog, covering a two week period in August 1970 was a far cry from Noah and the two Sengwa rhino capture exercises. Nevertheless, it offered a change from the routine tasks which, these days, seemed to eat up most of Rupert's time. A respite from the control duties and the removing of the increasing obstacles in the way of progress and development. There were waiting lists now, of farmers wanting someone from the Game Department to come out and destroy troops of crop-raiding baboons and monkeys, jackals suspected of being rabid, quelea flocks devouring the wheat crops, and the lions, leopards, hyenas and crocodiles taking their toll of livestock. Scattered amongst these tasks belonging to the roving warden were the poaching investigations and the fish poisoning investigations and the inspections of the hide and leather merchants' operations around the country. All in all his tasks seldom strayed from the routine duties which, it appeared, would occupy his time until his retirement. Rupert's spirits would lift when a specific problem was dumped in his lap only after farmers or other departmental personnel had failed to solve it. Like the leopard in the Mtoko area which evaded all efforts to destroy it during its depredations of the cattle. Though Rupert, with his trap cage and goat bait, failed to catch it, he succeeded in worrying it enough so that it departed from the area. There was also the lone hyena in the Inyanga district, which was very well educated in the way of gin traps and poison and shooting platforms and, which, single-handedly, caused stock losses valued at £1 880 on two farms alone, before Rupert came along and sorted out its cattle-killing habits.

But these challenges were few and far between now, and the only factor emerging from the mundane control duties which particularly pleased Rupert was that at least he was still out in the field. Still able to traverse the country and keep out of the mainstream of civilisation. Keep out of the way of the 'coke and buns' brigade! Still able to enjoy the sound of the rain on a canvas tent. Still able to enjoy the sound of roosting francolin and guinea fowl at sunset. And still able to pitch his camp, sometimes, in areas where he could listen to a hyena serenade, or the sawing rasp of a leopard on its nocturnal wandering, or the throat rumble of contented, feeding elephants. City life, headquarters, with its accompanying suffocating mantle of officialdom, was still anathema to him. A short, terse letter, sealed and marked 'Confidential', delivered to his desk during one of his brief spells in Salisbury summed it all up as far as Rupert was concerned. It was from his regional warden:

Warden Fothergill.

Dress Orders

It has been reported to me that you were out in the streets in Salisbury this morning, 28 June 1971, in uniform, but wearing no headgear. You will therefore submit a written explanation to me for your complete disregard of Circular 29/70, which reflects badly on yourself, me as your regional warden as well as the department as a whole.

Operation Warthog took Rupert back to the area of the Sengwa River, not at its wide convoluted junction with Lake Kariba but further inland, close to the narrow causeway which spans the Sengwa Gorge, surely one of the most economical construction tasks ever undertaken in the country, with some four yards of concrete bridging the deep water-sculpted gorge far below. Five and a half hours' bush track travel from the conglomeration of buildings that is Gokwe, by five-ton green Game Department truck to the Sengwa Research camp.

Over a period of two weeks, Rupert made three trips cross country to the Kyle Game Reserve, introducing a new warthog population to the area. Thirty one warthogs were trapped and hauled from their antbear hole havens and were penned and crated and translocated. This time there was no bright-eyed, brown mongrel barking its capture instructions. In place of Crackers were the personnel of a much-expanded Game Department and Rupert had little more to do than nursemaid his charges across into a new breeding area.

* * * * * * * * * *

In July 1972 he retired from the Department of National Parks and Wildlife Management. The lean, rugged 60-year-old Game Department veteran still made an imposing figure among the people gathered for the farewell presentation downstairs at the Salisbury Civil Service Club. His wife still retained her typical English country looks; and her laugh was as infectious as ever. The farewell gifts of a silver tea service and a framed copper firescreen would be a welcome addition in the house at the end of the shady, tree-lined avenue. The new surf rod would be an equally welcome addition to Rupert's fishing gear; already he had plans for embarking on another fishing expedition, to the wild, remote, beautiful coastline of Portuguese East Africa.

The fishing and prospecting trips would become the highlights of his retirement years, brief respites away from the claustrophobia of suburbia and part-time ivory weighing duties and other trivial tasks he sometimes carried out for his past employers. There were no pets or other orphans of the bush now, at his house amidst the leafy, shady trees. Apart from the parrots and the guinea fowl. He was proud of his collection of wild parrots, which both occupied his aviary and roamed at will over his garden, and the chirring cackle of guinea fowl echoed comfortingly from the bottom of his garden in the mornings. Over the fireplace a David Shepherd print of a herd of elephant vied for pride of place with a mounted tiger's head for which he had exchanged an alligator's head, in some obscure transaction during years gone by.

There is little doubt that without his drive, devotion to duty and heavy personal involvement, Operation Noah would not have been the great success that it was, and it was largely due to his efforts that Rhodesia earned its proud game conservation status which it now bears among even the most ordinary citizens overseas. It is no exaggeration to say that his work on this operation made his name a legend both at home and abroad. Because of the reputation he built up, Rhodesia has had a fine ambassador in the realisation of its policy of public education of the value of wildlife to the nation. His personality and presence have been of great value in the giving of talks, film shows and other means of propaganda among bodies such as schools, conservation associations and similar organisations.

The cause of wildlife conservation will be poorer by the loss of this quiet, unassuming but dedicated supporter and worker, in achieving its aims and objectives.

This was part of a press release signed on behalf of the Director of Rupert's Department ...

FLASHBACK. Kariba, November 1960. A storm-lashed, black night. Lightning. Forked. Jagged. Splitting the sky apart in its blue-white, crackling hiss to the ground. Thunder. Heavy artillery cracks. Reverberating off the escarpment and booming back over the lake. The inland sea of this new Kariba Lake convulsed and foamed, whipped and lashed by the gale-force winds. Later, the storm would be acknowledged as being the worst since the lake had begun to form, a year ago. Two rainy seasons ago. The full force of the storm hit Mike van Rooyen as he cleared the protecting bulk of Cementation Point and the small green Game Department boat, the *Warthog*, tossed and pitched on the swirling, rushing water. In the storm-blackened night he aimed the prow at where he estimated Long Island should be, over five miles away, squinting against the stinging, driving rain. In the lightning flashes he searched the churning waves ahead for half-submerged trees and, prematurely, he knew, for the bulk of the island. Looking back, a few faint twinkles of light were all that denoted the centre of Kariba, hazy and obscure in the pouring rain. For the umpteenth time he regretted being out here in the filthy weather and considered turning back. But Rupert's instructions echoed through his brain. *Make sure you get back tonight. We've got a busy day tomorrow.* And the rescue leader's instructions were not easily disobeyed. Earlier, Mike van Rooyen had ferried Archie Fraser across to Kariba after one of his visits to the game rescue operation. At the Kariba base he had snatched a quick drink with Boyd Reese and then, with the monthly pay for the men, mail, and some supplies, had set off back to the temporary base on Long Island. It was only when he had hit open water that he realised just how bad the storm was.

Mike van Rooyen was unashamedly frightened. The storm was getting worse. The waves were getting bigger. The bottom of the boat was awash. And the throttle of the outboard motor, always contrary, puttered and gurgled as if on the verge of giving up the ghost. The ranger concentrated on tacking as best he could into the maelstrom of the storm-thrashed waves. More water cascaded into the boat. Letters and paper money floated and eddied around his feet. He removed his bush hat and tried to bale some of the water out, simultaneously imploring God to get him out of this mess. Get him out of this floundering, sputtering little boat and allow him to reach dry land. Any land. Any small piece of a haven of dry land. The storm raged on. Mike alternatively baled and nursed the outboard. There seemed to be no response to his prayers. Desperately, he searched for a tree. Any one of the thousands of half-submerged trees which jutted up out of this new lake. In the glare of the lightning bolts a bare, treeless expanse of white water mocked him. Come on, he intoned, if there's no land to be had I'll settle for a tree. Just one tree to hang on to. Any kind of tree. I'll be good forever after, I promise. But there was only the rain and the thunder and the lightning, and the waves smashing over the boat.

He realised that the petrol drum was afloat, swirling around the bottom of the boat, kept near him only by its connecting tube to the motor. Another wave cascaded over him and he saw several pound notes go with it. Heart in his mouth, he shook the tank. It was very light. Almost empty. He nearly sobbed. How on earth was he going to refill the tank from the spare jerrycan, on his own, aboard the tossing, pitching water-filled *Warthog*? The boat was sluggish now, responding reluctantly to his touch on the tiller. He started baling again, and began to wonder if he would ever again see daylight. He saw it as he tossed a hatful of water over the side, into another high wave. A pinprick of light. There, over his right shoulder. Mike van Rooyen stared, rubbing water out of his eyes. It was still there. A light! It was hard to tell how far away. Maybe 100 yards. Or maybe a mile. But it was a light. And he had nothing else on which to pin his hopes! Heedless now of the angle of the waves, of trying to tack with the white horses pounding him, he swung the boat around. Aiming for the light. The *Warthog* was beginning to list, unresponsive to the controls, wallowing reluctantly onwards. The ranger peered through the rain. The light was still there. Closer now. Was it closer? Or was his mind willing it so? The rain was not so strong now. But the waves were still coming. And the wind bullied and gusted. Then the boat was going down. Sinking. Succumbing at last to the water pouring over its gunnels. And

Mike van Rooyen was floundering, treading water, wondering where the empty petrol tank was. So that he could use it as a raft.

"Mike! Mike!" Van Rooyen did not believe his ears. Then it came again. Someone was calling him. And then he recognised the voice, and knew what the light had been. Rupert had somehow heard the distant straining hum of the motor. He had been lying awake under a bucksail listening to the storm. So he lit a hurricane lamp and padded through the rain down to the shore. Whoever was out there on the lake sounded as if they were not doing too well. Then the engine sound changed, straining harder, becoming louder, and he realised that whoever it was, and it *must* be Mike, had missed Long Island and was now heading back to it. The noise faded. He went into the lake and started swimming. Aiming for where he'd last heard the engine. There in the waves and the rain and the howling wind he found Mike van Rooyen, and slowly the two men battled their way to land.

Morrungulo, Mozambique coast. April 1975. An endless vista of curving, white, sand beach. Fringed by palm trees on the landward side and the frothy, white-edged, turquoise sea on the other. A fisherman's paradise. Rock cod, barracuda, sailfish, marlin and mako shark. A clean, unpolluted, champagne-sparkling, clear ocean. Crayfish and oysters on the jagged, black, snaggle-toothed reefs. Prawns and crabs in the estuaries and the mangroves. Solitude. Peace. Therapy. A campsite, simple bamboo and thatch shelters, nestling beneath the overhead canopy of coconut palms. A tropical breeze rustling the palm fronds and nudging a green-brown coconut from its cluster. The dull thump, as it hits the ground, echoes through the large, cool, dim glade.

It is two months before this country will take its independence from the Portuguese colonial powers which have haphazardly governed the territory for the last 400 years. A handful of Rhodesians, a score or so, are visiting this small Indian Ocean paradise before the event takes place.

Access to this part of Africa in the foreseeable future is unlikely. It is late afternoon. The camp area is quiet, deserted. Everyone is out fishing, or beachcombing or generally playing in the ocean. For some reason Rupert has not gone out with his companions on this day; out over the horizon to try for the big fish which live on the edge of the Mozambique Channel. He is pottering around their camp, drinking a mug of tea and working on one of his reels. With his increasing deafness he does not hear the cries at first, over the sand dunes, blending with the sound of the high tide surf pounding the beach. Then the shouts reach him. Female. Distant. From the ocean. The retired game warden loped into an easy stride, away from the permanent shade of the palm trees and on to the beach. Bright, late afternoon sunlight. The sand clutching, hindering. There, almost 200 yards out, caught by the current, an elderly lady, part of one of the family groups, is drifting atop an inflated car tube, being swept out into the bay.

Rupert flung aside his shirt and sandals and waded into the surf. He felt the pull of the current immediately, tugging at his legs. He pushed on. Deeper. And then he was swimming, and it was easy, for he was going with the current. Coming back would be another story. Even without the woman on the tube it would be a hard struggle against the current. She was further out now, small on the tube as it balanced atop a swell. He remembered the fins they had seen, grey black triangles, frequently out here at high tide. He pushed those thoughts away.

He got her back to shore, after what seemed like an eternity. It had been a battle. Once or twice he wondered if he would make it.

He was 62 then.

A month later, on May 26, working on his Land Rover, he collapsed from a heart attack at his home in Salisbury.

This story of a man whose commitment to wildlife bridged a conservation era, started with a telegram.

An obituary, in TIME magazine, June 9, 1975, short and precise, ends it.

> **Died.** *Rupert Fothergill, 62, Rhodesian game ranger who headed "Operation Noah", a five year (1959-63) rescue effort that saved more than 6 000 warthogs, monkeys, snakes, lions, elephants, rhinos and other wild beasts from the rising waters of a man-made lake behind the Kariba Dam on the Zambezi River; of a heart attack; in Salisbury, Rhodesia.*